AF560276

PARADIGMS OF DISSENT AND PROTEST: SOCIAL MOVEMENTS IN EASTERN INDIA (*c.* AD 1400–1700)

Paradigms of Dissent and Protest: Social Movements in Eastern India

(*c.* AD 1400–1700)

BASANTA KUMAR MALLIK

MANOHAR
2004

First published 2004

ISBN 81-7304-522-4

Published by
Ajay Kumar Jain for
Manohar Publishers & Distributors
4753/23 Ansari Road, Daryaganj
New Delhi 110 002

Typeset by
Kohli Print
Delhi 110 051

Printed at
Lordson Publishers Pvt. Ltd.
New Delhi 110 007

for

Supriya,
Bapu & Niku

Contents

Preface

PRE-COLONIAL eastern India witnessed a profound transformation in social and cultural life of the people. Orissa emerged as a pioneering proud region during this time with the efflorescence of regional language and literature, growth of gigantic temples, art and architecture. There was a great deal of progress particularly in the realm of socio-cultural life of the people. The most important development that took place during fifteenth and sixteenth-century Orissa saw the social resurgence of the radical *Sudramunis*, who tried to stir the social milieu with the tenor of protest and reform, which has hitherto remained more or less unnoticed by the historians.

The Bhakti movement during this time as a focus of spiritual attention, gave rise to a new concept of divinity. The Krishna cult that sprang up in the Gangetic valley marked a high-point of this process of transformation, centred on Krishna's romantic life; the concept of *bhakti* under the spell of Sri Chaitanya emphasized a more loving and lovable aspect of the God Vishnu, in the form of Lord Jagannatha of Puri.

I have been, stimulated by the assumption that the notion of social stratification of medieval Orissa, her society and culture is a fertile subject for scholarly inquiry. I have intended to analyse the different nuances between the culture of the èlite and that of unlettered or semi-educated commoners. The sources on which the present study is based were created by the intellectual èlite who had monoply in the field of literacy, and education and also the literary sources created by the common men. In humble endeavour I have tried to look into the medieval world not only through the eyes of the 'èlites' but also from the vantage-point of the common people.

This work, emanated from a revision of my Ph.D. thesis 'Social Protest and Popular Movement in Medieval Orissa (*c.* AD 1450–1600)' written at Jawaharlal Nehru University, New Delhi. I owe a debt of gratitude to my esteemed teacher and supervisor Professor Muzaffar Alam whose invaluable guidance, inspiration and constant advice—oral or written—were indispensable for this work. I fall short of words to express my gratitude to him. I am also grateful to Professors Satish Chandra, Romila Thapar, Bipan Chandra, Harbans Mukhia and Dilbagh Singh, my esteemed teachers at the Centre for Historical Studies, JNU, who were generous enough to discuss with me matters relating to research methodology and issues relating to research problems. I also record my debt of gratitude to Professor Hermann Kulke, University of Kiel, Germany, then Visiting Professor at the Centre for Historical Studies, JNU, for his kind discussions with me of some questions concerning the present study. I am grateful to Professor Chittaranjan Das, Professor Krushna Charan Sahoo of Bhubaneswar and Professor Asutosh Patnaik, PG Department of Oriya Language and Literature, Utkal University, Bhubaneswar, for several valuable suggestions. I am thankful to Mrs Renuka Mohanty for her kind permission to use the fascimile cover pages of a few medieval Oriya books printed in Bengali script from the book of late Surendra Mohanty in the appendix of this book. Last, but not least, I am thankful to my wife Supriya for the hearty co-operation and support that I received from her during the period of my engagement in this work. I am grateful to the Manohar Publishers & Distributors for undertaking timely the publication of this book.

Vani Vihar
Bhubaneswar
26 January 2002

BASANTA KUMAR MALLIK

Abbreviations

AHRS	:	Andhra Historical Research Society
BOHRJ	:	Bihar-Orissa Historical Research Journal
DC	:	Directorate of Culture, Orissa
EI	:	*Epigraphia Indica*
IO	:	*Inscriptions of Orissa*
IHQ	:	*Indian Historical Quarterly*
IHR	:	*Indian Historical Review*
IESHR	:	*Indian Economic and Social History Review*
JASB	:	*Journal of Asiatic Society of Bengal*
n.d.	:	No date
OHRJ	:	*Orissa Historical Research Journal*
OSA	:	Orissa Sahitya Academy
PIHC	:	*Proceedings of the Indian History Congress*
POHC	:	*Proceedings of the Orissa History Congress*
RP	:	Radharaman Pustakalaya
SII	:	South Indian Inscriptions

Introduction

PRE-COLONIAL Indian society was broadly characterized as an unequal and hierarchical society. The specific forms of economic, social and cultural hierarchy and inequitable growth of power in India were based upon the varna system. The proliferation of castes also enriched the age-old varna system and strengthened the system of social hierarchy. This growth of inequitable power structure was legitimized by the religious concept that led to the development of the cultural hegemony of a few over the masses.

Following such a system of privileges for some and deprivation for many on the basis of birth, the varna ideology was contested at all times and in all places though in an uneven manner, over the entire region. Since the main anchor of the social system in India was religion in its dominant Brahminic tradition,[1] challenges to hierarchy largely came from within the same socio-religious framework. Beginning with the Ajivikas and Sramanas nearly 2,500 years ago, the subcontinent's history is replete with inadequately researched, anti-hierarchical socio-religious and cultural manifestations. Pan-Indian heterodoxies such as Buddhism, Jainism and the Bhakti movement, regional sects, such as Veersaivism, Sikhism, Kabirpanth and numerous other local movements, to a greater or lesser degree, were expressions of anti-hierarchical aspirations and values.[2]

However, the Bhakti movement of medieval India had a great bearing on shaping Indian society, culture, religion and literature. In the north as well as in the south, in the east and west, a large number of mystics and *bhakta-kavis* took to writing and acts of social reform. Almost all of them were *sadhakas* (meditators) and wanderers in the name of God and in the service of the people. They were often opposed to the establishment, and all authoritarian monastic orders. They also strongly criticized all sectarian zealotry and caste discrimination in society. All of them emphasized relevance of religion in social life, in the spheres of human aspirations and social relationships.

The *bhakti* teachers, like those of the devotional cults, came from a diversity of backgrounds. Many were artisans by origin or belonged to the class of less prosperous cultivators. Occasionally, Brahmins also joined the Bhakti movement, but by and large its followers were from the lower order of society.[3]

What is remarkable about the medieval Indian *bhakta-kavis* is that most of them belonged to the lowly classes and it was among these very classes they preached. Kabir (AD 1440–1518), the most outstanding of them was a weaver of Varanasi, and Ravidas, his contemporary, a cobbler of the same city. With Nanak (AD 1469–1539), who was a grain merchant, they formed a kind of trinity among the leaders of the monotheistic movement. Another contemporary of theirs was the devotee Sain, a barber and village menial. Dhanna was a Jat peasant from Deoli in Rajasthan. Dadu, a contemporary of Akbar and the teacher of the Dadupanthis was a cotton-carder. Haridasa (AD 1645), the teacher of Niranji's was a Jat slave. Namadev, a calico-painter from Maharashtra who lived in the fourteenth century was apparently recognized by the monotheists as one of their precursors.[4] He provided stimulus and inspiration even from so long a distance to what became a great religious movement among the common people of Punjab.

Gora was a potter by caste and craft. Chokhamela, an untouchable *bhakta-kavi* from Maharashtra was killed by collapse of Mangalvedhe town-wall for the construction of which he had been pressed by *corvee*, old as he was. The Paithan Brahmin Eknath (AD 1590) to whom we owe the text of *Jnaneswari* as well as many fine Marathi poems went outside of set conventions to break the crudest restriction of untouchability. Another distinguished *bhakta-kavi* Tukaram, the sixteenth-century Kunabi peasant and petty grain-dealer survived the grim famine, the unrelenting jealousy of contemporary folk-poets and the contemptuous hatred of Brahmins, ultimately to drown himself in the river.[5] Srinath (*c.* AD 1350–1450), another Telugu poet of Andhra

Pradesh (then a part of the Gajapati empire), treated differently from the Sanskrit scholars, was subjected to humiliating punishments and ill-treatment by the orthodox sections of society.[6]

These reformers representing a general movement were by no means confined to their region and language. The generally painful tenor of their lives shows that they were in opposition to the social hierarchy and did not care to exercise the art of pleasing the ruling class. 'Their stress on equality and condemnation of caste and ritual observance was certainly much greater than is to be found in any contemporary Islamic preaching. . . . In a beautiful verse, composed in the name of Dhana Jat, the fifth guru of the Sikhs (Arjun) insists on God's special grace upon such lowly worshipper.'[7] The concept of *Panjpiare* in the Sikh Khalsa in the seventeenth century corroborates their religious interaction towards a reform. The *Panjpiare*, the beloved five disciples of Guru Govind Singh, symbolized the social diversity of caste and class like the *Panchasakhas* of Orissa. For example, among the *Panjpiare* Daya Ram was a Khatri from Lahore; Dharam Dass a Jat from Hastinapur; Mokham Chand, a washerman from Dwaraka; Sahib Chand, a barber from Bidar; and Himat Rai, a water-carrier from Jagannathpuri. Thus, the social diversity of the *bhaktas* has revolutionized the concept of caste rigidity and the bhakti tradition of medieval times.

In the present work, I have endeavoured to analyse various aspects of the socio-religious movement that took place in eastern India with particular reference to medieval Orissa. The movement, developed particularly in the coastal Orissa and in course of time, its impact was seen in other parts of eastern India. The medieval Oriya *bhakta-kavis,* popularly known as *Sudramunis,* hailed from the lower order of society and propagated the ideas of *bhakti, sunya* and *nirguna* using the popular dialects. Their discontent against the contemporary society, priests, ruling class and their sincere effort for scholarly inquiry are clearly discernible in their writings. Their struggle has been generally characterized as a 'Social Protest Movement' that spread over different regions of eastern India including Orissa, Bengal and Assam. They protested against the authority of the 'four pillars' of the contemporary society.

First of all, they protested against the discriminating social structure (i.e. caste, untouchability, low status of Sudras and women and their deprivation of knowledge).

Secondly, they opposed the intellectual hegemony of the Sanskrit language and as a mark of protest they created parallel regional literature.

Thirdly, they criticized the religious impositions and various externalities like priesthood, rituals, pilgrimage and idol-worship.

Fourthly, they raised their voice against the political authority and dominance of the ruling class. They, however, worked for the common people and wrote in the peoples' language, advocated equality between the *raja* and *praja* and propagated *bhakti* for worshipping personal deities.

The nature of their 'dissent and protest' can be understood better with a look at the socio-cultural background of the period. The contemporary society, religion and culture remained completely under the spell of Brahminism with the growth of gigantic temples,[8] establishment of Brahmin *sasanas* and the patronization of Sanskrit literature in Orissa during the period: tenth-eleventh century. The scriptures remained entirely under the domination of Sanskrit, which served the official and professional language of a minority group in society that had monopolized education. Sanskrit enjoyed absolute primacy in the hierarchy of languages. For a long time it was the only written language, but even when its monopoly had been challenged and literary vernaculars developed alongside it, Sanskrit maintained a privileged position. It was seen as the sacred language guaranteeing unity of faith and salvation. It was believed that God could specifically be addressed in the medium of the *debabhasha,* i.e. Sanskrit. The layman did not know Sanskrit and to be literate, one had to know Sanskrit. Accordingly, the division of the people into literate and unlettered or semi-educated, a notion of late antiquity remained decisive. The former were the educated, those who knew Sanskrit; the latter were largely unlettered and few semi-educated, were understood as persons knowing merely their crude native tongue. In spite of education acquired by a few non-Brahmins in the medium of their mother-tongue, they were not considered to be knowledgeable, or educated, since value was attached to birth but not to merit in Indian society then.

The èlite of medieval Orissa succeeded in barring the common people from education and the means of recording their thoughts and mood. The common people, generally non-Brahmins, were often referred to as the Sudras,[9] *hina* (lowly)[10] and *mudha-jana*[11] (stupid), for direct access to scriptures was denied to them. In consequence, an èlitist view of medieval culture, based only on the thoughts of the so-called high-born—theologians, philosophers, poets and historians became firmly established and dominated scholarship. Bharata Muni of the first century AD attributed to the language of the common people of Odra as *bibhasha* (sub-language). The name he gave to it was Oudri or Udrabhasha.[12] The Sanskrit scholars considered Oudri, a *bibhasha* till as late as the twelfth century.

The Brahmins, besides performing religious ceremonies, acted as the foci of culture. It was they who taught the people the immense benefits of listening to the Puranas. Since the common people were not allowed to read the Puranas, *Purana-pandas* read out and explained to them the contents of the Puranas which were all written in Sanskrit. Apart from supernatural elements, the Puranas emphasized social norms as well as social sanctions or penalties for violating them. This was a clever and convenient way of maintaining social cohesion, and also of socializing young minds in the traditional social system. Over and above was the *Mukti-mandap*, an assembly of orthodox Brahmin pundits within the premises of the Jagannatha temple. This was the highest authority in socio-religious matters, and its verdict was enforced, if necessary under the authority of the king. *Mukti-mandap* was also a place of religious discourse which only the Brahmins could carry on and which only their brethren and the king listen.[13]

The *bhakta-kavis* of medieval Orissa played the most vital role in generating the spirit of equality and human dignity. They undermined the established tradition of writing scriptures and Puranas in Sanskrit and started composing them in the language of the common people, i.e. Oriya. They endeavoured to abolish the superstition preached by the orthodox priests and propagated that God could also be prayed to in their colloquial language, and worshipped in their heart and mind filled in with *bhakti*. Sudramuni Sarala Dasa, a cultivator and poet, composed the Oriya *Mahabharata* (late fifteenth century) in Jhankar village of the present Jagatsinghpur District, Sudramuni Balarama Dasa wrote the *Ramayana* in Puri, *Bipra* Jagannatha Dasa wrote the *Bhagavata* in Puri (both in sixteenth century) and another Sudramuni Achyutananda Dasa (sixteenth century) composed the *Harivamsa*, in his Nembal village of Cuttack District, quite far away from the royal court.

The orthodox pundits of medieval Orissa however, did not appreciate these efforts to render the main epics and Puranas into the vernacular by the *munis* of the Sudra or non-Brahmin communities.

Among the non-Brahimns those who were engaged earlier in worshipping the local deities were called the *munis*. Since they belong to the Sudra castes they were called *Sudramunis*. The *bhakta-kavis* had to face a lot of criticism and humiliation from the learned Brahmins, and to protect themselves against hostile criticisms they appear to have dedicated all their writings to the gods and goddesses they believed in. They have also characterized themselves with due humility as illiterate, uneducated, ignorant, low born, sinners, of the Sudra caste, etc., and have requested the wise èlite of the contemporary society to forgive them for their works.[14] The anti-caste pronouncements are very much conspicuous in their writings. Renouncing all original caste surnames they used *'Dasa'* after their names meaning servant or slave to god and goddesses. By doing this, they in a measure protested against different caste surnames, the discriminatorial character of the Brahminical order.[15] The *munis* did not remain satisfied only by rendering the Sanskrit works into Oriya, they also attempted to participate in the Vedanta discussions held at the *Mukti-mandap* of the Jagannatha temple of Puri. Amongst them the most outspoken and revolutionary, namely, Balarama Dasa and Achyutananda Dasa challenged the Brahmin pundits as regards the right of the Sudras to study Vedas and Dharmasastras, which were a complex and contradictory synthesis of two different levels of culture. In this work, there is an attempt to analyse both the traditions in their dialectical aspect, for the works of the èlites and the *Sudramunis* existed as the inseparably linked poles of a unified cultural universe.

The advent of Sri Chaitanya in Orissa in AD 1510 and his long stay in Puri till he breathed his last in AD 1533, marked an important period in the resurgence of the Bhakti movement in Orissa. He popularized the degenerated Radha-Krishna cult and spread the movement through *samkirtan* (collective worship and recitation of hymns) and *nagarkirtan* (religious processions from city to villages). The *prema bhakti* propagated by him gained momentum and made Orissa a stronghold of the *bhakti* faith. There was a flow of two streams of Vaishnavism in Orissa: one was the Utkal Vaishnavism led by the *panchasakhas* of whom four were *Sudramunis,* and the other was Gaudiya Vaishnavism led by Chaitanya. Both the groups of Vaishnavas respected and influenced each other in course of their movement. This had a remarkable impact on the socio-cultural life of the people of Orissa. It has been argued by some scholars that the *panchasakhas* or five associates, namely, Balarama Dasa, Jagannatha Dasa, Ananta Dasa, Yashovanta Dasa and Achyutananda Dasa were born at different places of Orissa in different times and they were not friends or did not work together.[16] They have been dealt with in this work as the *panchasakhas* with a shared sense of their rich cultural tradition and common perspectives of social reform in medieval Orissa.

The *bhakti* cult was widely popular as it laid stress on issues like egalitarianism, unity of godhead, dignity of man's actions, simple devotion, and protest against rituals and priesthood. All the schools of thought belonging to the genre of *bhakti* believed in the existence of a God supernaturally revealed to man. The chief attribute of this movement was the attitude of the soul with regard to the Supreme Being.

There were two eminent schools of *bhakti* cult popularly known as *sagunas* and *nirgunas*. The teachers of the *saguna* school of thought believed in the presence of God with all human attributes. According to them, God is like a man with supernatural qualities. The *sagunas*, who enriched Hinduism, believed in the authority of the Vedas and did not like to challenge the traditions of the past. Chaitanya can be cited as a rare exception. Perhaps he was the only *saguna bhakta* who had actively led a progressive reform movement despite his adherence to the conventional religious modes connected with Vaishnavism.[17] But the *nirguna* teachers preached the formlessness of God. According to them God has no human attributes, it is *nirakara* or formless. They challenged the traditions of the past and tried to bring about a change in social order. The *panchasakhas*, although they believed in *nirguna* school of thought, sometimes accepted the *saguna* principles as a matter of compromise with the elements of the established power structure.

The period of this study is remarkable in the history of Orissa which witnessed the decline of the later Eastern Gangas and rise of the Suryavamsi Gajapati kings (AD 1435–1540). Gajapati Kapilendra Dev founded the Suryavamsi dynasty and during his glorious rule (AD 1435–67) the Orissan empire was extended from the Ganges in the north to the Kaveri in the south. The importance of the period of the Gajapati kings should not be judged only from the viewpoint of their aggressive imperialism. The period is extraordinarily important for the rise of an awakening movement in the field of Oriya language and literature, devotional music, painting and sculpture, etc., which were closely associated with the Bhakti movement.

Regional state formation in late ancient Orissa was closely linked with the patronisation of local deities in the conquered areas and the construction of huge temples for the royal legitimization. The temple of Lord Jagannatha (twelfth century) of Puri was constructed during this period and in course of time it became a great centre of learning and education in medieval times. A large number of Sanskrit scholars from different corners of India came to this place and participated in various theological and philosophical discourses. In the eleventh century, while Chodaganga Dev was ruling over Orissa, Ramanuja, the founder of the Vishistadvait philosophy, came to Puri and preached his ideas.[18] Jayadeva (mid-twelfth century) composed his *Gita Govinda*, during this period. The Radha-Krishna concept was popular as one of the perennial streams of Vaishnavism in Orissa and Bengal.[19] Chodaganga Dev also took interest in the construction of the Jagannatha temple in the twelfth century. According to tradition, Vidyapati a great poet of Mithila, also came to Orissa during this time. Ramananda came to Puri at the end of the fourteenth century and preached his philosophy. Kabir visited it in the early fifteenth century and preached his doctrine of equality based on lofty humanism.[20] Tulsi Dasa[21] and Guru Nanak[22] also visited Puri during the early phase of the sixteenth century and preached their respective ideas. In the middle of this century, Guru Nanak's son, Sri Chandra, the founder of the Udasi Sampraday and Vallabhacharya, the founder of the Shuddhadvaita (pure monism), also arrived at Puri to preach their religious viewpoints.[23] Thus, Puri had acquired the status of a great pilgrimage centre of religious significance by the sixteenth century, and therefore, the *panchasakhas* and Sri Chaitanya made it the nucleus of their movement.

The sources on which the present study is based were created by the contemporary *bhakta-kavis* writing in vernaculars, and on the inscriptions and some archaeological evidences of the period under review.

The epigraphic source of the period consists of the copper-plate grants and temple inscriptions. I have used the relevant copper-plate grants from the period of Anantavarman Chodaganga Dev, dated AD 1082 to Gajapati Kapilendra Dev (dated AD 1435–67). Notable among the temple inscriptions are those of the Lingaraj temple at Bhubaneswar, the Jagannatha temple at Puri and the temples of Mukhalingam, Drakshashram, Palur, Srikurmam and Simhachalam, the places which were the spheres of influence of the Ganga and the Gajapati rulers. The inscriptions, generally, were written in Sanskrit. We find that they are also sometimes mixed with Oriya terms. Almost all the epigraphs are dated; years are more often regnal years or refer to the Saka era. Their paleography also helps to determine their period. The contents of the copper-plate grants follow a definite pattern where the details of the donor, donee, conditions of the grants and years of the grants are mentioned. The Orissa State Museum has published six volumes of inscriptions under the title *Inscriptions of Orissa*[24] which are very much helpful in studying the socio-economic and political history of the region.

Besides political aspects, the inscriptions provide information on the territorial expansion, Brahminical settlements, development of trade and urban centres. They also contain references to land tenure, land measurements, land-grants and land revenues. Evidence regarding social life available in epigraphic sources is rather meagre. A few scattered references to the social structure and different castes and communities are found in them. The archaeological sources are mainly the sculptures depicted in the temples of Lingaraj at Bhubaneswar, Jagannatha temple at Puri and the Sun temple at Konark. These sculptures provide us information regarding dress, ornaments, music and dances of medieval Orissa. We have also got some references to the Vaishnav monuments and sculptures in the Mayurbhanja District of Orissa.[25]

The regional literature of the period is the principal source of our study. The literature of the period generally is scattered in a variety of Oriya, Sanskrit, Bengali and Persian literatures.

Madalapanji (sixteenth century AD), the chronicle of the Jagannatha temple is an important literary source for depicting the socio-economic life of the people as it contains valuable references to state's income, expenditure, land administration and famines of Orissa.[26]

The *Mahabharata* of Sarala Dasa (fifteenth century AD) is a remarkable source of information for the study of the socio-economic life of medieval Orissa. It contains information regarding the glorious victories of Kapilendra Dev, origin of the cult of Lord Jagannatha, the economic condition and socio-religious life of the people. Besides this, there is an attempt to discuss various aspects of socio-religious, political and economic thoughts of Sarala Dasa which are enormously relevant to the present days. Some topographical and geographical information of the period is also available in the *Sarala Mahabharata*.[27]

The next important Oriya literary writings of the period are the works of the *panchasakhas* who flourished in the sixteenth-seventeenth centuries. Among these works *Jagamohan Ramayana*[28] and *Lakshmi Puran*[29] of Balarama Dasa (sixteenth century) provide information about the social life, condition of women and the Sudras and the poet's attitude towards the king, priests and common men. The Srimad *Bhagavata* of Jagannatha Dasa (sixteenth century), mainly a theological work, throws light on society, religion, culture and the value system. This work also influenced remarkably the society, literature and culture of the later period.[30] *Govindachandra* of Yasovanta Dasa deals with the philosophy of the Natha Yogis and it is still sung by the Natha mendicants.[31] The *malikas* (prophecies) of Achyutananda Dasa depicting conflict and tensions in society were written in the form of predictions for future. The *Harivamsa*,[32] the *Gopalanka Ogala*,[33] and the *Kaivarta Gita*[34] of the same author were composed to enhance the social status and self-respect of the lower classes.

Besides this, Dibakara Dasa's *Jagannatha Charitamrita*[35] (seventeenth century), Rama Dasa's *Dardhyata Bhakti*[36] (eighteenth century), Iswara Dasa's *Chaitanya Bhagavata*[37] (early seventeenth century), Vrindaban Dasa's *Chaitanya Bhagavata*[38] (seventeenth century) and Madhav Dasa's *Chaitanya Vilasa*[39] (sixteenth century) provide biographical details about the *bhakta-kavis* of contemporary society. Bhima Dasa's *Bhakti Ratnavali*,[40] Chaitanya Dasa's *Nirguna Mahatmya*[41] (seventeenth century) and Salabega's *Bhakti Poetry*[42] (seventeenth century) are the indispensable sources of Bhakti movement of the period under review.

Many Sanskrit literary texts of the period contain rich references to the socio-religious life of Orissa. Jayadeva's *Gita Govinda*[43] (twelfth century), Viswanath Kaviraj's *Chandrakala Natika*[44] (fourteenth cen-tury) and the *Saraswati Vilasa*[45] ascribed to Purushottam Gajapati, Murari Gupta's *Chaitanya Charitamrita*,[46] Kavi Karnapura's *Chaitanya Charitamrita* and Ray Ramananda's *Jagannatha Vallabha Natakam*[47] are important among them.

The Bengali works, namely, *Chaitanya Charitamrita*[48] (sixteenth century) of Krishnadasa Kaviraja and *Chaitanya Bhagavata*[49] of Vrindaban Dasa are the biographical sketches of Sri Chaitanya. Lochana Dasa's *Chaitanya Mangal*[50] (sixteenth century) and Jayananda's *Chaitanya Mangal*[51] throw light on the reign of Prataprudra Gajapati and his association with Vaishnavism.

The Persian accounts such as Al-Biruni's *Tarikh-ul-Hind*[52] (eleventh century) give us information about the social organization, caste, communities, religion and beliefs of eleventh-century India and some references to Orissa as well. *Tabaquat-i-Nasiri*[53] (thirteenth century) of Minhaj-ud-din-bin-Siraj-ud-din and *Tarikh-i-Firuzshahi*[54] (fourteenth century) of Shams-i-Shiraj refer generally to the Muslim invasion of Orissa. But they also make incidental references to the economic condition of the people. Abul Fazl in his *Ain-i-Akbari*[55] (sixteenth century) has given an account of the rent-roll, land assessment, economic data regarding output and price and administrative units of the then Orissa. On these materials also we have drawn selectively for purposes of discussion of the social and economic history of the period.

The present work has been divided into four chapters. In Chapter 1, I have analysed the socio-economic and cultural background of the regional state formation in late ancient or early medieval Orissa, and examined various socio-cultural and economic factors responsible for the transformation of tribal chiefdoms into the monarchical kingdom. The process of Hinduization/Kshatriyaization and the patronization of the local cults and tribal deities was the mainstay behind the regional state formation. I have discussed the crown-priest relationship, growth of priestly power in the Gajapati era (AD 1435–1540), and constant land-grants to Brahmins, state officials and other dominant non-Brahmin classes which led to the rise and growth of monarchical kingdom.

In another section, various aspects of the medieval Orissan social structure have been lucidly illustrated. The social order was caste-ridden and legitimized by the dominant Brahminical religious doctrines. The continuity of land-grants helped to rise an intermediary class consisting of the priests, nobles and temples. The establishment of tax-free Brahmin *sasanas*, a remarkable feature of the medieval Orissa, implies the alliance between the Brahmins and Kshatriyas to have their share in administration, economic resources and political power. I have also analysed the condition of primary producers, royal patronage to Sanskrit literature, the causes of social inequality, appropriation and deprivation which led to the rise of the protest movement in medieval Orissa.

In Chapter 2, I have elucidated the background to the emergence of the rise and growth of the written Oriya literature from the Oral tradition. Sudramuni Sarala Dasa, the pioneer of the protest movement changed the established tradition of writing epics in Sanskrit and started composing them in the vernacular, very much close to the crude spoken language of the people. The Oriya

Mahabharata was his *magnum opus*, in addition to other creations like *Vilanka Ramayan* and *Chandi Puran*. I have studied his innovative writing of Puranas and Dharmasastras in vernaculars, departing from the set pattern of *puranic* compositions as a form of social protest. Sarala Dasa's socio-religious outlook, his resentment against the social order, his theory of the Jagannatha cult, his political philosophy, his attitude towards kingship, priesthood, women and Sudras and his contribution to the moral uplift have been lucidly presented. His popularity and impact on later *bhakta-kavis* have been also explained. Arjuna Dasa, the author of *Ramabibha*, Chaitanya Dasa, the author of *Nirguna Mahatmya* and Markanda Dasa, the author of *Keshav Koili* immediately followed the tradition of Sarala Dasa and contributed to the growth of Oriya literature.

Chapter 3, is an attempt to discuss various factors leading to the rise of a non-conformist movement against the established social order. The Sudramuni's movement which gained momentum following the tradition of Sarala Dasa during sixteenth century, has been the mainstay of discussion in this chapter. I have brought to light the socio-religious and political views of the *panchasakhas*, their effort of scholarly inquiry, their criticism of orthodox religion and *sastras*; authoritarianism and impositions, as well as their contribution to shape the society and literature. The role of the *panchasakhas* in updating women and Sudras and endowing them with 'self-respect' has been emphasized. They endeavoured to establish a new social order based on universal brotherhood, equality, reason and humanism. The objectives of their teachings and significance of their protest have been given special attention in this chapter.

Chapter 4, explicates the spread of *premabhakti* of Sri Chaitanya and his popularization of the Radha-Krishna cult in Orissa. Sri Chaitanya accepted disciples from all sections of society, irrespective of their caste and creed. He reached out to the common people through *samkirtan*, *nagarkirtan* and his creative devotional music. People of all denominations were able to assemble at one place for the purpose of *samkirtan*. Chaitanya's attitude towards caste, priesthood, disciples and his *samkirtan* consisting of mass-singing, chanting, dancing, common prayer and *nagarkirtan* has been critically appraised. I have also brought out the similarities and differences between the streams of Utkal Vaishnavism and Gaudiya Vaishnavism, which spread over Orissa under the period of this study.

The period between fifteenth and seventeenth centuries has been a remarkable era in the history of eastern India, that witnessed the cultural resurgence movement. The writings and teachings of Sudramuni Sarala Dasa and the *panchasakhas* invoked the wrath of the dominant vested interests and therefore, some of the writers and their followers were imprisoned, and a few even tortured, whereas some others were banished from their own areas. But they endeared themselves to the common folks by their genuine emphasis on egalitarianism. They did not want to found a new religion, nor did they advocate a particular sectarian zealotry; they formed a different faith and protested against the evil features of the contemporary social order and struggled to reform it with the objective of bringing about social harmony, universal brotherhood, social equality and stability. Their egalitarian philosophy and humanitarian approach bear significant relevance to the present day's society.

NOTES

1. The use of the adjective 'Brahminic'/'Brahminical' is not meant to imply an ideology that is confined only to one particular social group but rather a set of values, ideas, concepts, practices and myths that are identifiable in the literary tradition and social institutions.
2. Romila Thapar, *A History of India*, vol. I, Penguin Books, Harmondsworth, 1966, pp. 65–9, 214–16, 260–5, 308–13.
3. Ibid., p. 308.
4. Irfan Habib, 'The Historical Background of the Popular Monotheistic Movement of the 15th–17th centuries', in B. Prasad (ed.), *Ideas in History*, Asia, Bombay, 1969.
5. D.D. Kosambi, *Myth and Reality*, Popular Prakashan, Bombay, 1962, pp. 33–4.
6. C.V. Ramachandra Rao, 'The Later Eastern Gangas: The Suryavamsa Gajapatis and Telugu Language and Literature', in H.C. Das et al. (eds.), *Krsna Pratibha: Studies in Indology*, vol. II, Sundeep Prakashan, Delhi, 1994, p. 377.
7. Irfan Habib, *Essays in Indian History: Towards a Marxist Perception*, Tulika, New Delhi, 1995, p. 175.
8. Amidst numerous temples of Orissa the main temples which influenced religion and culture were (i) the Lingaraj temple (eleventh century) at Bhubaneswar, (ii) Lord Jagannatha temple (twelfth century) at Puri and (iii) the Sun temple (thirteenth century) at Konark.
9. Cf. p. 26 nn 28 and 29, *Vedantasara Gupta Gita*, Union Printing Works, Cuttack, 1910, p. 2.

10. Idem.
11. Idem.
12. Chittaranjan Das, *A Glimpse into Oriya Literature*, Orissa Sahitya Akademi, Bhubaneswar, 1982a, pp. 11–12
13. R.K. Das, 'Social Protest in Medieval Orissa', in *Proceedings of Indian History Congress* (*PIHC*), 41st Session, Bombay, 1980, p. 341.
14. K.C. Panigrahi, *Sarala Dasa*, Sahitya Akademi, Delhi, 1975, pp. 17–18; Chittaranjan Das, op. cit., 1982, pp. 49, 62; and see also note 85 of Chapter 2.
15. Surendra Mohanty hints at the viewpoint that the pre-Aryans have been identified as *'Dasas'* in the *Rigveda*. Since the *Bhaktidharma* based on Krishna *bhakti* was prevalent mostly among the people of a non-Sanskritized society, the poets and preceptors of this society identified themselves with the title '*Dasa'*, which appears to be correct from the standpoint of the process of Hinduization in Orissa. See Surendra Mohanty, *Oriya Sahityar Madhyaparva O Uttar Madhyaparva*, Cuttack Students Store, Cuttack, 1995, p. 19.
16. Natabar Samantaray, *Sakhahina Panchasakha* (Oriya), Swadhina Press, Berhampur, 1975, pp. 6–9.
17. Krishna Sharma, *Bhakti and the Bhakti Movement: A New Perspective*, Munshiram Manoharlal, New Delhi, 1987, p. 25n.
18. A.B. Mohanty (ed.), *Madalapanji*, Prachi Samiti, Bhubaneswar, 1940, pp. 49–50.
19. S.N. Rajguru, *Inscriptions of Orissa*, vol. III, pt. II, Directorate of Culture, Orissa, Bhubaneswar, 1966, p. 294.
20. Existence of the 'Kabir Chaura Math' at the *Swargadwar* of Puri suggests the visit of Kabir to Puri. The Hindu institution Chauramatha, named after saint Kabir, also reminds us about the Hindu-Muslim mutual impact.with the effort of Kabir. Also *vide* Rama Dasa, *Dardhyata Bhakti*, pts. I and II, Dharmagrantha, Store, Cuttack, n.d., pp. 132–40.
21. Rama Dasa, op. cit., pp. 229–37.
22. Amar Singh, 'Guru Nanak in Orissa', in M.N. Das (ed.), *Sidelights on History and Culture of Orissa*, Vidyapuri, Cuttack, 1977, p. 424.
23. Ibid., p. 425.
24. S.N. Rajguru, *Inscriptions of Orissa*, vols. I–III, Directorate of Culutre, Orissa, Bhubaneswar, 1966.
25. N. Vasu, *Archaeological Survey of Mayurbhanja*, vols. I and II, Calcutta University, Calcutta, 1911.
26. A.B. Mohanty (ed.), op. cit., 1940.
27. *Sarala Mahabharata*, Radharaman Pustakalaya, Cuttack, 1968.
28. Balrama Dasa, *Jagamohan Ramayan*, vols. I–VII, Dharmagrantha Store, Cuttack, n.d.
29. Balarama Dasa, *Lakshmi Puran*, Sanyasi Pustakalaya, Berhampur, n.d.
30. Jagannatha Dasa, *Srimad Bhagavata*, skandha I–XII, Orissa Jagannatha Company, Cuttack, n.d.
31. Yasovanta Dasa, *Govinda Chandra*, Cuttack Printing Company, Cuttack, 1927, p. 56.
32. Achyutananda Dasa, *Harivamsa*, Dharmagrantha Store, Cuttack, 1970.
33. Achyutananda Dasa, *Gopalanka Ogala*, Orissa Jagannatha Company, Cuttack, 1990.

34. Achyutananda Dasa, *Kaivarta Gita*, Radharaman Pustakalaya, Cuttack, 1956.
35. Dibakara Dasa, *Jagannatha-Charitamruta*, Bada Oriya Math, Puri, 1963.
36. Rama Dasa, *Dardhyata Bhakti*, pts I and II, Dharmagrantha Store, Cuttack, n.d.
37. Ishwar Dasa, *Chaitanya Bhagavata*, 1st edn., Utkal University, Bhubaneswar, 1953.
38. Vrindaban Dasa, *Chaitanya Bhagavata*, Utkal University, Bhubaneswar, n.d.
39. Madhav Dasa, *Chaitanya Bhagavata*, A.B. Mohanty (ed), Utkal University, Bhubneswar, 1962.
40. Bhima Dasa, *Bhakti Ratnavali*, pts. I and II, Vishnupuri, Cuttack, 1964.
41. Chaitanya Dasa, *Nirguna Mahatmya,* Prachi Samiti, Bhubaneswar, 1927.
42. N. Mishra (ed.), *Bhaktakavi Salabega* (Oriya), Grantha Mandir, Cuttack, 1979.
43. Jayadeva, *Gitagovinda Mahakavyam,* Orissa Sanskruta Akademi, Bhubaneswar, 1999.
44. Viswanath Kaviraj, *Chandrakala Natika.* S.N. Rajguru and Sarbeswar Das (eds) Orissa State Museum, Bhubaneswar, 1958.
45. Purushottam Dev, *Saraswati Vilas.*
46. Murari Gupta, *Chaitanya Charitamrirta*, Amrita Bazar Patrika Office, Calcutta, 1931.
47. Ramananda Ray, *Jagannatha Vallabha Natakam*, Radharaman Press, Murshidabad, 1921.
48. K. Kaviraj, *Chaitanya Charitamrita,* Cuttack Printing Company, n.d.
49. Vrindavan Dasa, *Chaitanya Bhagavata*, Haridas Seth, Calcutta, 1923.
50. Lochan Das, *Chaitanya Mangal*, Ramanarayan Vidyaratna, Murshidabad, 1913.
51. Jayananda, *Chaitanya Mangal*, Bangiya Sahitya Parishad, Calcutta, 1901.
52. Al-Biruni, *Tarikh-ul-Hind* (tr. Edward C. Sachau), Atlantic Publisher, New Delhi, 1990.
53. Minhaj-ud-din-bin-Siraj-ud-din, *Tabaquat-i-Nasiri* (tr. Major H.G. Raverty), Gilbert & Rivington, London, 1881, pp. 587–92.
54. Shams-i-Shiraj, *Tarikh-i-Firoz Shahi*, Bib. Ind., Calcutta, 1890.
55. Abul Fazl, *Ain-i-Akbari,* vol. I (tr. H. Blochmann), Asiatic Society of Bengal, Calcutta, 1873, pp. 122, 306, 326, 340.

CHAPTER 1

Political and Social Setting

THIS CHAPTER sets a background to our main discussion which bears a close relation with the origin and trends of the radical social movement that took place in Orissa during the period between fifteenth and seventeenth centuries. The torch-bearers of the movement were mainly the *Sudramunis* who launched their protest against the discrimination and deprivation of man on the basis of birth, through their writings of the Puranas and other religious poems in the vernacular. They criticized the evils of contemporary society and emphasized on equality and happiness of all mankind. They tried to arouse mass consciousness almost in opposition to the dominant Sanskritic culture and ruling elements of the time. However, this period was an era of the radical social movement with a profound bearing on religious ideology, growth of language and regional literature and a cultural movement with the development of art, painting, dance, music, and architecture.

The political and social setting of medieval Orissa could be better explained with the background of the processes of social transformations in her early historical period. The process of transition to agriculture and subsequently, the emergence of a stratified state society may be a proper perspective of the discussion. The Kalinga war (261 BC) and the inclusion of Kalinga in the Mauryan empire provide the beginning point for such a discussion, there is not much of source material for the preceding period. However, the process of the extension of agriculture and the peasantization of the natives seem to have made notable progress during the period *c.* AD 350–600.[1] A series of dynasties, issuing land grants, emerged in different principalities of Orissa during the said period.

With the Kalinga war early Orissa emerged to the full view of history. Major Rock Edict XIII and two special edicts, one at Dhauli and the other at Jaugarh provide us a glimpse of the nature of Asokan rule and conditions prevailing in Orissa. The large number of deceased and the captured people of Kalinga war as mentioned in the Rock Edict XIII is more than suggestive of the fact that Kalinga of the third century BC was a well populated geographical entity. The two special edicts elucidate the administrative policy of Asoka in the newly conquered province of Kalinga. It was governed from two headquarters, one at Tosali (Sisupalagarh) and the other at Somapa (Jaugarh). Asoka's effort to provide a civilized administration seems to have been, at best, restricted to the coastal Orissa and the predominant primitive tribal people appear to have been outside the pale of civilization. The reference to *avijita anta* in the Jaugada inscription may suggest that there were some unconquered tribes in or near Kalinga. The *atavikạs* who find mention in Asokan Edicts largely remained untouched. The *atavika* land comprised roughly the present Districts of undivided Koraput and Kalahandi in Orissa and of Bastar of Madhya Pradesh.[2]

The time of the emergence of organized political structure in Orissa can be definitely assumed since the time of Kharavel (second half of the first country BC). The Institution of kingship emerges with Kharavela and the Mahameghavahan rule seems to have synchronized with the intensification of the process in deltaic Orissa that had set into motion during the preceding period. The emergence of the social stratification with the functional hierarchy operating within the socio-economic and political structure. In the Hatigumpha inscription, Kharavela refers to the restorative and rebuilding activities at Kalinganagar, the arrangements for water-supply (irrigation), entertainment of the people with music, dance and festivities, on one occasion, the remission of taxes and endowing the Jain monks and their establishments clearly suggest the transition to a state society with the king as the pivot, who could collect taxes, remit them and make gifts and endowments. Also significant are the terms, e.g. *lekha* (writing), *rupa* (coinage), *ganan* (accountancy), *vyavahar* (law) and *vidhi* (administrative procedure) and titles *mahameghavahan* (Indra) and *aira* (destroyer of the foes) and the references to Brahmins and the consecration ceremony under Kharavela that indicate the increasing adoption of the northern Sanskritic culture.[3]

The kingdoms under Asoka and Kharavela in Orissa were more centralized than the later kingdoms in Orissa and they were also less rooted in and less linked with the local power structure. In Orissa both the empires, therefore, left only a few archaeological traces outside the central area around Bhubaneswar. But both kingdoms seem to have initiated in Orissa a political development on the local and sub-regional level.[4]

The history of early Orissa, i.e. from AD 350 to AD 600 is very much significant from many standpoints. The period witnessed the rise of a number of dynasties and small kingdoms in different pockets of Orissa, with each one of them bestowing land grants on Brahmins and religious establishments. It also brings to focus the rise and growth of private ownership in land and the subordination of the peasantry to the landlords. Royal patronage to Brahmins goes as far back as the fourth century AD during the rule of the Matharas. The Korasondha grant of Vishakha Varman is the earliest such grant found in Orissa.[5] Thereafter, the Brahmin settlements multiplied in Kalinga, Villages were declared as *agraharas* and donated to Brahmins. Land grants to Brahmins and religious establishments,[6] implies large scale agrarian expansion a process which must have had important bearing on the social process and structure.

The inscriptions show that the kings intended to establish Brahmin colonies known as *sasanas*. The Brahmins might not have been pioneering cultivators themselves but surely some of them looked after the management of land and helped in bringing virgin soil under cultivation. They also seem to have ushered in the acculturation process in tribal belts. Here one may cite the Rithapur plates of Bhattavarman where the ideal of protecting cows and Brahmins along with the subjects has been cherished. The ruler desires the prosperity of these three categories (*Swasti Go-brahmana prajabhya siddhirastu*). Here it may be noted that the Suripuram plates of Anantavarman record the gift of a thousand cows. The emphasis on the importance of cattle in the forest tracts of the Nalas should be appreciated in the context of agrarian expansion and the spread of Brahminic culture. The Brahmins patronized Vedic learning and performed the *agnistoma* and other sacrifices. The adoption of Sanskrit as the official language and there the popularization of Dharmasastras, which is borne out by the quotations of verses from Dharmasastras in Mathar records, clearly drive home the role of Brahmins in disseminating the Sanskritic culture.[7]

The migration of Brahmins to Orissa forms an interesting feature in the socio-cultural life of this region. It is observed that Orissa came in contact with the Sanskirtic culture before Kalinga war (261 BC) as we notice the reference to Brahmins in Kalinga in the Rock Edict XIII of Asoka. So it may be presumed that the Brahmins started migrating to Orissa during the fifth or fourth century BC.[8] It is said that in early medieval times the priests were invited by the princes to inhospitable tracts to strengthen their power against hostile populations and generally Brahmins were granted land within not more than hundred miles of their original homes.[9] It also happened in case of early medieval Orissa as its rulers invited Brahmins, particularly, from Ahichhatra[10] (Barely), Kolancha[11] (Banaras), Atidha[12] (Ayodhya), Tirabhukti[13] (Tirhut), Magadh,[14] Kamarupa[15] (Assam),Varendra[16] (north-Bengal), Radha[17] (Burdwan), Madhyadesa,[18] Sravasti,[19] Takari,[20] Apilomuliri,[21] Gangabadi,[22] Madhura,[23] Sravasti,[24] and Taremba.[25] Takari was situated either in Madhyadesa or in Sravasti, where as Madhyadesa and Sravasti have been identified with Uttar Pradesh. The large Brahmin migration as far as epigraphic evidence is concerned took place during the regions of Bhauma King Subhakara[26] and Ganga King Devendravarman.[27] Their numbers were two hundred and three hundred respectively. The Somavamsi King Yayati Keshari invited ten thousand Brahmins from north India to perform ten *asvamedha yajnas* (horse sacrifice) at Jajpur where the stone steps at the Vaitarani river are still called Asvamedha Ghat.[28] This legend contains a historical tradition about systematic settlement of a large group of Brahmins under the Somavamsis which continued till the Ganga and Gajapati Periods.

Orissa provides an excellent example of a continuous and stepwise territorial integration. In its early history, Orissa emerged for a short period as the province of the great empire of the Mauryas in the third century BC and in the late first century BC was the centre of a short-lived empire under King Kharavela. Apart from a few historically isolated archaeological finds in the neighbourhood of Bhubaneswar, we possess little evidence to understand the legacy of these early empires in the early centuries AD. In any case, the process of indigenous state formation began only four centuries after the vanishing of Kharavela's kingdom on the sub-regional level with an obviously different character. The basis of the principalities and small kingdoms of Orissa of the early centuries AD usually were 'nuclear areas' near the heads of the deltas along the coast of Bengal or, further upstream, in the riverine basins. The most significant economic feature of these nuclear areas was irrigated rice cultivation. They were usually separated by mountains with jungles which are still inhabited by the aboriginal tribes.[29]

As far as our historical knowledge goes, these 'nuclear areas' were under small Hindu *rajas* who ruled their territory with the help of newly settled Brahmins according to the Hindu *sastras*. The early inscription of these *rajas* make it clear that most of them originated from one of the tribes which surrounded these nuclear areas. For example, the Banai plate refers to Vinita Tunga, a Tunga ruler as *Ashtadash Gondmahadhipati*, i.e. the lord of the eighteen tribes known as Gonds.[30] Again the charter of the Sulki ruler Kulastambhadeva addresses him as *Sakal Gond Mahadhinath,* i.e. the lord of all Gonds.[31] These two terms mentioned in these grants suggest the existence of Gond as important political force during this period. In the seventh century AD, a line of rulers of Hinduized Sabar origin established its rule in south Kosal with Sirpur (in the District of Raipur) as the capital. Raja Tivaradev of this line was very powerful in the eighth century AD.[32] Similarly the Sailodbhavas (late sixth century-early eighth century) and the Bhaumakaras (eighth-tenth centuries) also flourished as important rulers had tribal origins. However, security and legitimation of Hindu rule under these circumstances depended largely on the loyalty of these tribes which was enhanced through the acknowledgement of one of the tribal deities as tutelary deity by the new *raja* families. Examples are the God Gokarneswar, who was worshipped on the Mahendragiri mountain as the tutelary deity by the Gangas of Kalinganagar and Stambheswari, the 'Lady of the Pillar' who was acknowledged both by the Sulki kings (a dynasty of the ancient Saulika tribe) and the Bhanjas of central Orissa.

The early history of these nuclear areas and their rulers is largely unknown. But in the middle of the fourth century AD, Samudragupta during his conquest of the Dakshinapath (southern region) defeated three chiefs of western Orissa (Dakshina Kosal) and on his march further south four chiefs or small *rajas* on the coast between the Mahendragiri and the Godavari rivers. Though we do not know much more than their names and their location, Samudragupta's famous Allahabad pillar inscription shows that at least in those portions of Orissa which he had passed through there existed many small principalities in the middle of the fourth century AD. However, it is mainly after the downfall of the Gupta empire in the early sixth century that the development of the nuclear areas of Orissa are available in the indigenous epigraphic sources. We know about four such nuclear areas on the Orissan coast, there in the valleys of the various rivers flowing into the Bay of Bengal and one on the upper plains or the high lands of Orissa. During the second half of the first millennium AD the following 'nuclear areas' developed from south-west to northern on the coast of Orissa:

(i) *Kalinga*, located in the delta area of the Nagavali and Vamshadhara river in the Srikakulam District of northern Andhra Pradesh. Though outside Orissa proper, Kalinga was of great importance for the further development of Orissa after it had become the nuclear area of the eastern Gangas at the end of the fifth century AD. Their capital Kalinga Nagar was situated on the bank of the river with the significant name 'bearer of the dynasty' (*vamsa-dhara*).

(ii) *Kangoda Mandal*, situated on the western coast of the Chilika lake and in the lower valley of the Rishikulya river is identical with present-day undivided Ganjam District. It was the homeland of the Sailodbhava dynasty since the late fifth or early sixth century AD and was elaborately described by the Chinese pilgrim Huen-t-sang in the early seventh century.

(iii) *Dakshina Tosali* (Utkal), in the southern Mahanadi delta had been the centre of the Mauryan province of Kalinga with its capital at Tosali (or Dhauli) near Bhubaneswar and also of Kharavela's empire with its capital at Kalinganagar, near Bhubaneswar. Though for a short period in the late sixth century AD small dynasties tried to establish themselves here (e.g. the Vigrahas), Dakshina Tosali remained for centuries the bone of contention between neighbouring dynasties. The Mahanadi delta as a whole was too large to be ruled and defended by the early small medieval kingdoms.

(iv) *Uttar Tosali* (Odra), situated in the northern delta area of the Mahanadi and in the Brahmani delta is identical with the modern undivided Cuttack and Balasore Districts. Its chronological and territorial demarcations against Odra and Utkal which later came to be known in this area are still disputed. After short-lived dynasties in the late sixth and early seventh centuries (Manas and Dattas) the most important dynasty which came up in the region was the Bhaumakaras since the late seventh century.

In the valleys of the rivers Mahanadi and Brahmani three important nuclear areas were situated.

(v) *Dakshina Kosal* comprised in its Orissan part mainly the fertile plain of the Mahanadi valley, the region between the present Hirakud reservoir and Sonepur, and included the Tel valley south of Sonepur. Since the early sixth century, parts of Dakshina Kosal, together with some of its neighbouring tracts, were ruled in succession by the Sarabhapuriyas, Panduvamsis and the Somavamsis. The latter became most important for the whole of Orissa when they conquered coastal Orissa.

(vi) *Khinjali Mandal* lying between Dakshina Kosal and coastal Tosali in the less prosperous Baudha valley region of the Mahanadi. It was ruled by a Bhanja dynasty in the eighth and ninth centuries.

(vii) *Kodalaka Mandal* in the lower Brahmani valley is the present Dhenkanal District formed the home of Sulki dynasty (eighth-ninth centuries).

In the high lands of Orissa we know of several smaller nuclear areas of early principalities. Most important among them was :

(viii) *Khijjingakotta* in the present-day Mayurbhanj District of north Orissa with Khijjing as its capital, famous for its temples was ruled by another Bhanja dynasty since the eighth century. To the west of Khijjing in the surrounding of the later feudatory state of Keonjhar, epigraphic findings (*Sitabhinji* and *Asanepat*) prove that this whole area was under the control of some otherwise unknown Bhanja kings as early as the fourth-sixth centuries AD.[34]

The history of mediaeval Orissa from the sixth to the sixteenth century is characterized by a stepwise yet continuous process of territorial integration of these nuclear areas. During the fifth and sixth centuries none of the rulers of these areas was able to extend his power permanently into a neighbouring nuclear area. In all cases, their power was still confined to their own homeland. Obviously the socio-economic development of these nuclear areas had not yet reached a stage which permitted a considerable extension of their political power. It was only in the seventh century after Orissa had been drawn temporarily into the great north Indian power struggle between Harsha, Sasanka and Pulakesin II, that the Sailodbhavas of Kangoda were able to extend their power into Dakshina Tosali or today's Puri District. The next step towards territorial integration took place under the Bhaumakaras of Uttar Tosali in the eighth century. They extended their sway from their capital Jajpur over the whole coastal region of present-day Orissa including the northern parts of Uttar Tosali, Dakshina Tosali and Kangoda in the south. Furthermore several rulers of smaller nuclear areas in the hinterland acknowledged their sovereignty (e.g. the Sulkis of Kodalak Mandal and the Bhanjas of Khinjali Mandal). The main achievement of the Bhaumakaras, however, was the permanent unification of three nuclear areas (i.e. Uttar and Dakshina Tosali and Kangoda) under one rule.

The next step of territorial integration took place in the tenth century AD. When the Somavamsis of Dakshina Kosal conquered Khinjali Mandal and coastal Orissa and unified them for the first time with their homeland in western Orissa. Thus they ruled over the three riverine nuclear areas (Dakshina Kosal, Khinjali and Kodalaka Mandal) and the three coastal areas (Uttar and Dakshina Tosali and Kangoda). However, their kingdom fell apart in the eleventh century when a branch again began to rule independently over its western parts.

In *c.* AD 1112, King Anantavarman Chodaganga, one of the Eastern Gangas of Kalinganagar in Kalinga, conquered central Orissa and extended his rule in the following decades from modern Midnapur District in West Bengal up to the northern bank of the Godavari in Andhra Pradesh. His career marked the beginning of the great regional kingdom of Orissa under the Gangas (AD 1112–1434) and the Suryavamsis (AD 1435–1568). Under their rule the four major coastal nuclear areas, i.e. Uttar and Dakshina Tosali, Kangoda and Kalinga were permanently integrated. Their sway over the peripheral coastal areas of *Dandabhukti* (Midnapur) and south Kalinga (Vizagapatnam) was also unchallenged. The lower riverine nuclear areas of the Mahanadi and Brahmani rivers were also ruled directly, whereas Khinjali Mandal and particularly Dakshina Kosal in the upper Mahanadi valley were only temporarily conquered.

In AD 1435 Kapilendra, an army officer and son of a local chieftain (*Nayaka*), usurped the throne and established the Suryavamsa dynasty. He became the most powerful king of his time in the whole of India under him and his two successors the Orissan empire extended from the Ganges down to the Krishna and temporarily even to the Kaveri in the far south.

However, the wonderful feature of the political phenomenon at the beginning of the Suryavamsi dynasty was Kapilendra's success in his usurpation of the throne. All the previous dynastic changes had taken place after a successful military conquest, led by an already established king who was in full command of the means of his own dynasty. Each conqueror from the Sailodbhavas to Chodaganga emerged by uniting his own homeland with the conquered areas and thus carrying on the stepwise process of territorial integration. Kapilendra on the other hand seized power without domestic troops of his own and was able to keep it against a strong opposition of members and followers of the overthrown dynasty. And what is most surprising against all expectations is that the Orissan kingdom did not disintegrate into the previous nuclear areas. Thus, the process of political integration came to be complete under Kapilendra Dev with a modified development of administrative system.[35]

The territorial integration was supplemented and supported by *cultural integration,* which operated mainly through religion and language. Regional traditions became the backbone of this cultural integration and communication. The integration of local traditions into regional tradition meant that local loyalty become supplemented by a regional loyalty.

The core of this regional tradition was the cult of Jagannatha who was acknowledged by the kings of Orissa since the thirteenth century as their overlord (*samraja*). The cult of Jagannatha became a part of the royal policy and legitimation which operated and integrated on several levels. We may briefly discuss :

In large parts of Orissa we can trace at least four 'levels' of divinity. The 'imperial' level is represented by Jagannatha, the 'Lord of the World'. The cult of Jagannatha itself integrates various aspects of Hinduism prevalent in Orissa, i.e. Vaisnavism, Saivism, Saktism and tribal or village cults, and to some extent even aspects of Buddhism.

The 'regional level' of Orissa finds its expression in the concept of the 'Five Deities' (*Panchadevatas*) which integrates the most important cults of Orissa, i.e. Siva-Lingaraja of Bhubaneswar, Durga-Viraja of Jajpur, Vishnu-Jagannatha of Puri, Surya of Konark and Ganesh-Mahavinayak at a place of the same name in north Orissa. Three of the *Panchadevatas* had very distinct association with the ruling dynasties of Orissa: Viraja and Lingaraja were the tutelary deities of the Bhaumakaras and Somavamsis respectively, and Jagannatha of the Ganga dynasty. Surya was included because of the monumental sun temple of Konark, built in about AD 1250. Ganesh is worshipped as Mahavinayak in a flat unhewn stone in the sanctorum of a classical temple and represents the dominant tribal aspect of Orissa's religion among the *Panchadevatas*.[36]

On the third 'sub-regional' level we find a group of very powerful indigenous goddesses, many of whom have been the tutelary deities of the former feudatory states of Orissa. Most of them are still worshipped in aniconic idols which bear witness to their pre-Brahminic origin. The most important among them form a group of the 'Eight Mothers' (*astamatrika*). The link between these 'Mothers' and the state deity is described symbolically through the picture of a great tent, Jagannatha being the tent pole, and the Eight Mothers representing the tent's pegs. The *astamatrikas* or eight Mother Goddesses have been identified to be Carccika in Banki, Sarala in Jhankada, Viraja in Jajpur, Hingula near Talcher, Samalai in Sambalpur, Vimala in Puri, Bhagavati in Banapur and Mangala in Kakatpur.[37]

Below these 'sub-regional' deities we find on the local level the village goddess (*gramadevatas*). Clusters of local village deities are often associated with the nearby sub-regional deities, though their relations are less codified than the inter-relations of the sub-regional and regional deities.

Apart from their horizontal integration these four levels are linked vertically too, inasmuch as Jagannatha as state deity is also a member of the 'Five Deities' and 'Viraja-Durga' at Jajpur, who belongs to the same regional group, figures also prominently among the sub-regional 'Eight-Mothers'. All these gods and goddesses of Orissa are furthermore interlinked in a very elaborate system of ritual relations which finds its expression in a very dense network of pilgrimage as a major factor of the cultural integration of various nuclear areas of Orissa into a cultural unity.

The legitimization of the political unification or territorial integration of the nuclear areas was accomplished by the process of Hinduization or Kshatriyaization of the tribal culture in early Orissa. The riverine nuclear areas were usually under the rule of chiefs or *rajas*, who were either independent or only temporarily and nominally subjugated by foreign rulers. These little *rajas* claimed to organize their rule according to Hindu law books (*sastras*). Somadatta, who ruled in northern Orissa (Utkal and Dandabhukti) during the first quarter of the seventh century under the suzerainty of Sasanka of Bengal, mentioned in his Midnapur inscription that he followed the *Manusastra*.[38] These centres of the nuclear areas were encircled by a number of tax-free *agrahara* villages which had been donated by the *rajas* to Brahmins who formed the elite of the administrative and ritual functionaries. These Brahmins of the court-circle together with those Brahmins who had been settled in the outer areas certainly had a deep influence of (Hindu) law and (*royal*) order. It was mainly due to their influence that these nuclear areas were gradually integrated into the all-India sphere of Sanskrit learning and hitherto unknown temple architecture, both indispensable paraphernalia of future Hindu kingship. The most significant economic feature of these fertile riverine nuclear areas was peasant agriculture based on irrigated rice cultivation.[39]

The association of the 'state' with 'religion' in Orissa may be traced back to the times of Kharavela. In the second half of the fourth century AD this association became more intense and widespread. This process of political development of certain nuclear areas began in the fifth century when donations of whole villages to Brahmins became more and more frequent. It was certainly fully developed in the late sixth century. The inscriptions bear evidence of a steadily increasing number of these principalities and small sub-regional kingdoms. Under Matharas, Kalinga became a centre of Vedic sacrifice. The Matharas patronized Vedic scarifices and Bhagavata religion to gain legitimacy in the newly emerging socio-religious pattern.[40] In central Kalinga (of the Ganjam District) there existed clearly thirty-six Brahmin-villages during the fifth century.[41] Other indications for the extension of this process in eastern India were land-donations not only to individual Brahmins, but also to temples and monastic institutions,[42] and the first construction of Hindu stone temples.[43]

During this gradual development Brahmins played an important role. They defined and codified the duties of the tribes, as the *Mahabharata* nicely put it 'reside in the domination of the (Aryan) Kings'. According to the *Mahabharata* they should lead the life of a 'recluse living in the forest . . . and serve their king . . . dig wells and give water to thirsty travellers, give away beds and make other reasonable presents upon Brahmins'.[44] It was the task of those Brahmins to whom villages in remote areas had been donated to propagate this ideal for their own and for their king's sake. The grantee in this way brought new knowledge which improved cultivation and inculcated in the aborigines a sense of loyalty to the established order upheld by the rulers.[45]

Whereas usually this indoctrination sustained an unstable pacification of the tribes in the outer areas, it caused their partial integration in those more central areas which were already penetrated by pockets of Hindu peasants. This partial integration was achieved through their gradual inclusion into the lower strata of the caste system, paradoxically usually as 'outcastes' and/or through their inclusion into the militia of the Hindu court. This process has been characterized as Kshatriyaization—a social change 'from above' which was initiated in tribal areas by the Kshatriyas, i.e. zamindars, chiefs or *rajas,* to strengthen their claim to legitimacy in the society and to broaden the base of their economic and political power.[46]

The process of 'Hinduization and integration' was the mutual need of the time. This, in fact, developed out of interdependency between the Hinduized *rajas* and the tribal population of ancient Orissa. Both ways of partial integration (inclusion in the caste system and into the militia) deeply influenced Hinduism and the means of legitimization of Hindu royal power in these partly Hinduized areas. The inclusion of the tribal groups into the Hindu caste system initiated, on the village level, a *process of Hinduization of their deities.* The assignment of military duties to tribal or semi-tribal groups, often led to royal patronage of the dominant autochthonous deities of the respective area.[47]

The main reason for this royal patronage was that even a fairly Hinduized court, in tribal or partly Hinduized surroundings, was highly dependent on military and economic support and political loyalty of the tribes. Royal patronage of autochthonous deities seems to have been an essential presupposition for the consolidation of political power and its legitimization in the Hindu-tribal zone of Orissa whether the Hinduized chiefs or Hindu *rajas* had ascended from the local tribes or whether they had entered the respective areas as roaming freebooters, most of them accepted the dominant autochthonous deities of their territories as family and tutelary deities of their principalities. For example, Goddess Mani Nageswari (Lady of the jewel serpant) of Ranapur, Siva-Gokarnaswamin of Mahendragiri (deity of Sauras accepted by the Gangas), Stambheswari (Lady of the Pillar) in south of Sonepur and in various parts of Orissa and Goddess Bhattarika of Baramba were the family and tutelary deities of different royal dynasties of those respective principalities, to mention a few.[48]

The politically and economically highly developed nuclear areas yielded sufficient surplus crop for the establishment and the maintenance of a sub-regional power and its gradual extension into the tribal border areas. Looting expeditions against neighbouring peoples often led to a temporary conquest of the adjoining nuclear areas. But the rise of a sub-regional principality to a regional kingdom, comprising several nuclear areas and its lasting establishment presupposed a permanent participation in the agrarian surplus of the conquered nuclear areas. Often enough the defeated *rajas* became the feudatory *rajas* (*samantas*) of the conqueror.[49]

The history of the Hindu places of Pilgrimage (*tirtha*) is inextricably linked with the *bhakti* faith. In its origin, in older times, the ideal of salvation through intense devotion (*bhakti*) to a personal deity became a powerful religious movement in south India from the late sixth century onwards. It was mainly through this Bhakti movement that forms of orthodox Brahminic Hinduism in a continuous process of two-way communication came down to the villages. The folk devotionalism of the rural centres also travelled to royal headquarters (capital) and urban centres truly to be accepted by the High Hinduism of the elitist order. Various autochthonous deities in a long and gradual process of Hinduization were included into the pantheon of *bhakti* Hinduism.[50] *Bhakti* also turned out to be the true religion of the peasant society within the highly developed nuclear areas. The *Bhakti* religion with its emphasis on personal faith and self-sacrifice became the best religion to hold this type of society and its state together.[51]

The fact that Hinduization was particularly frequent and intense in medieval times has two main reasons: first, the rising *Bhakti* cults brought a new religious impetus which, emphasizing the omnipresence of the divine, was universalistic in its outlook. Secondly, its new institutions, the temples, became agents of Hinduization and received royal patronage. The Jagannatha temple of Puri is a striking example of such a development. It is one of the most important temples of India, patronized by many kings enshrining a deity of tribal origin. The fame of the temple within the Hindu world has grown considerably since medieval times, and the peculiar iconography of its main images still testify to the important role which Hinduization must have played in the formation of the Jagannatha cult.[52]

The legend of the Puri temple, the Indradyumna legend, is that the deity was originally worshipped by the aboriginal Sabar chief Viswavasu in the woods, and only later on miraculously appeared in Puri. The tribal origin of the figures is emphasized by the existence of a special group of priests, the *Daitas,* who are considered to be the descendants of the original tribal worshippers. As the *Badus* in the Lingaraj temple of Bhubaneswar, the *Daitas* are specially entrusted with those services implying a close contact with the figures for instance, bathing, dressing or moving them. Tradition and the present practice clearly indicate the tribal origin. The peculiar shape of the Jagannatha figure, as has been shown, not because such figures are typical of tribal religion, but because such figures are typical products of the process of Hinduization.[53]

A survey of Narasimha in the Jagannatha cult showed that both Narasimha and Jagannatha are intimately linked and were identified at an early stage. Even today a Jagannatha figure is found to be worshipped as Narasimha. From the important role which Narasimha plays within Hinduization in eastern India and his special relationship to tribal deities represented by wooden posts, it could be concluded that the Jagannatha figure was the result of the process of Hinduization, where a tribal deity represented by a wooden post was identified with Narasimha.[54]

Most of these tribal cults in Orissa, which were important enough to be Hinduized, were related to a female deity, who protected the men, ascertained the fertility and accepted blood sacrifice. Such a connection between a tribal goddess and Durga may start on a purely tribal level. The Van Durga (Durga of the Woods) of many Khond villages of Orissa, who is also identified with Durga or Kali, in her main aspect, may herself be associated with that group of goddesses who like Mangala, Pitabali, Hingula and Stambheswari play an important role within the folk religion and regional traditions of Orissa. Most of these are none but aboriginal deities who were Hinduized in earlier times. Though not appearing in Brahminical all Indian theology they were acknowledged as members of the documented theology of the society in whose contact the tribes lived.

These goddesses are widely worshipped at different levels all over Orissa. Pitabali is found in multi-caste villages, as also in almost entirely tribal villages in the Khond *mahals*. Mangala is worshipped almost in every village every Tuesday on the open road, if there is no shrine for her. She has an important temple in Kakatpur which also plays a role in the Jagannatha cult. Hingula is also widely worshipped in the villages, especially in the scorching summer (April/May) when fires are setup and also fire-walking is performed in her honour so that she may be satisfied and not cause the outbreak of fires during the hot season. She has an important shrine in Gopalprasad near Talcher. Bauthi is worshipped, particularly in the villages of Sonepur region. The Goddess Stambheswari, or Oriya Khambeswari (Lady of the pillar) is known in Orissa since about AD 500. She was the tutelary deity of the Sulki and the Bhanja dynasties and is still widely worshipped in western Orissa. Iconographically the Stambheswari cult is linked with wooden posts. But not everywhere. The goddess may also be worshipped in the form of stones. In the shrine at Bamur, in the Angul area, Khambeswari is represented by a simple stone worshipped daily by the *dehuris* of the Suddha caste, a caste of tribal affiliation.[55]

At the 'Village level', a deity of tribal origin may be worshipped as—or be associated with the worship of the village goddess *gramapati* or *gramadevi*. Her cult is of 'tribal' typology : the goddess is represented by a uniconical symbol, who often can hardly be distinguished from its surroundings and is only occasionally worshipped with animal sacrifices by a non-Brahmin priest.[56]

The legend has similarities with the Tara Tarini legend: the goddess appears in a low-caste family, disappears suddenly by making an order to be worshipped by a low-caste or tribal people on the spot. The phenomenon of the body of the deity cut into pieces suggests the idea of human sacrifice or at least Tantrik practices. In its present form, the legend does not account for the peculiar nature of the image, but only for the affiliation of those, who are not Brahmins and call themselves *Sudramunis*. They worship the goddess according to a formula adopted to a Vana Durga, and offer her non-vegeterian *bhoga* cooked by them. On the occasion of Dasahara goats are sacrificed and the *bhoga* cooked by these 'Sudra' priests is taken by all castes.

The most important example is found in the Khambeswari temple in Aska, Ganjam District of Orissa. The legend of the temple is very similar to the second legend of the Tara Tarini temple. As told by the priest Ramachandra Muni, once upon a time a Risi Khambamuni used to live there in the forest. The goddess Khambeswari appeared to him in a dream and expressed the desire to be worshipped by him.[57] These traditions suggest that the tribal priests came to be regarded as *munis* previously, but when they were considered to be Sudras in the process of Hinduization, they were called *Sudramunis*.

Now, the Saiva typology of Hinduization may be taken into consideration. The most famous *Swayambhulinga* worshipped in

Orissa is the Lingaraja in Bhubaneswar, whose temple was built in the eleventh century.[58] The temple has two classes of priests. The Brahmins and a class called Badus, who are ranked as Sudras and said to be of tribal origin. Nevertheless, they are not only priests in this important temple; their duties bring them in the most intimate contact with the deity whose personal attendant they are. Only Badus are allowed to bathe the Lingaraja and to adorn him and at the time of festivals when the god, represented by his *chalanti pratima* leaves the temple only the Badus may carry this movable image. Without them, it is said the 'God cannot move a step'. The Badus are, of course, not allowed any contact with the *bhoga*—indeed they have to leave the *garbhagriha* when it is offered to the god by a special class of the Brahmin attendant.[59]

The temple legend, given in the Sanskrit *Ekamra Purana*, a text probably composed in the fourteenth century and written texts like the *Svarnadri Mahodaya* and the *Ekamra Chandrika* corroborate and explain the tribal origin of the cult. They indicate that the deity was originally under a mango tree, hence the name Ekamra and it was not seen as *linga* in the first two ages, *Satya* and *Treta*. In the *Dwapar* and *Kali* ages it revealed itself as *linga* but had no temple. The Badus are described by the legend as tribals (*sabaras*) who originally inhabited the place and worshipped the *linga* under the tree.[60]

In the present context, two results of the brief survey of the Saiva typology of Hinduization are relevant. First, the cult of Bhubaneswar which competed with Puri for regional dominance is a Hinduized cult. Secondly, it could be shown that the Saiva typology of Hinduization in Orissa is mostly a secondary development, connected with the uniconical *murti* of the *Swayambhulinga*.[61]

The political process of early medieval India has been identified within the framework of the interdependence between the 'temporal power' and 'sacred domains'. To point out the relationship between these two domains, if temporal power needed 'legitimization' from 'spiritual' authority, so did human agents of spiritual authority required sustenance from temporal power.[62] The case of early medieval Orissa is quite synonymous with this idea whereas the legitimization of political power was determined through the collaboration of the kings and priests. The concept of *bhakti* also played a remarkable role as an instrument of integration. *Bhakti* paved the path to the political legitimization in two ways, for example: (a) introduction of the divine theory of kingship and (b) the overlord-feudatory relationship between the 'sacred-domains' and the 'temporal power'. Of course, the Matharas declared themselves *maharajas* and claimed the title of 'Lord of Kalinga', but in contrast to them, the Nalas professed the theory of divine origin of kingship. Kings like Arthapati frequently bore the epithet 'Bhattarpe' signifying the sense of divinity. The Gangas related themselves to their deity in an overlord-feudatory relationship.[63] This process is illustrated by the stages through which the cult of Jagannatha emerged as the central cult in Orissa and the ritual surrender of temporal power to the divinity by King Anangabhima Dev. The centrality of the cult in relation to others in this process implied the centrality of its agents as well.[64] Through the process of the interdependence between 'temporal power' and 'spiritual domain' not only the political power of those kings was legitimized, but also Lord Jagannatha was Hinduized and the Brahminic hegemony was enhanced by the cult of Jagannatha.

The famous Puri deity was identified with the Brahminic deity 'Vishnu-Purushottam' and 'Vishnu-Jagannatha' sometime in the late eleventh century. But the mode of worship of this Purushottam Jagannatha was not yet completely Brahminized and the non-Brahmin priests were not adept at Brahminic rites.[65] It is corroborated by the fact that even at the present time one comes across the non-Brahmin priests, called *Daita* and *Sudha* as well as the non-Brahminic traits in the services of Lord Jagannatha.

The patronage of the Gangas took the shape of (a) making land grants and other gifts to Lord Jagannatha,[66] (b) construction of the temples of Jagannatha at the different places of the empire,[67] (c) accepting Vaishnavism as their personal faith,[68] and (d) accepting Lord Jagannatha as the sovereign of the empire which was the climax of the trend.[69]

The position of the non-Brahmin priests declined since the popularity of Lord Jagannatha spread outside of the Ganga empire. Pilgrims from all over India started visiting Puri and they expected a Brahminical shrine, i.e. a Brahminic deity worshipped by the Brahmin priests in accordance with the Brahminical mode of worship. To satisfy the feelings of these pilgrims and to make Lord Jagannatha a great deity of the Hindu dharma, it became imperative to strengthen the Brahminical elements in the cult. This Brahminic acceptance of Lord Jagannatha presupposed Brahminization of the shrine which must have taken place between the tenth and fourteenth centuries AD.[70] It was not that the process of Brahminization of the deity went on without protest. Ramanuja faced a vehement protest from the non-Brahmin priests because of his attempt to introduce the Brahminic mode of worship at the shrine. In spite of the possible support of the monarch, Ramanuja had to abandon his attempt and flee during the night.[71] Whatever may be the opposition the Brahminization of the shrine was inevitable in course of time.

The Brahminic version of the Indradyumna legend as found in different Sanskrit Puranas written between AD 1312 and 1370 suggests again that the process of Brahminization, with its corollary appointment of the Brahmin priests started prior to that date. This is corroborated by the account of Anangabhima-III (*c.* AD 1216–39) as has been recorded in the *Madalapanji*.[72]

The non-Brahmin priests neither could resist the appointment of the Brahmin priests for the fear of losing all India acceptance of their cult and consequently their position and power, nor could they welcome the Brahmin priests with outstretched hands (as it spelled the increasing dominance of the Brahmin priests in the affairs of the cult, hence their doom). They were prepared to make the best of the situation and had to recognize unwillingly the priestly status of the Brahmin priests in the cult of Jagannatha. The whole picture now underwent a transformation and the position of the king became lower at least theoretically in comparison to the elevated position of the priests who assumed the role of spokesmen for Lord Jagannatha.[73]

It is very significant that the Gangas who were Saivas for centuries had switched over to Vaishnavism sometime after the conquest of Orissa proper by Chodaganga Dev in their zeal to patronize the cult of Jagannatha. But it seems the later Gangas were not prepared any more to accept the overlordship of Lord Jagannatha and to rule as his deputy, as is evident from Narasingh Dev's (IV) return back to the Saiva fold. There were, it seems, reactions to the influential position of the priests of the Jagannatha temple. It appears also that the later Gangas tried to control the temple or mode of administration as a counter-measure to priestly influence and power. But it was too late and the priests were not willing to part with their power and position, their influence and freedom of action. They were not prepared to allow the king to control the priests among whom the non-Brahmin priests must have been quite dominant, to meddle with the administration of the temple. Their reaction was very sharp.[74]

In *Sarala Mahabharata* we find the non-Brahminic version of the Indradyumna legend in contrast to the Brahminic version of the same found in some other Sanskrit Puranic texts.[75] It appears that in this non-Brahminic version of the Indradyumna legend written by Sudramuni Sarala Dasa, the non-Brahmin and Brahmin priests of Lord Jagannatha have been represented by Sabara Jara and Brahmin Vasu.[76]

As the legend goes, when the *daru* (a log on which Jagannatha's image to be carved out) was lifted, the Sabara could lift it easily while the Brahmin could lift it with difficulty. This suggests that the log lifting capability was the measuring rod to determine a group's proximity to Lord Jagannatha and its position in the cult hierarchy. Therefore it was believed that the non-Brahmin priests are nearest to Lord Jagannatha and hence have the highest position in the hierarchy. In contrast, the Brahmin priests have occupied the middle position, and the lowest position has been assigned to the king of Orissa.[77]

There is also another evidence to show the superiority of the non-Brahmin priests to the king of Orissa. According to Sarala Dasa the Sabaras were the first and original worshippers of Lord Jagannatha. King Galaba of Orissa, under the suspicion that the Sabaras had concealed the deity Neela Madhava, killed many Sabaras. In consequence, the Lord equating the Sabaras with his sons cursed that the line (*vamsa*) of Galaba will be completely extinct despite the fact that he was a devotee.[78] This is a significant point. Furthermore, it may be correctly presumed that King Galaba faced defeat at the hands of Sabara Jara. The Lord himself reunited both of them which symbolized the assimilation of the Aryan and non-Aryan cultures in the land of Orissa. From the narration the Jara's descendants have been claiming a status superior to that of the king.[79]

From the description of Sarala Dasa it would be clear that the struggle for power between the non-Brahmin and Brahmin priests and the king was conspicuous. Struggle for power would come to an end if and when the king surrendered to the priests and accepted their superiority in the cult hierarchy demanded the non-Brahmin priests. This practice is being carried out from generation to generation. Now all rituals are of course symbolic of the past culture.

The Jagannatha cult in a unique way fulfilled the essential functions for a mighty state cult of a regional Hindu empire. These were: (i) the vertical, (ii) the horizontal legitimation, and (iii) the ability to unite the various sub-regional nuclear areas of the multi-centred Orissan empire through a regional loyalty.

Another important function of a state cult of a medieval Hindu empire was to cope with the centrifugal feudal forces through the three 'ritual counter-measures', i.e royal patronage of (i) pilgrimage places (*tirthas*), (ii) of Brahmins, and (iii) through the cult of new imperial temples. The Jagannatha cult was more appropriate for this type of ritual policy. The lasting success of Chodaganga's and Anangabhima's deed most probably was based on the fact that, contrary to the ritual policy of the Colas, no new, purely Brahminic cult was chosen for the new state cult. Instead, Chodaganga and Anangabhima chose an autochthonous cult whose *kshetra* since the tenth century had already become a centre of pilgrimage of inter-regional fame. Through the construction of the new imperial Jagannatha temple in Puri and the dedication of the empire to its deity the economic means invested in an important place of pilgrimage were directly utilized for the formation of a state cult. Large scale settlement of Brahmins in Jagannatha's *kshetra* and its hinterland and land donation all over the empire enhanced the wealth and greatness of the *tirtha* which attracted more and more pilgrims from Orissa and all over India. The new centralized ritual structure of the state cult at Puri was thus combined with the network of Jagannatha's pilgrims and the traditional channels of ideological transmission.[80]

The king-Brahmin alliance reached a climax during the rule of the Gajapatis. Since the Brahmins (Priests) were the custodians of Lord Jagannatha and they monopolized over the 'spiritual domain' and the kings derived their legitimacy with the help of priests, the interdependency or so to say an alliance developed between them. This alliance has been explained by following different traditions still prevalent in Orissa. According to popular tradition, the last of the Ganga kings, Bhanudev IV being issueless was very much worried as regards the question of his political heir. One day he prayed to Lord Jagannatha to let him know who would succeed him to the throne of Orissa. Then Lord Jagannatha told him in a dream that the beggar boy he would observe in front of the Vimala temple in the premise of the Jagannatha temple the following day was his choice to succeed him to Orissan throne. Accordingly, when the king went there the next day he found a beggar boy named Kapila Rauta, who first was a cowherd, then a thief and finally had become a beggar in Puri at the appointed place. He took Kapila Rauta alias Kapilendra to his palace with him and adopted him as his son who became the king of Orissa in due course.[81]

But according to *Gangavamsanucharita* by an eighteenth-century poet Vasudeva Rath, Kapilendra, the founder of the Suryavamsa usurped the throne.[82] *Bhakti Bhagavata* by Jayadeva written in the sixteenth century AD during the reign of Prataprudra, grandson of Kapilendra, more or less supports this theory when it says Kapilendra ascended the throne with the support of the nobility of the lord and founded the Suryavamsa.[83] Had Kapilendra been the adopted son of Bhanudev IV there was no necessity of taking the help of nobility to ascend the throne and he could have continued the line of Gangavamsa instead of founding a new dynasty namely, Suryavamsa. So he was not an adopted son of the last Ganga king Bhanudev IV as the *Rajbhoga* section of the *Madalapanji* seeks to establish. Thus it appears there is truth in the remark of *Gangavamsanucharita* that Kapilendra usurped the throne. It may further be articulated that Kapilendra's father Jageswar was a *nayaka*[84] and with every possibility Kapilendra himself being a *nayaka*, was also one of the commanders of the Ganga army.

So it may be believed that the legendary tradition recorded in *Rajabhoga* section of the *Madalapanji* has been deliberately created in which Kapilendra's usurpation of the throne has been ignored and his early career has purposefully been painted black. It may be argued that this tradition was created when *Rajabhoga* was compiled for the first time, i.e. in late sixteenth century AD or thereabout. Persons without any claim to the throne becoming king through the grace of a deity is a well-known and popular motif and it is extremely unlikely that the priest-compilers of *Rajabhoga* used this very motif simultaneously in three different cases while narrating how Chodaganga, Kapilendra and Purushottam became kings unless these legendary traditions were already prevalent. It seems then that these traditions were created at different times, most probably during the reign of Chodaganga, Kapilendra, and Purushottam respectively, in order to legitimize the accession of these monarchs.[85]

We may now look at the price Kapilendra had to pay for the support provided to him by the priests and how it enhanced their power and prestige. We know that early imperial Gangas dedicated their empire in favour of Purusottam-Jagannatha and accepted his overlordship which was immensely beneficial to the priests. But it is remarkable how the last imperial Gangas changed their policy and did not acknowledge the overlordship of Lord Jagannatha and how they even tried to interfere in the affairs of the Jagannatha cult. These policies of last Ganga rulers were very much disliked by the priests and they were in search of an opportunity to turn the situation in their favour. Kapilendra Dev appeared at this end and in contrast to the policy of those last Ganga kings, he rededicated the Orissan empire in favour of Lord Jagannatha, accepted the *sevaka* status in the hierarchy of the cult and lavishly patronized the Brahmins.[86]

Afterwards the priests also intervened again successfully in the selection of the successor to the throne of Kapilendra Dev. According to legendary traditions, Kapilendra Dev had eighteen legitimate sons and one illegitimate son named Purusottam who was not the rightful heir to the throne. But Purusottam succeeded to the throne and could protect it against the challenges of the other sons of Kapilendra Dev only because according to these traditions, Lord Jagannatha wanted it to be so and overruled the claims of the other sons of Kapilendra Dev.[87]

As we have already discussed the tradition and the situation concerning the accession of Kapilendra Dev and Purusottam Dev and it is ascertained from different sources that the priests created the tradition primarily to acquire more power and prestige for them and secondarily to legitimize the accession of those kings. It appears that Purusottam had to accept a relatively lower position than that of the priests in the cult hierarchy in return for their support for his accession and it seems he had to agree to the institution of *chherapahanra*, the ceremonial sweeping of the car of the three deities during the car festival. This ritual duty was assigned to him as a *sevaka* (servant) of Lord Jagannatha which clearly indicated his inferior position in the cult hierarchy. Since a sweeper *sevaka* was considered to belong to the lowest category.[88] This apparently was the price Purusottam had to pay in return for the support he got from the priests.

Although King Purusottam was dissatisfied with the growing power of the priests of Lord Jagannatha, he could not take any action against them; he rather preferred to adjust with the situation. He wanted to control the priests and therefore he thought to patronize the Brahmins other than Puri priests. The earlier Somavamsi and Ganga kings of Orissa patronized the Brahmins as a matter of state policy and established Brahmin villages. Kapilendra made land grants lavishly in favour of the Brahmins. Purusottam also established fifteen Brahmin *sasanas* near Cuttack and also made tax-free land-grants. Prataprudra's association with Sri Chaitanya and extension of patronage in his favour was of a mutual help.[89] Thus, there was a remarkable alliance between the kings and the Brahmins which, in fact, furthered successfully the system of mutual help and benefit to each other.

However, it may be asserted that acceptance of tribal deities as family and tutelary deities was a desideratum for a state formation in tribal tracts in Orissa. The most important process which was generated by these socio-economic and cultural changes was the emergence of a class society of which the king was the pivot. Significantly, the aboriginal and autochthonous tribals in this area certainly were experiencing the process of integration and assimilation into a caste peasant base through the adoption of agriculture as well as cultural norms of the Brahminical Sanskritic culture.[90]

II

The social formation in early medieval Orissa need to be elucidated in the perspective of political developments in the region during the same period. The process subsumes the assimilation of tribes into the Brahminic fold and their consequent peasantization. This development in turn created new prerequisites, for example, the accommodation of tribal deities in the Brahminic pantheon and as well as their ascendancy to levels of high ritual elaboration. It was in a way a concession and compensation to the tribal culture for the disorganization of its social and economic life by the dominant Brahminic culture, which was used to aid the process of state formation.[91]

There is a glaring difference of the varna structure of society between the northern India and that of early medieval Orissa. The orthodox fourfold varna society which became the hallmark of northern India in the early historical period and was articulated in the socio-economic matrix of the Gupta period was late to develop in Orissa. Ultimately when it crossed the frontiers and diffused into this region, it could not take the same form and operate with the same intensity in Orissa, as it did in the north.

In detail, the difference was as follows. First and primarily, the tribal population was predominant in Orissa. Secondly, Orissa, excepting the coastal region, did not have wide rich alluvial plains to uphold and to provide the economic base for such a social order or stratification pattern. While the alluvial plains of the Ganges region provided a strong economic base which could uphold a highly stratified feudal social structure, the latter in turn vigorously reinforced the varna society and the feudal economic system, as the means for surplus extraction. This interdependence developed by the very logic of the given socio-economic order. Possibly they probably could not afford the luxury of having a rigid, multi-tiered stratification pattern with a sizeable section of the society engaged in production. The unproductive, surplus appropriating èlite had to be within manageable limits in this formative period, characterized by the initiation of agricultural and rural expansion.[92]

The generous land grant in early Orissa deeply influenced the process of the development of the State and society. The Matharas ruling in south Orissa during the fourth-fifth centuries are recorded to have given land grants to Brahmins and other State officials. The important officials found in the land-grant charters were *amatya* (minister), *kumar-amatya, talavara* (revenue), *desakasapatala* (record keeper), *mohapratihara* (chamberlain), *ajna bhogika* (registrar), *dutaka* (ambassador), *mahabaladhikrita* (supreme head of army), *mahadanda nayaka*, *dandanayaka* and *dandaneta* (judiciary officials).[93] The point of interest is the increasing occurrence of the feudal titles like *mahasamanta, samanta, maharaja*, etc., in the records of the late fifth and sixth centuries AD.[94] The Sailodbhavas in the seventh-eighth centuries continued the trend. Many secular assignees comprising vassals and officials emerged as distinguished land-holders during the period of Bhaumakaras and Somavamsis.

There were different categories of vassal land-holders in Orissa, e.g. *bhupal, bhogi, bhogirupa, mahabhogi, brhadbhogi, mahattara, mahamahattara, samanta, mahasamanta, mahasamantadhipati, rajni, rajyanaka* or *ranaka, rajaputra* and *rajaballabha*. Most of them seem to have been given military obligations and to have lived on the revenues assigned to them.[95] We have as yet no statistics with which to establish the relative status and rank of land-owning elements but we can have an idea of the function of a few officials by corroborating evidence from Orissa's neighbouring regions, that of Bengal during the Gupta and Post-Gupta period. The process of the rise of the *mahattaras* and *samantas* is evident from a set of sixth-century inscriptions from the Vanga subregion of Bengal. The first plate of the time of Dharmaditya records the land-sale transactions which were made before the *visaya-mahattaras* of whom eighteen are mentioned by name. The *mahattaras* are thus seen for the first time functioning at the level of the executive office of a *visaya* (District). The functions like measurement and demarcation of land were then carried by *kula-vara* or *jana-kula-vara* which could be constituted by the *karanika* officials. These *karanika* officials were designated as *visayadhikarana* and *jyesthadhikaranika* at the District level. However, more detailed evidence of the Egra copper-plate of the time of Sasanka from the Midnapore District (once upon a time a part of Orissa and now a border District between Orissa and Bengal) reveals a cross-section of the rural elite of the period. From some new terms like *mahamahattara, pradhan* and *mahapradhan* used in the records in relation to probably both Brahmin and non-Brahmin landholders it would appear that the hierarchical ordering of rural landholding elite had become much more complex by the seventh century.[96]

A number of inscriptions indicate that many grants were made in forest region under the Bhanjas, the Somavamsis and the Gangas. The practice of land grant was intensified especially under the Gangas. The *nayakas* and *paikas* emerged as significant non-Brahmin landowners. *Nayakas* seem to have been powerful local leaders who ruled like semi-independent lords in the peripheral areas of the Ganga empire. They were selected on the basis of their military ability and local influence and were also assigned some territories with special land-rights and duties. The *paikas* constituted the local militia and they served under the *nayakas* at the time of the war. In lieu of salary in cash, they were assigned land for cultivation and their maintenance. The Brahmins were granted land both in settled and forest regions. The main reason for grants particularly in the backward areas must have been the desire to bring them under cultivation and to acculturate the tribal people of the newly conquered regions. Besides this, another purpose of these land grants was the establishment of Brahminic pockets in the kingdom, who helped the consolidation of the ruling dynasty without weakening the central authority. The Brahmin donees in Orissa cannot be considered to be a group of feudal landlords weakening the central authority, rather they contributed to strengthening the power and influence of the king. The study of the land-system of medieval Orissa shows that there were three categories of landholders: (i) the king, who had a major share of land and who was regarded the ultimate authority in this respect as head of the kingdom; (ii) traditional landholders; and (iii) landholders like Brahmins, officials and temples created through land grants.[97]

Land grants to Brahmins and the extension of agriculture and rural expansion had the attendant consequence of the transformation of the autochthonous tribes into Sudra castes, a process which was carried out simultaneously along with their peasantization.[98] The postulation that in the early medieval period in course of Brahminization in the backward areas the local tribal people were transformed into Sudras and their chiefs absorbed as Kshatriyas into the Hindufold seems to be valid in the Orissan situation.[99]

Thus appears the emergence of two-tiered social structure in early medieval Orissa which needs more elaboration. An analysis of the absence of a Kshatriya varna in south India reveals that the tribal chieftains and/or Hinduzied *rajas* claiming Kshatriyahood lost their status as soon as they lost their political dominance.[100] A similar thing seems to have happened in Orissa too. The numerous autochthonous ruling families, for example, the Sailodbhavas, the Bhaumakaras, the Tungas, the Bhanjas, the Sulkis, the Sarabhapuriyas, etc., in early medieval Orissa were of tribal origin[101] and their pretensions to Kshatriyahood seems to have disappeared with the loss of their political power. They could not give rise to a viable Kshatriya varna. In Orissa there was no ancient Kshatriya class to provide the base and therefore, the varna could neither take deep roots nor flourish. The present-day *khandayats* (the wielder of swords/controller of *khandas*, the administrative units) who stake claim to Kshatriyahood are after all a militia-cum-cultivator caste, whose origins may be traced to the medieval period, possibly to the Ganga-Gajapati times. A proper analysis of all possibilities would reveal their tribal antecedents.[102]

A number of epigraphs show that birth in the high ranking Sudra castes was not at all considered low, since in ritual practice Sudras ranked only next to the Brahmins. There were many Sudra rulers who appeared as zealous patrons of the Brahmins and *varnashramdharma* and expressed pride in having been born from the feet of Lord Vishnu and some of them even assumed the Brahminical *gotras*.[103] Raja Ramachandra Deva, who belonged to the late sixteenth-century Orissa, has been described as *Sudra-nrupati* (Sudra-king) in the Srijanga inscription.[104]

However, the extension of the varna system to the predominantly non-Brahminical areas of the south and the east meant categorization of peasant communities such as the Vellalas, the Kammas, and the Kalitas of Assam and Orissa as Sudras, despite some feeble attempts at gaining Kshatriya status owing to the strong position of these communities in the agrarian structure of the regions. These areas had two clearly identifiable varnas on the basis of their functions, the Brahmin and the Sudra; the category of the Vaishya emerged only occasionally in times of trade and that of Kshatriyas could not take deep roots.

The changes in the economic and social life in northern India had much to do with the decline of trade and the decay of towns, which led to a decline of the Vaishyas, who gradually came to be associated with mercantile and urban-based activities. In the meantime the Sudras had emerged to be farmers and agriculturists. It may be presumed that the Vaishya varna did not arise in Orissa because during the period when Orissa experienced 'Brahminization' the distinction between the Vaishyas and Sudras had already got blurred or confused in northern India.[106] What seems possible in the Orissa context is that the indigenous tribal population was integrated to the Brahminical social order mainly as Sudras and lower castes, rather than as lowly Vaishyas in order to emphasize their servility.[107] However, it may be added that the blurring of the distinction between Sudras and Vaishyas and the absence of a viable Vaishya varna might have made the Sudra status acceptable to the aboriginal without much reluctance. Besides, in the Orissan situation, as we shall notice in the following pages, there was no rigid polarization of the society, quite unlike the picture that obtains in the south during the same period. In contrast, the ruling class made conscious efforts to integrate the tribes and accommodate their culture.[108]

Following the improvement in the economic and social status of the Sudras and the decline of the overseas trade, many of the Vaishyas and Sudras left their traditional professions and worked as civil and military persons. The Ganjam plate of Vajrahastadev III dated AD 1068, refers to a *Nayaka* Gokana who was a Vaishya *vamsodbhava*.[109] An epigraphic record at Simachalam, dated AD 1382, mentions one Gurudasa of *vaisyakula* serving as *mahasenapati*.[110] According to a charter issued in the year 526 of the Ganga era under Madhukamarnava, son of Anantavarman, three villages were together formed into a *vaisyagrahara* and it was granted to one Erapa Nayak son of Manci Nayak of the Vaishya caste.[111]

In spite of many inhibitions imposed by the Smriti literature, many Sudras promoted themselves to the status of Kshatriyas and many of them also claimed the Vaishya status. The artisans and the craftsmen got a higher status, patronized by the ruling chiefs. Many Sudra menial labourers were attached to the temples. A stone inscription of

Govinda Senapati registers grant of land to a group of persons for their daily service to the temple like sweeping, lime washing and for supply of earthen pots.[112] Many Sudras were also appointed to the position of commanders and were assigned the *nayakaship*.[113] From this it appears that military service also extended to the Sudra and Vaishya communities in medieval Orissa and they were paid the grant of land and village assignments. Not only that, we will also notice in the forthcoming chapters, that the Sudras achieved remarkable progress in the field of learning and literature in medieval Orissa. Sarala Dasa, a Sudramuni composed the *Mahabharata*, a monumental work in Oriya literature, Sudramuni Balarama Dasa composed the Oriya *Ramayana* and another Sudramuni Achyutananda Dasa earned his name by writing the *Harivamsa* in Oriya. Their works earned popularity among the masses.

This upward mobility of the Sudras and the new stratification of the society is also found in the emergence of different trends of religious movements. The development of the Sakta-Tantrik cults, Vaishnavism and the Natha cults virtually helped to decline the Brahminical caste hegemony in society. These new religious movements assimilated Sudras and tribals into their fold. Many Tantrik teachers and *siddhacharyas* of the medieval period were from the Sudras, tribals and untouchables. In the seventh-eighth centuries, these *siddhas* composed many folk-poems in the regional broken dialects called *charyapadas* and they were popularly called as *dombipa, tantipa, sabarapa* and *luipa,* etc.,[114] which suggest that they were treated like fathers/teachers of different communities.

Despite the absence of the viable Kshatriya and Vaishya varna for that matter, we still find references in the characters of the regional ruling families where they vociferously proclaim themselves to be the defenders of the *varnashramdharma* and fourfold varna order. This is more pronounced in case of the Bhaumakaras and the Somavamsis. What is strikingly absent in all the charters is the categorical mention of the four varnas. It may be interpreted that in doing so they were clearly trying to gain vertical legitimacy in society and the acceptance of their rule. In Orissa while the fourfold varna order continued to remain the ideal, i.e. what ought to be the two-tiered structure with its division into castes and the numerous intermediary functional castes came to constitute the functional reality.[115]

The predominant position of the Brahmins in Orissan society since the days of the Matharas is a well established fact. What needs emphasis is that as in northern India here too there was a proliferation of Brahmin castes on the basis of different identities. The migration of Vedic Brahmins must have created divisions in their marks owing to differences at their levels of ritual purity and pollution.[116] Many of the Brahmins in Orissa, in course of the tribal acculturation and peasantization process, might not have been able to avoid physical labour completely and such Brahmins then must have stood degraded in the eyes of those who did not engage in manual labour. The presence of the tribal priests and their recognition as degraded Brahmins must have further complicated the Brahmins being deprived of ritual functions in society carried out other professions like horse-trade (*ghoda-banjara*),[117] agriculture and gardening,[118] and mason as and artistic works.[119] Besides, there is evidence of Brahmins being engaged in many prestigious and powerful occupations. They officiated in different capacities, e.g., as *mantrin* (minister), *senapati* (commanders), *akasapatalika* (record keeper), *dutaka* (ambassador), *utkirnaka* (engraver), *mahattara* (village headman), *lekhaka* (writer of public documents), *ranaka* (a feudatory status) and *mandalika* (governor).[120] These diversified occupations must have been of great relevance in triggering off stratification within the Brahmin fold and consequently it must have stimulated caste proliferation within this category.

The most remarkable development in medieval Orissa was the emergence of a distinguished and dominant functional caste namely, Karanikas or Kayasthas. They did exist and proliferate occupying possibly in several cases an ambivalent position in the seemingly two-tier varna structure. The earliest reference to the Kayasthas is found in the *smriti* of Yajnavalkya. The *Vedavyasa Smriti* includes them among Sudras along with the barbers, potters and others.[121] Constant transfer of land and land revenue to Brahmins, officials and temples needed a large number of writers and record keepers to draft documents and to maintain them. In the initial stage literate members of the higher varnas were recruited as Kayasthas or scribes to meet the fiscal and administrative need of the expanding state. But gradually the scribes were recruited from the Sudra and Vaishya communities.[122] We have references to terms like *lekhaka*, *karanika*, *akasapatalika* and *pustapala*, etc., but the inscriptions of Orissa do not indicate anything about the existence of a separate caste such as the Kayastha prior to the tenth century AD.[123] They emerged towards the eleventh century AD,[124] during the period of the Somavamsis. It seems that during the Somavamsi and Ganga rule, with the increasing rate of the number of land grants and the intensification of the feudal system, the Kayastha as a distinct caste came to emerge. During the period of the later Eastern Gangas they emerged as a dominant caste and adopted local names as Karanikas or Karanas. Some of them rose to high positions, occupied both civil and military posts, received land grants, held *nayakaships* and feudatory status.[125]

A striking feature of rural stratification and hierarchy developed in early medieval Orissa in consequence of the rural settlements and extension of agriculture following the massive land grants. After the decline of the Gupta power the composition of the executives at the level of the *vithi-adhikaran* and *visayadhikaran* came to be changed and new rural notables like *maha-mahattara* and *mahapradhan* emerged through the proliferation of the *agrahar* based Brahmin landholders. Simultaneously, there was a considerable proliferation of officials who came to appropriate much of the functions of *adhikaranas*. The Khalimpur record lists among various social groups, *maha-mahattaras* and *mahattaras* in association with *adhikaranas*, they are distinguished from *prativasis* (ordinary residents) and *kshetrakaras* (cultivators), but stratification within individual villages was now overlaid by another hierarchical pattern reflected in the massive proliferation of official designations.[126]

There had emerged another situation which must have structured relationships within a number of rural settlements. The situation was caused by a proliferation and clustering of *agrahara/sasan* type of settlements. In the newly created *Brahmapuras* (Brahmin *sasanas*) different communities were settled, obviously for the purpose of ensuring varieties of services to temples and Brahmins. The sizes of plots given to them in return for expected services may reflect the relative social, but not necessarily varna status of these communities. The pattern of land grants also led to the stratification between the artisan class and other service communities: while individual carpenters, masons and black-smiths each received two *patakas* of land, the individuals of other service communities like *malakar* (florists), *tailika* (oil-man), *kumbhakar* (potter), *karmakaras* (menials) and *carmakaras* (tanners) and so on each received only one-half *patakas*. Apart from the service communities, there were three major categories of grantees in a village which possessed either a temple or a *math*. The Vedic Brahmin scholar attached to the temple or the *math* was the first category of grantees who received ten *patakas* of land. Secondly, other Brahmins of *mahattar* category attached to temples or *mathas* received not more than two *patakas*. This was even less than the shares received by a Kayastha whose varna status was considered lower than that of the Brahmin. The carpenters, smiths, and artisans were put far above other service communities in terms of their share in land and although this may be construed to indicate greater relevance of their services to the newly created *Brahmapuras* or Brahmin *sasanas*. It is more likely that the differentiated ordering of the various communities in this particular situation derived largely from the pattern of differentiation already in existence in rural society.[127]

We find terms like *grihaswami* and *grihadhyaksha* in the Jairam copper-plate[128] and the term *kutumbin,*[129] in another record of fifth-sixth centuries AD. These terms may imply the householders and/or the well-to-do peasant householders. Among the other functional castes mention may be made of the *kumbhakara* (potters), *kamsyakara* (bronzesmith)[130] and the Bhaumkara epigraphic records mention three more castes, *viz.*, *tantavaya* (weaver), *gokula* (cowherds) and *saundhika* (distiller).[131] The inscriptions, sculptural relics and temple architectural remains of the period endorse the existence of engravers, sculptors, masons and quarrymen. What attracts attention is the fact that there is no positive record of the untouchables in this period. The Dombas, Panas and Candalas of today might have made their beginning in a later period. Those aboriginals who remained on the fringes of the Hindu society and yet were not fully absorbed by it seem to have been reduced to these categories.[132]

As regards the position of women in medieval Orissa, the sources do not provide adequate information. From the sculptural representation on the Satrughneswar group of temples it may be inferrred that some women excelled in the art of dance and singing. The stray information that we receive is all about the status of the women of royal classes. Kalyana Devi of the Sailodbhava dynasty is known to have patronized the Jaina saints.[133] Bhaumakara record reveals that widowed queens and daughters of the deceased kings ascended to the throne and ruled over the kingdom. They also made land grants to Brahmins and religious establishments.[134] We do not come across the evidence of *sati* before eleventh-twelfth century in Orissa.[135] In case of Bhumakaras it was conspicuously absent. Women education appears to have been limited to a few women of the higher strata of society. *Sarala Mahabharata* (fifteenth century) is a remarkable source of reconstructing the social history of Medieval Orissa. It reflects the existence of the patriarchal social order with the presence of child-marriage, concubinage, prostitution, *parakiya* relations and other age-long traditions determining lower status of women subordinate to their male counterparts.[136] Nevertheless, the status of women in Orissa seems to have been better than that of their sisters in northern India, due to continuity of the tribal heritage and legacy for a long period of time.[137]

The socio-economic and cultural scenario so far perceived clearly suggest a paradigm of deviation from the north-Indian pattern of social structure. The Orissan context is, therefore, a brilliant case of regional variation. However, the proliferation of Brahmin and Sudra castes and the rise of the Kayastha-karanas have to be viewed in the overall emerging peculiar feudal context. The period of our study witnessed the process of interaction and assimilation between the autochthonous tribal population and the dominant elilte that altogether developed a new social relationship. Early medieval Orissa experienced a process of Hindu-tribal continuum and not a 'sustained displacement' of the aboriginal from their homeland a process which formed the basis of the regional kingdoms. Not only the Brahmins were the donees of the land grants. Gradually, some aboriginal chiefs were also transformed into feudal vassals. Thus, the system gave rise to a typical feature of feudal land relations, which developed out of a tribal aboriginal background in which the tribal-heritage of land system had not completely disappeared although the aboriginal chiefs could assimilate themselves into the Hindu way of life. In search of legitimacy and to redress the sense of deprivation of the tribes-turned peasants, religious compensation was offered to them by the ruling class. The rise of Saktism and the cults of various Mother Goddesses,[138] Tantricism and Buddhist Tara amply reflect on the emerging and existing realities. The most striking example of the Hindu-tribal continuum is that many tribal deities underwent a process of Hinduization along with the parallel development of chieftainship to Hindu kingship.[139] Both tradition and practice indicate the tribal origin of god Lingaraja of Bhubaneswar and Lord Jagannatha of Puri, the two famous Hindu deities of Orissa. Both these temples have two categories of priests, of which the Badus in Lingaraja and the Daitas in the Jagannatha temple are considered to be of tribal origin. They come into close and intimate contact with the deities like bathing, dressing and moving them. They are the personal attendants of the *deities*.[140] The cases of the Badus and the Daitas along with the thirty-six functional castes in the service of the temples of Orissa, present brilliant illustrations of the conscious attempt by the ruling class to cultivate and win over the tribal subjects. Thus, the issue of Brahmins monopolizing the gods and their temples in Orissa is strikingly missing.[141]

If agricultural and rural expansion constituted the economic factor and the two-tier varna order made up the social factor, then religion was the ideological factor in the emerging socio-economic pattern. However, as in the south, the history of religion in Orissa during this period, does not synchronize with a mushrooming of temples and *tirthas*. It is a history of the Hinduization of the tribal deities, a process which not only served to legitimate the Hinduized kingship but also tried to divert attention from the social conditions emanating from the new production relations. Although temples in Orissa appeared under the Somavamsi and Gangas, that development did not contribute in a major way to the study of our period under review.[142]

The process of change in early medieval rural society is thus seen to consist in the understanding of 'peasants units' of production, the agglomeration of which would perhaps constitute a problem of communal rights within a rural settlement. B.D. Chottopadhyaya observes that social tensions emerged when there was intervention of the political power in rural settlements, either for making grants or for enlarging its revenue base. The tension may be between political power and the autonomously organized agrarian units or between State agents such as Brahmin landholders, temples or secular assignees and the original rural social groups.[143] The expansion of the land grants (in form of *brahmadeyas, brahmapuras, sasanas* or *agraharas*) mode of agrarian system into the clan settlements certainly would have dissolved the primitive agriculture on the one hand and the transformation of clan settlements on the other. Such a process could hardly have been peaceful.[144] Besides this, transfer of the village to a donee not only with various types of dues but also with artisans like weavers, brewers, cowherds and menial subjects created another kind of disturbance in the rural set-up. The practice was followed by the Bhaumakara rulers for about one hundred years from the middle of the ninth century AD and also by their feudatories, the Bhanjas and Tungas. This practice prevailed in Orissa on a far wider scale and for a long period of time. Hence it may have been found necessary on account of the scarcity of working population for running the rural economy. But such grants reduced the villagers to the condition of semi-serfs, producing surplus for the benefit of the donee beneficiaries. Secondly, the donees monopolized on the waste land and other local resources within the geographical boundaries of this assignment and stopped the villager's free-access to these resources which were, once upon a time, traditionally owned by them. The villagers, could therefore, no longer easily reclaim the jungle land for cultivation. On the other hand as the families of the beneficiaries would multiply there would be a natural tendency to appropriate the fallow land for their use, thus depriving the peasants of their natural right to expand into the waste land. This was bound to lead to unequal distribution of land in the villages, the lion's share going to the donees and their descendants. Moreover, they had the additional advantage of being vested with numerous fiscal rights which, in course of time gave them practical ownership of land.[145]

From the aforesaid discussion it may be concluded that medieval society of Orissa provides a new feature altogether. It undermined the concept of traditional society based on Dharmasastras and led to the emergence of a number of new functional social groups and adjusted within the two-tiered framework of social structure. Because of changes in economic and social life due to agricultural and rural expansion, power and status of the new group of dominant land-owning elite, there emerged new functional social groups such as landlords, priests, civil and military officials, *karanikas*, traders, peasants, artisans, etc., cutting across the traditional varna system. The Brahmins actively aided the process of State formation and acculturation into the Sanskritized set-up and simultaneously emerged as intermediaries in the feudal set-up. Little wonder, the Brahmins were highly respected and even worshipped by the king.[146] The Brahmins even played the role of king-makers. So the defence, protection and adulation of the Brahmins was a tacit recognition of their role in the socio-economic system. Keeping in view these developments one may assume that the system was successful and effective by the Brahmin-Kshatriya (transitional Kshatriya) alliance. Because this period is characterized by the State formation based on peasantization of the tribes. Social stratification does not seem to have been complex or rigid owing to the strong tribal legacy. However, it appears reasonable to infer that the relations between the non-producing landowning èlite on the one hand and the actual Sudraized toiling peasantry, on the other were not entirely harmonious. The distinct paradigm of the 'Social Protest movement' may be cited here in that the upward mobility of the Sudras and the emergence of the *karanikas* as dominant èlite challenged the Brahminical hegemony of society, religion and culture in medieval Orissa. Despite the differences and cleavages between them their co-existence and inter-relationships have been rightly characterized as 'antagonistic cooperation'.[147]

NOTES

1. B.P. Sahu, 'Ancient Orissa: The Dynamics of Internal Transformation of the Tribal Society', *Proceedings of Indian History Congress* (*PIHC*), 45th Session, 1984, p. 148.
2. Ibid., pp. 149–50.
3. Ibid., pp. 150–1.
4. H. Kulke, *Kings and Cults: State Formation and Legitimation in India and South-East Asia*, Manohar, New Delhi, 1993, p. 1.
5. *E.I.*, vol. XXI, pp. 23–5.
6. B.P. Sahu, op. cit, 1984, p. 153; See also R.C. Misro, 'Brahmanas as Created Landholders in Early Medieval Orissa: An Epigraphic Study (*circa* AD 400–1000)', in H.S. Patnaik and A.N. Parida (eds.), *Aspects of Socio-Cultural Life in Early and Medieval Orissa*, Utkal University, Bhubaneswar, 1996, pp. 1–12.
7. B.P. Sahu, op. cit. 1984, p. 154.
8. Biswarup Das, 'The Migration of Brahmins to Orissa', *Proceedings of the Orissa History Congress* (*POHC*), Berhampur, 1977, p. 35, see also D.P. Patnaik, 'Aryanization of Orissa', *Orissa Historical Research Journal* (*OHRJ*), vol. VII, no. I, 1958, pp. 51–5.
9. R.S. Sharma, *Social Change in Early Medieval India* (*c.* AD *500-1200*), Devraj Chanana Memorial Lecture, Peoples Publishing House, Delhi, 1969, p. 5.
10. *EI*, XXXV, pt. II, p. 102.
11. *JBORS*, II, p. 409; *IHQ*, XXI, p. 216.
12. *JBORS*, LXIV, p. 123.
13. *JBORS*, XVII, pt. I, p. 17.
14. Ibid., VI, p. 484.
15. *JBORS*, II, p. 273.
16. *JBORS*, XII, p. 292; *EI*, XXIV, pt. II, p. 99.
17. *EI*, XXVII, pt. VII, p. 330; *JBORS*, IV, p. 168.
18. *EI*, XXII, p. 137; *JBORS*, II, pp. 54 and 401.
19. *EI*, III, no. 47, p. 357; XII, p. 240.
20. Ibid., III, no. 47, p. 347; XXIX, p. 81.
21. *EI*, XII, no. 36, p. 322.

22. *EI*, XXIV, p. 137.
23. *EI*, XXII, p. 137.
24. *EI*, XXVIII, pt. VII, p. 323.
25. *OHRJ*, vol. III, no. 2, p. 67.
26. *EI*, XV, no. III, p. 1.
27. *IA*, XIII, p, 273.
28. K.C. Panigrahi, *Itihasa O Kimbadanti,* Utkal University, Bhubaneswar, 1962, p. 10; S.K. Panda, *Medieval Orissa: A Socio-Economic Study*, Mittal Publication, New Delhi, 1991, p. 78.
29. H. Kulke, 'Fragmentation and Segmentation versus Integration? Reflections on the Concepts of Indian Feudalism and the Segmentary State in Indian History', *Studies in History*, vol. IV, no. 2, 1982, pp. 255–6.
30. *JBORS,* IV, p. 239.
31. Ibid.
32. *JASB,* VI, p. 357.
33. H. Kulke, 'Early State Formation and Royal Legitimation in Late Ancient Orissa', in M.N. Das (ed.), *Sidelights on History and Culture of Orissa*, Vidyapuri, Cuttack, 1977, p. 110.
34. H. Kulke, op. cit., 1982, pp. 256–8.
35. Ibid., pp. 258–60.
36. Ibid., pp. 260–1.
37. H. Kulke, op. cit., 1993, pp. 125–6; see also Jagabandhu Samantrai, *Carccika Mahatmya*, Gopalpur, 1968, pp. 6ff.
38. S.N. Rajaguru (ed.), *Inscriptions of Orissa* (*IO*), vol. I, pt. II, Orissa State Museum, Bhubaneswar, 1958, p. 143.
39. H. Kulke, op. cit., 1993, p. 3.
40. B.P. Sahu, op. cit., 1984, p. 154.
41. *IO*, vol. I, pt. II, pp. 25ff.
42. Kanas Inscription in *EI,* XXVII, p. 328.
43. K.C. Panigrahi, *Archaeological Remains at Bhubaneswar*, Orient Longman, Calcutta, 1961, p. 28, dates the oldest temple in Bhubaneswar around AD 575, i.e. of Satrughneswar group.
44. *Mahabharat* (*Santiparvam*), LXV, tr. Ray, VIII, p. 146.
45. R.S. Sharma, *Indian Feudalism* (*circa* AD 300–1200), 2nd edn., Macmillan, Delhi, 1980, p. 281.
46. H. Kulke, op. cit. 1993, pp. 5, 90–2 (particularly the chapter titled 'Kshatriyaization and Social Change—A study in the Orissa Setting',) pp. 82–92.
47. Ibid., pp. 5–6.
48. Ibid., pp. 6–7 (for details see Kulke's chapter titled 'Tribal Deities at Princely Courts: The Feudatory Rajas of Central Orissa and their Tutelary Deities (*Istadevatas*)', pp. 114–36).
49. Ibid., p. 9.
50. Ibid., p.10.
51. D.D. Kosambi, *Myth and Reality,* Popular Prakashan, Bombay, 1962, p. 32.
52. A. Eschmann, 'Hinduization of Tribal Deities in Orissa: The Sakta and Saiva Typology, in A. Eschmann et al. (eds.), *The Cult of Jagannatha and the Regional Tradition of Orissa*, Manohar, New Delhi, 1986, p. 80.
53. Ibid., p. 100.

54. Ibid., p. 116.
55. Ibid., p. 85.
56. Ibid., p. 87.
57. Ibid., p. 93.
58. K.C. Panigrahi, op. cit., 1962, p. 164
59. A. Eschmann, op. cit., 1986, p. 97.
60. K.C. Panigrahi, op. cit., 1962, p. 219.
61. A. Eschmann, op. cit., 1986, pp. 96–7.
62. For details see B.D. Chattopadhyaya, 'Political Processes and the Structure of Polity in Early Medieval India', in H. Kulke (ed.), *The State in India (1000–1700 AD)*, OUP, Delhi, 1997, pp. 195–232.
63. B.P. Sahu, op. cit., 1984, pp. 93, 113.
64. B.D. Chattopadhyaya, op. cit., 1997, p. 210; see also H. Kulke, op. cit., 1993, pp. 93–113.
65. G.N. Dash, 'The Evolution of the Priestly Power: The Ganga Vamsa Period', in A. Eschmann et al. (eds.), op. cit., 1986, p. 160.
66. A.B. Mohanty (ed.), *Madalapanji*, Prachi Samiti, Bhubaneswar, 1940, pp. 29–30.
67. Ananta Basudev temple of Bhubaneswar is the only existing Jagannatha temple of this period. From Nagari plates of Anangabhima Dev III it was deduced that he constructed another temple for Purushottam in Cuttack which was also a Jagannatha temple, *EI*, XXVII, pts. V and VI.
68. H.K. Mahatab, *History of Orissa*, vol. I, Prajatantra Prachar Samiti, Cuttack, 1959, p. 179.
69. H. Kulke, 'Kshatriyaization and Social Change: A Study in Orissa Setting', in S. Devadas Pillai (ed.), *Aspects of Changing India: Studies in the Honour of Prof. S.G. Ghurye*, Bombay, 1976, p. 5.
70. G.N. Dash, op. cit., 1986, p. 163.
71. Ibid., p. 158.
72. A.B. Mohanty (ed.), op. cit., 1940, pp. 27–34.
73. G.N. Dash, op. cit., 1986, p. 164.
74. Ibid., p. 165.
75. A.B. Mohanty (ed.), *Sarala Mahabharata, 'Musali Parva'*, Chaps. 8–12, Bhubaneswar, 1958.
76. Ibid., Chap. 12, pp. 106ff.
77. G.N. Dash, op. cit., 1986, p. 167.
78. A.B. Mohanty (ed.), op. cit., '*Musali Parva*', Chap. 9, 1958, p. 83.
79. Ibid., p. 85.
80. H. Kulke 'Jagannatha as the State Deity under the Gajapatis of Orissa', in A. Eschmann et al. (eds.), op. cit., 1986, p. 200.
81. A.B. Mohanty (ed.), *Madalapanji*, 1940, pp. 42ff, quoted in G.N. Dash, in. A Eschmann et al. (eds.), op. cit., 1986, p. 209.
82. P. Mukharjee, *History of the Gajapati Kings of Orissa*, Kitab Mahal, Cuttack, 1981, 1953, p. 19; R. Subramanyam, *The Suryavamsi Gajapatis of Orissa*, Andhra University, Walitar, 1957, p. 32.
83. G.N. Dash, op. cit., 1986, p. 209.
84. *EI*, vol. XXXIII, 1959, pp. 125ff.
85. G.N. Dash, op. cit., 1986, p. 210.

86. Ibid., pp. 211–12 and 219.
87. Ibid., p. 212.
88. Ibid. , p. 213.
89. Ibid., p. 220.
90. B.P. Sahu, op. cit., 1984, pp. 155–6.
91. B.P. Sahu, 'Social Morphology and Physiology of Early Medieval Orissa (*c.* AD 400–1000)', *PIHC*, 44th Session, 1983, p. 133.
92. Ibid.
93. N.K. Sahu, *History of Orissa*, vol. I, Bharatiya Publishing House, Delhi, 1980, p. 96.
94. B.P. Sahu, op. cit., 1984, p. 156.
95. R.S. Sharma, op. cit., 1980, p. 230.
96. B.D. Chottopadhyaya, *Aspects of Rural Settlements and Rural Society in Early Medieval India*, K.P. Bagchi & Co., Calcutta, 1990, pp. 49–52.
97. S.K. Panda, 'From Kingdom to Empire: A Study of the Medieval State of Orissa under the Later Eastern Gangas (AD 1038–1434)', *Indian Historical Review* (*IHR*), vol. XVII, nos. 1 and 2, 1990, pp. 50-8.
98. Suvira Jaiswal, 'Studies in Early Indian Social History: Trends and Possibilities', in *IHR*, vol. VI, nos. 1 and 2, 1980a.
99. R.S. Sharma, *Sudras in Ancient India*, 3rd edn., Motilal Banarsidass, Delhi, 1990, pp. 340–4; H. Kulke, op. cit., 1977, pp. 110–14; and B.P Sahu, op. cit., 1983, p. 135.
100. Suvira Jaiswal, 'Studies in the Social Structure of the Early Tamils', in R.S. Sharma (ed.), *Indian Society: Historical Probings*, 2nd edn., Peoples Publishing House, New Delhi, 1977, p 145. Also see Jaiswal, op. cit., 1980, pp. 36–7.
101. H. Kulke, op. cit., 1977, see also S.K. Panda, 'Changes in the Pattern of Social Stratification in Medieval Orissa (*circa* AD 1100–1600)', in H.S. Patnaik and A.N. Parida (eds. , op. cit., 1996, p. 30.
102. B.P. Sahu, op. cit., 1983, p. 135.
103. Suvira Jaiswal, 'Changes in the Status and Concept of the *Sudra Varna* in Early Middle Ages', *PIHC*, 41st Session, Bombay, 1980b, p. 116. See also R.S. Sharma, op. cit., 1980, pp. 268–9. The Sudra rulers such as those in Saurastra, Avanti, Arbuda and Malwa along with the traditional Sudra, Abhira and Mlechha rulers, all are described as reigning in the regions of Sindhu and Kashmir, and are assigned by Pargiter to the fourth century AD.
104. A.N. Parida, 'Kaivarta Gita: Eka Samkshipta Adhyayan' (Oriya), in K.S. Behera (ed.), *Sagar O Sahitya* (Oriya), Dasarathi Pustakalaya, Cuttack, 1993, p. 196.
105. Suvira Jaiswal, op. cit., 1990, p. 116.
106. R.S. Sharma, op. cit., 1969, pp. 11–12.
107. Suvira Jaiswal, op. cit., 1980b, p. 39.
108. B.P. Sahu, op. cit., 1983, p. 136.
109. S.K. Panda, op. cit., 1996, p. 31.
110. *South Indian Inscriptions* (*SII*), vol. VI, no. 335.
111. R.S. Sharma, op. cit., 1980, p. 231.
112. *OHRJ*, vol. II, nos. 3 and 4, pp. 46-8.
113. For details see S.K. Panda, 'Nayaka System in Medieval Orissa', in K.K.

Dasgupta et. al. (eds.), *Sraddhanjali: Studies in Ancient Indian History*, Delhi, 1988, pp. 92–107.
114. K. Mohapatra (ed.), *Charya Gitika* (Oriya), Cuttack, 1976, p. 8.
115. B.P. Sahu, op. cit., 1983, p. 136.
116. Ibid., p. 137.
117. *SII*, vol. V, nos. 1080 and 1176.
118. A.B. Mohanty (ed.), *Sarala Mahabharata* (*Madhya Parva*), Bhubaneswar, 1968, p. 14; Balarama Dasa, *Jagamohan Ramayan* (*Lanka Kanda*), Cuttack, n.d., p. 205.
119. *Inscriptions of Orissa*, vol. III, pt. 2, no. 280, p. 347.
120. *EI*, vol. IV, pp. 314–18, see U. Subudhi, 'A Study of the Brahmanas of Ancient and Early Medieval Orissa form Epigraphic Sources (*c.* 350–1100 AD)', in *Proceeding of Orissa History Congress*, 1980, pp 18–24.
121. A.P. Shah, *Life in Medieval Orissa* (*circa* AD *600–1200*), Chaukhambha Orientalia, Varanasi, 1976, pp. 129–30.
122. S.K. Panda, op. cit., 1996, p. 32.
123. A.P. Shah, op. cit., 1976, p. 130.
124. *EI*, vol. XXIX, pp. 188–9.
125. *EI*, vol. III, p. 224; *EI*, vol. XXXII, pp. 311–16; see also *Journal of the Andhra Historical Research Society*, vol. VI, p. 208.
126. B.D. Chottopadhyaya, op. cit., 1990, pp 53–4.
127. Ibid., pp. 55–7.
128. D. Das, *The Early History of Kalinga*, Calcutta 1977, p. 268.
129. Ibid.
130. Ibid., p. 269.
131. U. Subudhi, *The Bhaumakaras of Orissa*, Punthi Pustak, Calcutta, 1978, p. 114.
132. B.P. Sahu, op. cit., 1983, p. 138.
133. S.C. Behera, *Rise and Fall of the Sailodbhavas*, Punthi Pustak, Calcutta, 1982, p. 187.
134. U. Subudhi, op. cit., 1978, pp. 115–16.
135. A.P. Shah, op. cit., 1976, p. 140.
136. K.C. Sahoo, *Literature and Social Life in Medieval Orissa*, Pustak Sadan, Ranchi, 1971, pp. 62–3.
137. B.P. Sahu, op. cit, 1983, p. 139.
138. Ibid.
139. For example, the cults of Vana Durga, Mangala, Hingula, Charchika, Tarini of Ghatagaon, Kenojhar; Tara Tarini of Berhampur, Ganjam; Kichakeswari of Mayurbhanj, Samalai of Sambalpur are existing still with tribal heritage.
140. H. Kulke, 'Royal Temple Policy and the Structure of Medieval Hindu Kingdoms', in A. Eschmann et al. (eds.), *The Cult of Jagannatha and the Regional Tradition of Orissa,* Manohar, New Delhi, 1986, p. 130.
141. For details see A. Eschmann, 'Hinduization of Tribal Deities in Orissa: The *Sakta* and *Saiva* Typology' and 'The Vaishnav Typology of Hinduization and the origin of the Jagannatha', in A. Eschmann et al. (eds.), op. cit., 1986, pp. 79–98 and pp. 99–117, respectively.
142. B.P. Sahu, op. cit., 1983, pp. 140–1.

143. B.D. Chattopadhyaya, op. cit., 1990, p. 10.
144. Rajan Gurukkal, 'Non-Brahman Resistance to the Expansion of the Brahamadeyas: the Early Pandya Experience', *PIHC*, 45th Session, 1984, p. 161.
145. R.S. Sharma, 'The Land System in Medieval Orissa (*c*. AD 750–1200)' (Appendix 1) to *Indian Feudalism*, Macmillan, New Delhi, 1980, pp. 234–5.
146. S.C. Behera, op. cit., 1982, p. 181.
147. B.P. Sahu, op. cit., 1983, p. 141.

CHAPTER 2

The Dissenter within: Sarala Dasa and his Oriya *Mahabharata*

THE UNEQUAL distribution of land and emergence of different castes on the basis of functional hierarchy led to the growth of social stratification resulting in the proliferation of not only the classes of rich and poor, but also the social groups educated and unlettered. The common people were looked down upon and degraded as lowly and illiterates since the Puranas, and Dharmasastras were written in Sanskrit and they were deprived of Sanskrit knowledge. The *puranapandas* (a section of Brahmins) used to read out and explain the Sanskrit texts to the unlettered common people and collected money in return. Thus, socio-educational deprivation of the common people continued for a long time and their spoken language was considered to be *bibhasha* (not fit to be used for religious texts) at least till the fifteenth century.

In course of time, the common people endeavoured to form the scripts of their own spoken language and composed devotional songs in praise of gods and goddesses. Fifteenth century was an era of the political and cultural awakening in the history of Orissa. Gajapati Kapilendra Dev during this time achieved political glory for Orissa by extending his empire from the Ganges to Kaveri and his contemporary poet Sudramuni Sarala Dasa rephrased the epics of all-India character in the language of the common people of Orissa. He was the pioneer of the movement and, in fact, his literature was the literature of protest against the domination of a section of people who monopolized learning Puranas, Dharmasastras and other religious texts as the only authorities on the sacred books and scriptuers. In

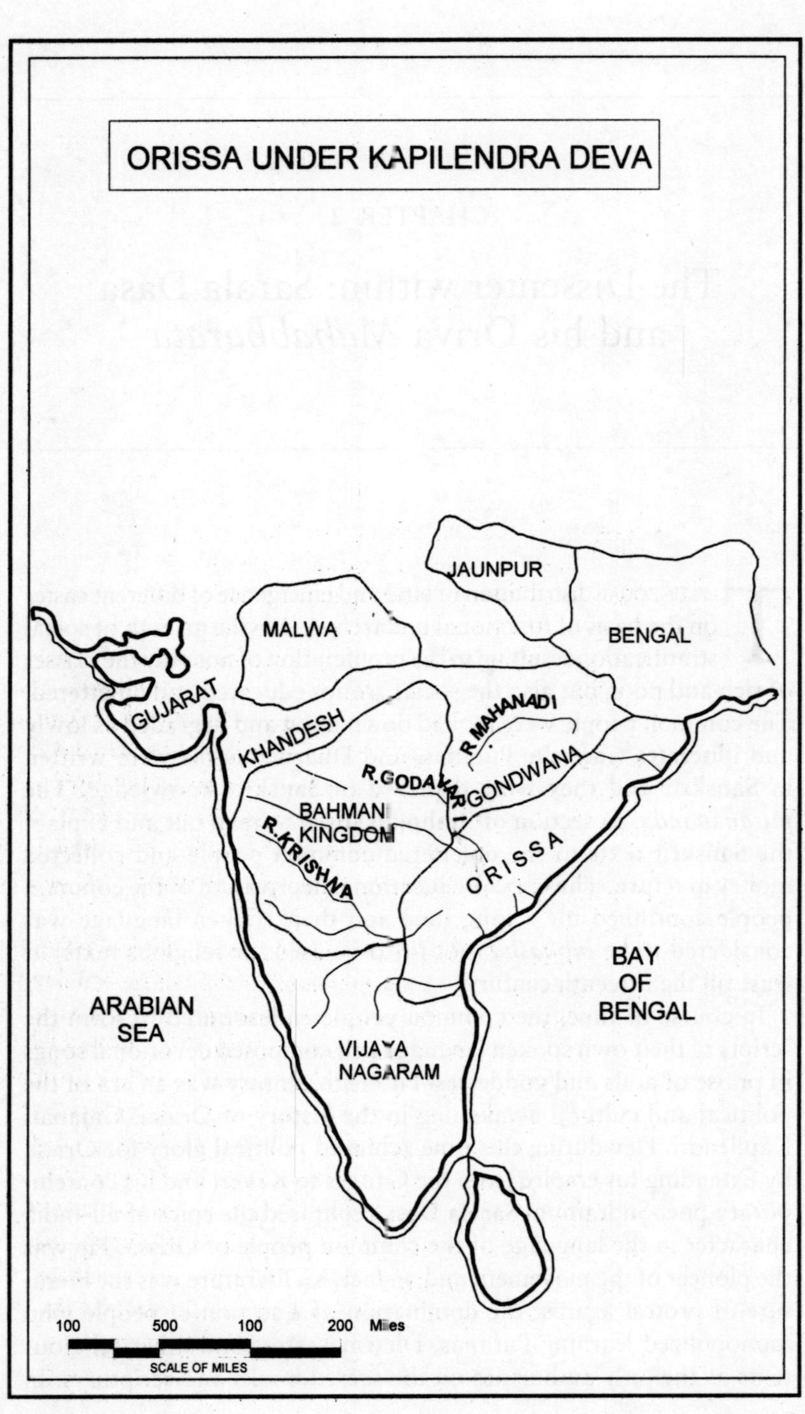
ORISSA UNDER KAPILENDRA DEVA
JAUNPUR
MALWA
BENGAL
GUJARAT
KHANDESH
R. MAHANADI
R.GODAVARI
GONDWANA
BAHMAN
KINGDOM
R.KRISHNA
ORISSA
BAY
OF
BENGAL
ARABIAN
SEA
VIJAYA
NAGARAM
100 500 100 200 Miles
SCALE OF MILES

this chapter, we attempt to discuss various factors responsible for the growth of Oriya literature and also the socio-political and economic thoughts of the poet Sarala Dasa, who shaped the Oriya language and literature and also commented on the contemporary social customs. Before we discuss the main themes of the chapter, it is necessary to understand the process of development of the Oriya script and language in the light of the general history of Indian languages and literatures.

In the history of Indian languages and literatures the sixth-seventh centuries were remarkably important. Although Sanskrit continued to be used by the ruling class at their higher administrative levels, the *apabhramsa* began to shape into several branches from this period. Although it is difficult to fix the beginning of regional languages, on the basis of the *Vajrayana* Buddhist religious writings from eastern India, proto-Bengali, proto-Assamese, proto-Oriya, proto-Maithili and proto-Hindi can be traced back to the seventh century.[1] The parent stock of languages in eastern India was certainly different from that of other Indian languages. We have earlier observed that Brahmins were invited from different north Indian regions and they were settled in different tribal tracts. In the tribal areas they introduced various forms of Sanskrit on the substratum of the existing Aryan and pre-Aryan dialects. The consequential interaction gave rise to regional languages. They helped develop and systematize local dialects into languages through the introduction of writing and eventually the composition of grammar based on Sanskrit.[2]

The local element in language was strengthened by the insulation of the local areas. On the break up of the Gupta empire arose several principalities which, in the context of the vast subcontinent, were confined to narrow territorial limits. This naturally hindered countrywide communications. Between sixth and tenth centuries, lack of communications between different regions is also indicated by the decline of both internal and foreign trade, which is shown by the striking paucity of coins in this period. It is, therefore, evident that too many principalities, little trade, and less inter-zonal communication created congenial conditions for the origin and formation of regional languages from the sixth-seventh centuries. The emergence of regional languages was paralleled by that of regional scripts. Obviously the regional script was the result of regional insulation and the availability of the locally educated scribes to meet the needs of local education and administration. The country did not have any wide political authority as that of the Mauryas, Satavahanas, Kushanas or Guptas to enforce the same script throughout.[3] So regional variations became pronounced.

Oriya as a language has its very first base in the Sabari or the Austric language. It has been nourished to subsequent shapes and forms by its contact with the Dravidian speech, enriched with the elements of Magadhi and Suraseni. Then it has been influenced by Sanskrit with the expansion of Sanskritic culture in Orissa.[4]

The history of the Oriya script and language can be traced back to the seventh century AD. The earliest use of Oriya words in Sanskrit inscriptions, discovered from a copper-plate grant of Madhav Verma of Khurdha (seventh century AD)[5] and the Manjusha copper-plate of Anantadeva Verma (tenth century AD)[6] bear the testimony of early development of the Oriya script and language as a vehicle of expression. As far as the eastern group of Indian languages are concerned, a breakthrough was made by some of the lower caste wandering *siddhas* of the seventh and eighth centuries who decided to depend on the spoken word as a medium of communication with the common people. Some of them Luipa, Sabarapa, Dombipa, Hadipa, Tantipa and Kanhupa were among the pioneers who sang and preached in 'Oriya', the people's own language, instead of, in Sanskrit.[7] The inhibitory gap between thought and speech thus narrowed and the *bhashas*, the spoken languages, took their second birth and came to be recognized as worthy media for all types of communication.

With the gradual development of script and language, the oral Oriya literature, which was transmitted from generation to generation came to be recorded by its admirers. The local poets also composed their songs, *bhajans* and *jananas,* and preserved them inscribing on the palm-leaves with a stylus. Bachha Dasa's *Kalasa Chautisa* was poetry of such kind considered to be written earlier than the writings of Sarala Dasa. Sarala Dasa's writing, in fact, was a major breakthrough in the history of Oriya language and literature and his literary creations were held to be a challenge against the Brahminical hegemony of knowledge and literature. Sarala Dasa is generally recognized to be the maker of the Oriya literature, by creating a perennial fountain of literary forms and traditions with distinct characteristics of his own that have come down to posterity as an ever-widening stream. Three of his epics, the *Vilanka Ramayana*, the *Mahabharata* and the *Chandipurana* are so far known and of them the *Mahabharata* is his *magnum opus*.

Sarala Dasa was born in an age when the society and literature of Orissa were taking a new shape. He played a vital role in contributing to its growth and development. His date of birth cannot be accurately determined, but can safely be placed in the second half of the fifteenth century AD.[8] The *Adi Parva* of his *Mahabharata* opens with a long invocation addressed to Lord Jagannatha of Puri who enjoyed then and is still enjoying unquestioned supremacy among the Hindu gods and goddesses. In course of this vocation which describes the manifold powers and qualities of Lord Jagannatha, the poet tells us that Maharaja Kapileswara with innumerable offerings and many a salutation, was serving this great deity and thereby destroying the sins of the *Kali* age. The reference leaves no doubt that Sarala Dasa started writing his *Mahabharata* in the reign of Kapileswara, otherwise known as Kapilendra Dev, the famous Gajapati king of Orissa who ruled from AD 1435 to 1467. Kapileswara has been described by the poet as the servant of Lord Jagannatha on account of the fact that this great deity had been conceived and regarded as the real king of Orissa since the reign of the Ganga King, Anangabhima Dev III (AD 1211–38). He formally dedicated his kingdom to Jagannatha and declared himself to be his deputy and first servant. This custom was followed by the subsequent Orissan kings who too conceived of their position in the State as the deputy and the first servant of this deity. Even now, the *raja* of Puri, the traditional representative of the Gajapati kings of Orissa, is the custodian and the first servant of the Jagannatha temple. In view of these facts Maharaja Kapileswara, represented as the first servant of Lord Jagannatha in the opening part of the *Sarala Mahabharata* can be no other than the Suryavamsi king of the same name. The contemporaneity of Sarala Dasa and Kapileswara (Kapilendra Dev) has been widely accepted.[9]

Sarala Dasa witnessed the highest pinnacle of political glory of Orissa under Kapilendra Dev, an Oriya legendary figure after Kharavela. In AD 1435 Kapilendra Dev staged a successful *coup d'êtat* and occupied the throne of the last Ganga King Bhanudeva IV. At this stage Kapilendra Dev was a *nayaka* in the Ganga army and it is said that he rose from the common ranks of Orissan people. He retrieved the prestige of Orissa and also in course of his reign lasting for thirty-three years, established an empire stretching from the Ganges in the north to the river Kaveri in the south. His achievements have been estimated by a historian as follows :

> Kapilendra's reign inaugurated a new epoch in the history of Orissa. Making his way to the throne from a humble position, Kapilendra carved out an extensive empire. As a warrior he displayed unusual energy and vigour of action. He defeated the Sultan of Bengal and extended the north-eastern frontier of his kingdom, up to the river Hughli. He also made extensive conquests in South India. Humayun Shah Bahmani, Saluva Narashimha and Mallikarjuna suffered defeat at his hands. His dominion extended for sometime from the mouth of the Hughli in the north to the Kaveri in the South. There can be hardly any doubt that Kapilendra was a great conqueror, even if we reject in the absence of any conclusive evidence, the statement of the Veligalani copper plates to the effect that Kapilendra successfully invaded Malwa and Delhi or that he proceeded as far as Hampi. The empire which he founded formed a bulwark against the Muslim kingdoms in northern India and the Deccan plateau. Orissa became the standard bearer of Hindu culture; and scholars like Vasudeva Sarvabhauma and religious teachers like Chaitanya came to live there. (Mukherjee 1981: 37)

During the rule of the Ganga and Suryavamsi kings military service was compulsory for all classes and castes in Orissa. Only the Brahmins were exempted from it, but even then, as several inscriptions testify, they also sometimes occupied commanding positions in the Orissan army. Militarism penetrated into the entire society and the local militia, mainly consisting of the *paika*-cultivators, was the mainstay of the Gajapati army.[10] Starting from the Brahmins to the drummers, all castes in Orissa are now found with numerous military titles which they had received during the Gajapati rule. It was a distinctive feature of the Orissa that the protection of the kingdom or its expansion was a responsibility which was shared by the entire population and not by a particular caste or castes. This is believed to have been a tribal heritage and it may be recalled that in 261 BC the people of Kalinga fought against Asoka with a rare collective zeal. However, most subjects joined the army of Kapilendra Dev irrespective of caste distinctions which was made then compulsory to keep up the glory of the Orissan kingdom.[11]

Lord Jagannatha was considered to be the nucleus of Orissan socio-political life and the Oriya soldiers fought unitedly in the battlefield after the name of Lord Jagannatha. Love for Orissan kingdom, however, ultimately generated a love for Oriya language, literature and culture. It was an inevitable consequence of the ferment created by the strong and vigorous rule of Kapilendra Dev.

Kapilendra Dev and his successors patronized the Brahmin scholars and Sanskrit literature, but they did not inhibit the growth of the Oriya literature. Kapilendra Dev and other Gajapati kings were learned scholars of Sanskrit but then they liked to compose Oriya songs. *Parashurama vijaya*, a Sanskrit drama ascribed to Kapilendra Dev also includes an Oriya song, which shows the sympathy of the king towards the Oriya literature.[12] It was a noble attempt to create parallel literature along with Sanskrit and incorporating an Oriya song in the Sanskrit drama like *Parashurama vijaya* ascribed to king Kapilendra Dev only to defend the noble endeavour from the opposition and criticism of the orthodox elements of contemporary society.

There are twelve Oriya inscriptions found at the *Jaya Vijaya* door of the Jagannatha temple Puri believed to have been inscribed during the period of Kapilendra Dev.[13] From this it is evident that Oriya language was accepted as an official language from the period of Kapilendra Dev. By this time Oriya language was enriched by constant interaction with Magadhi, Telugu and Tamil languages.

THE ORIYA *MAHABHARATA* AND ITS SUDRA AUTHOR

There were tremendous temptation which was expressed in almost every Indian language to compose the Puranic literature in vernacular during this period. By this time, the Oriya script had attained her full-fledged shape and the writers wanted to preserve the sacred events of gods and goddesses in the form of their own literature. Since the Brahmins, were still the devotees of Sanskrit literature and had perhaps an aversion to the spoken language and its literature, a poet from the lower rung of the social ladder came forward to accept the challenge of the time. Sarala Dasa was born in such conditions and in such propitious times. He very often tells us that he was an uneducated Sudra cultivator and a man of no importance. But the posterity will not accept his low self-estimation and will no doubt take him to be a man of vision, who responded to the call of the time and brought about a revolutionary change in Oriya literature. His predecessors in Oriya prose and poetry, though their achievements were small, had prepared the ground for Sarala Dasa. They flourished under the

Sanskrit loving Gangas and their literary ventures look like hesitant attempts—as yet unaccomplished task. But the popularity of little thing like Bachha Dasa's *Kalasa Chautisa* must have put into the heart of this semi-educated peasant poet, the necessary courage for the unprecedented endeavour of writing epics in a neglected tongue.

Sarala Dasa was born in the village of Jhankar in the District of Jagatsinghpur. His descendants are believed to be there scattered in the villages around. He was a devoted worshipper of the goddess Sarala whose temple still stands in the village of Kanakpur, about a mile from his native village. Not far from this village the poet's grave (*samadhi*) still stands under a spreading banyan tree, an object of devotion and respect to people all around.

The name of the poet as given to him by his parents was Sidheswara and in his earliest work *Vilanka Ramayana* he has described himself as such, but in his later works his name appears as Sarala Dasa. The poet himself explains several times the reason for this change and tells us that since he became a devotee and servant of the goddess Sarala, he came to be known as Sarala Dasa.

Sarala Chandi is stated by the poet to be the same as Hingula Devi; we must note that Hingula is a goddess of the aboriginal tribes and the name itself is a variant of the Mundari word '*shengel*' which signifies fire. That Sarala is identical with Hingula is what occurs in a colophon in his *Mahabharata*, Sarala Dasa was a Sudra and belonged to the Odra tribe. These Odra tribes are now known by the general name Oda-Chasa or simply as Chasa or Tasa.[14]

Though the biographical references given in the works of the poet are numerous they do not enable us to obtain a full picture of his life. In one verse of the *Drona Parva* he describes himself as the son of Yasovanta, and in another of the *Madhya Parva* he mentions his elder brother's name as Parasurama.[15] He very often tells us that he was uneducated and had no chance of going even to a village school. He had no opportunity of associating himself with the learned men, particularly with the pundits of the *sasanas*.[16] He calls himself a Sudra and a cultivator by profession. Thus he sang in his *Mahabharata*,

Sarala Dasa; the unlettered and unknowledgeable one,
the slave beneath the feet of Sri Chandi Sarala
There is a land on the left of the Goddess
that I cultivated by a plough
and sang different songs of cultivators.[17]

From the *Drona Parva* of his *Mahabharata* we know that he had children and grand-children, and he derived his living from his own paddy fields. There is, however, no evidence to show that he ever received any royal patronage.

What Sarala Dasa achieved through self-education, experience and untiring efforts have all been attributed to the grace of the goddess Sarala, the deity of his devotion and inspiration, and he has nowhere taken any credit for what he wrote. In the *Drona Parva* of his *Mahabharata* the poet says,

It is through the grace of the goddess Sarala that I have been able to make the invisible visible. I make no claim to the authorship of these lines, as I write only what she dictates to me. Ignorant from birth, hardly have been to a school, far from being a celebrity and not vested in *japas* or *mantras*, I write out merely that which comes to my mind, through her grace, sitting under this green banyan tree.

With unconditional humility he expressed himself to be lowlv and sang:

Sudramuni Sri Sarala Dasa, the unlettered one,
the slave beneath the feet of Sri Chandi Sarala
writes whatever she dictates to me.
Oh pious and wise men!
I have no fault in it.[18]

The poet very often has wished us to believe that what he composed in his epics, was dictated to him by goddess Sarala in the night and he merely transcribed her dictates to writing in the day time. A spirit of humility and intense religiousness pervaded the personality of the poet to such an extent that it is difficult to reconstruct a real picture of his real personality from his writings.

Complete surrender to a personal deity, conceiving Him/Her as the source of all knowledge and inspiration, was a common practice which Sarala Dasa shared with other poets of his age. All Oriya poets writing before the middle of the sixteenth century are found, in their works, to have designated themselves as '*Dasa*' meaning a slave or servant of a particular god or goddess. We have thus a long list of poets preceding and succeeding Sarala Dasa, whose names end with '*Dasa*' for example, Vatsa Dasa, Markanda Dasa, Balaram Dasa, Jagannath Dasa and Yasovanta Dasa, etc. None of them has accepted the surname of his caste. These poets also have shown an intense spirit of humanity and have declared themselves in their writings as uneducated, unwise, poor and the lowly.[19] They have said in no uncertain words that they composed their works for the benefit of 'the entire world', 'all people', and 'all creatures'.[20] Why did they do so? Because, they had launched a movement which was developing in opposition to the interest of the èlite and dominant section of society. They had expressed humbly to protect them from the criticism and anger of these elite and dominant classes. In the fields of religion and literature the spirit of humility was the order of the age, which Sarala Dasa shared in a greater degree.

Since time immemorial, goddess Hingula (later on Hinduized and called Sarala) was worshipped by the non-Brahmin Sudras. In Sudra society those who used to worship gods and goddesses were called *munis* (sages) similarly since Sarala Dasa worshipped goddess Sarala he came to be called *Sudramuni*. Sarala Dasa was the pioneer in undermining the tradition of writing religious texts in Sanskrit. As the writer of the Oriya *Mahabharata* he was expected to translate the Sanskrit original, or at least to follow it up closely, but he has done neither. Borrowing merely the bare outline of the original *Mahabharata* he has composed a *Mahabharata* with innumerable omissions, deviations and creations of his own.

The omission and additions are numerous in the Sarala *Mahabharata*. Some important differences between the Sanskrit *Mahabharata* and Sarala *Mahabharata* are illustrated here. Sarala Dasa has not even followed the general scheme of the original *Mahabharata* in dividing his *Mahabharata* into eighteen *Parvas* or books as will be evident from a comparison given below:

Sanskrit Mahabharata	*Sarala Mahabharata*
1. *Adi Parva*	1. *Adi Parva*
2. *Sabha Parva*	2. *Madhya Parva*
3. *Vana Parva*	3. *Sabha Parva*
4. *Virata Parva*	4. *Vana Parva*
5. *Udyoga Parva*	5. *Virata Parva*
6. *Bhishma Parva*	6. *Udyoga Parva*
7. *Drona Parva*	7. *Bhishma Parva*
8. *Karna Parva*	8. *Drona Parva*
9. *Salya Parva*	9. *Karna Parva*
10. *Suptika Parva*	10. *Salya Parva*
11. *Stri Parva*	11. *Gada Parva*

12. *Santi Parva*	12. *Kainsika* or *Aisika Parva*
13. *Anusasanika Parva*	13. *Nari Parva*
14. *Asramavasika Parva*	14. *Santi Parva*
15. *Mahaprasthanika Parva*	15. *Asramika Parva*
16. *Asvamedha Parva*	16. *Asvamedha Parva*
17. *Musala Parva*	17. *Musali Parva*
18. *Svargarohana Parva*	18. *Svargarohan Parva*

In these *parvas*, some of which are obviously his own creations and Sarala Dasa follows the bare outline of the *Mahabharata* story, but omits numerous mythological episodes, fables, incidents, wise sayings, morals, philosophical and dialectical discourses occurring in the original. He has disposed of the entire *Srimadbhagavata Gita* by only making a reference to it in two verses. It may be owing to the view that considered the *Gita* as a remarkable interpolation and that it belonged to the leisured class of the upper strata of society.[21] Besides this, Sarala Dasa has written his *Mahabharata* in a most simple and lucid manner. There are some stories which are either creations of his own imagination or adoptions of several stories current in his time. He describes a story about the origin of the *Mahabharata* war which is not to be traced in the Sanskrit *Mahabharata*. His story runs as follows.

The Kauravas and the Pandavas used to play a game known as *jhimiti* which involved a trial of strength between two persons of both the parties. The Pandavas always used to win the game because of the mighty strength of Bhima, which was never tolerated by Duryodhan, the eldest of the Kauravas. Duryodhan became jealous of the success of Pandavas and he started humiliating them in other ways. He knew that the Pandavas were not all the sons of Pandu, and so in order to humiliate them he addressed Yuddhisthira, Bhima, Arjuna, and Nakula respectively as the sons of Dharma (Sun), Pavana (Wind), Indra (Rain God) and Aswini Kumar (the doctor of heaven), as they entered into his court everyday. Bhima felt greatly insulted and one day shut himself up in his room without taking food and water. Requests of his mother Kunti and others to him to break his fast were of no avail and therefore the mediation of Sri Krishna was sought. When Sri Krishna promised to redress his grievance Bhima opened the door and explained to him his grievance. Sri Krishna smiled and said, 'You should retort by addressing Duryodhan as the son of Golaka' Bhima now got a secret weapon and wanted to keep the words 'the son of Golaka' in his memory by uttering them again and again. Nevertheless, he forgot them when he slept at night and then early in the morning searched frantically for them in every nook and corner of his house. At last his brother Sahadeva revived his memory.

Bhima on the following day entered the court of Duryodhan in a triumphant manner, and as soon as the king addressed him as the son of Pavana, he addressed him as the son of Golaka. Duryodhan did not understand the meaning of the term Golaka and with great anger he slept in his chamber without food and water. He opened the door when his mother promised to explain to him the meaning of the words 'the son of *Golaka*'.

Gandhari then narrated the story of her marriage with Dhritarashtra. She said that, since she was born on the last day of the dark fortnight which is a very inauspicious day, no king wanted to marry her, and those who even proposed to marry her, died immediately. On the advice of Vyasa her father Gandharasena first got her married to a *Sahada* tree (*strebulus asphera*) which in consequence withered immediately. After her first marriage with the *Sahada* tree she was married to Dhritaraṣhtra. Golaka is another name of the *Sahada* tree. After listening to the entire story Duryodhan said, 'You were then a widow and your father managed to marry his widowed daughter to my father. Therefore your father is my enemy'.

Duryodhan then nursed a great anger against his maternal grandfather Gadharasena and planned to take revenge on him and his one hundred sons. He invited his grandfather and uncles to his capital for a visit and imprisoned them together in a locked-up stone house. Duryodhan ordered that they should be supplied with food through a window, but it should be reduced everyday in such a way that after one hundred days the food supplied should be just enough for one man. In consequence of this terrible order many of the prisoners died after a few days, and the remaining ones held a conference to select the last survivor. The eldest son Sakuni being the best, ablest and most intelligent was chosen to be the last survivor and his father Gandharsena bequeathed to him the responsibility of taking terrible revenge upon Duryodhan and his family in the guise of friendship. He exhorted his son to start the *Mahabharata* war by turning, after his death, his wrist bones into the dice which would miraculously obey all calls from Sakuni.

The days passed on and Sakuni remained the only survivor in the prison house. One day, the maidservant, who supplied food to Sakuni, was passing that way and she saw the prince Duryodan sitting and laughing under a banyan tree. She caught the contagion of laughter and could not help laughing. The prince became furious and demanded, 'Why did you laugh?' 'As your Highness laughed', replied the maidservant humbly. 'Why did I laugh?' asked the prince again. The poor woman could give no reply. Duryodhan gave her one day's time to furnish a reply to his query failing which she was to be beheaded.

The fearful maidservant, while supplying food to Sakuni that day, told him about the terrible order of the prince and the previous circumstances connected with it. After listening to her, Sakuni instructed her to tell the prince that he was urinating under the banyan tree, and since innumerable tiny seeds of the banyan fruit floated in his urine, he laughed. The phenomenon of such tiny seeds producing such gigantic trees excited his laughter. The maidservant returned and told the prince exactly as she had been instructed by Sakuni. The prince refused to believe that the circumstances leading to his laughter could have been correctly guessed by a simple woman like her. So he demanded of her the name of the person who had instructed her. When she disclosed the name of Sakuni, Duryodhan personally went to the house of the stone, released him, took him with all honour to his palace and made him his prime minister. Sakuni in disguise became a great friend and well-wisher of Duryodhan but secretly planned his and his family's destruction. It was he who arranged the game of dice between Duryodhan and Yuddhisthira which ultimately led to the great Mahabharata War.

Another story of Sarala Dasa, not to be found in the original *Mahabharata*, is the story of a jackal, which occurs in the *Adi Parva*. Once upon a time, a pair of jackals lived in a jungle near the city of Sukanti where a large number of Brahmins lived. One day, the jackals while searching for food, found a newly born female-infant abandoned on the roadside by a young Brahmin widow. They took it to their house and nourished it with honey and fruit juice. As the infant grew up, they supplied her with all kinds of food collected from the neighbourhood. The girl, in course of, time became an extremely beautiful young woman, and one day she attracted the notice of King Bhagyavara of that kingdom while he was on a hunting expedition. The king fell in love with that young girl and wanted to marry her. Next day the king put forward to her jackal parents his proposal of marrying her. The jackal parents agreed to the proposal, but when the king wanted them to take their daughter to his place for marriage, they declined and insisted that the bridegroom must come to the house of the bride. The king then asked, 'How will you feed the bridegroom party?' The jackal put a counter question to him, 'Have you granted me rent-free land as you have done to your big Brahmins and big lords?' Sarala Dasa's description of the conversation between the king and jackal is very interesting which represents his satire on the king's fabulous land grant to Brahmins and other officials. He shrewdly criticized the king through a jackal that the king was not impartial and did not look after others excepting the Brahmins and the lords.

Next day the king came with a large, retinue and the marriage was solemnized amidst pomp and grandeur. At the end of the ceremony the bridegroom asked, 'Where is the dowry?' The jackal replied, 'All cultivated lands certainly belong to you, but I am the master of all waste lands. I now make a free gift of them to you by way of dowry. Get them cultivated.' In this version the poet has encouraged the king to get the uncultivated waste land cultivated so that poor peasants could be benefited and the agricultural produce be enhanced.

Sarala Dasa appears to have possessed very good knowledge of astrology, which he has exhibited in various parts of his work. He speaks of the characteristics of best horses and of the maladies from which they suffer. He gives the form of incantation with which snake-bites can be cured. He believed that through incantations, charms and tracts people could possess miraculous powers with which they could achieve whatever they desired.

Of his numerous deviations from the Sanskrit *Mahabharata* I mention one instance to illustrate the types of poetical fancies which Sarala Dasa has presented after being free from the original.

The fall of Salya, the last general of Duryodhan, practically brought the Mahabharata War to a close. Bereft of his brothers, best generals, allied kings and most part of his army, that were all destroyed in the continuous war, the proud Kaurava prince sat aghast on a stately elephant in the midst of the battlefield, mournfully surveying the terrible carnage still being perpetrated on the remnant of his army by the relentless Pandavas. There was no other way for him than to flee from the battlefield, but before doing so, he frantically searched for his only son, Lakshmana Kumar, who was also, in the thick of the fight, and fortunately found him out.

'Run away from the battlefield my son and hide your self in a forest', whispered the forlorn prince to his son. The boy being the son of a Kshatriya prince, was at first reluctant to leave the battlefield but had ultimately to yield to his father's advice. The Pandavas were, however, closing upon the remnant of the Kaurava army from all sides and there was no way to escape. While forcing his way through the Pandava army Lakshmana Kumar lost his life under the heavy blow of Bhima's terrible mace. Duryodhan could have no knowledge of his son's death.

After a short while Bhima met Duryodhan and gave a heavy blow to the latter's stately elephant which in consequence fell with its rider. Duryodhan then found an opportunity to hide himself inside the huge bell attached to the elephant's neck and thus remained concealed underneath the pachyderm's dead body. Searches by Bhima to find him out were of no avail.

Evening came and the fight was over for the day. The battlefield became still at night. Duryodhan realized that the night had fairly advanced and he crawled out from beneath the dead body of the huge elephant. But he was confronted with a river of blood, deep and wide with chariots floating like ships, dead elephants and horses like boats and corpses like rafts. For a while he stood bewildered and then thought of using one of the floating corpses as his raft to go to the other side of the river of blood. He saw the bodies of his valiant brother Dushasana, his great friend and general Karna, his instructor Drona and his trusted minister Sakuni, that came floating one after another in the river of blood. He lamented the death of each of them, describing their manifold qualities and powers and wanted to use each of them as his raft, but none could bear the weight of his body and his huge mace. Therefore in each attempt to cross to the other side he plunged into the river of blood. At last he saw a dead body, young and slim, bedecked with jewels, shining bangles and sparkling earrings, that came floating like a rising sun in the river of blood.

'Who are you, lovely one? Can you take me to the other side of the river of blood?' cried Duryodhan and sat upon it with his huge mace. The corpse floated like a canoe and by using his mace as oars, the desperate prince was before long on the other side of the river of blood. When he was safe, he wanted to recognize the face of the corpse which did so great a service to him but alas, he found it to be that of his only son Lakshmana Kumar. His paternal heart broke and he cried loudly. There was no time to lose. He hurriedly dug a trench with his mace and laid the body of his beloved son in it, and then ran to his palace.

The rest of the story is connected with Duryodhan's flight during the same night to the Vyasa Sarovara where he ultimately fought with Bhima and lost his life. The deviations which have just been given are numerous and each has received a distinct treatment in Sarala Dasa's *Mahabharata*. The departures of Sarala *Mahabharata* from the original were intended to communicate a definite message to the society. These departures had obvious social connotations. There was a widespread superstition that a person who weds a girl, born on the *Amavasya* (the last day of the dark fortnight) does not survive. Secondly, widow-remarriage was also another superstition which prevailed at all levels of society. We have noticed earlier that Sarala Dasa was a contemporary of Gajapati Kapilendra Dev, who organized the massive warfare to extend the frontiers of the Orissan empire. The large number of widows of the soldiers killed in the battlefield encountered social indignity and ostracization, besides their personal grief and suffering. By characterizing Gandhari in a totally different way the poet thus intended not only to discourage the superstition but also to cleanse the society of them. Since nobody wanted to have her as his spouse, on Vyasa's advice she was first married to a *Sahada* tree. Later, even though she became a widow, her marriage was solemnized with Dhritarashtra. The poet was not simply a poet but also a reformer. The limitations of his notions of reform, however, should not be overlooked. In a measure, he appears to have conceded the validity of one of the superstitions, namely, the fate of a person married to the *Amavasya kanya*, but the more significant message he conveyed forcefully was the 'remarriage of widows'.

In the second story Sarala Dasa has indirectly criticized the king through a jackal that the king was not impartial and did not look after all the subjects properly. In the foregoing discussion I have illustrated on the land grants made to the Brahmins and the State officials during the Ganga and Gajapati rules in Orissa. Sarala Dasa came of a peasant milieu and he himself was also a peasant. Being a peasant he must have gone through the toiling labour and insufficient resources to pass his days. He being a poet and a sensitive member of society, appreciated the implications of the extensive land grants made to the Brahmins and lords at the cost of toiling masses. Representing the miserable condition of the peasantry Sarala Dasa's disapproval of the discrimination was unequivocal which he intended to convey through the story of a jackal. In the same story, the jackal has gifted all the waste land in the form of dowry to the king, so that it could be cultivated. In this story the poet's discontent against the king and his suggestions for increasing agricultural produce are conveyed in a subtle way. The story does not delineate the poet's anguish and resentment over the prevailing discriminatory policy, there is also a suggestion for a positive approach to reclaim the waste land and bring it under cultivation.

The wicked man gets horrible punishment, the poet has shown it by describing the fate of Duryodhan on the last day of the Mahabharata war. The same day in the evening, Duryodhan faced difficulty in crossing the river of blood, when he was escaping from the battlefield. He used a corpse as the raft to cross the river and on later recognized the corpse that to be that of his lovely son Lakshmana Kumar. There was no time to lament although his heart broke down with sorrow and grief and immediately he buried his son there and escaped. In this story the poet gives us a message of peace and amity. To him, Duryodhan could have saved the lives of his brothers, generals, innumerable soldiers and his son Lakshmana Kumar by avoiding the war. Sarala Dasa believed in peace and advised very often to avoid war. Thus he has deviated from the original by incorporating these stories and many mundane phenomena in his *Mahabharata* which were not supposed to find place in a sacred religious text. The poet's departure from the original and his own way of writing evoked sharp criticism from the learned Brahmins, well-versed in sacred texts. It was to defend himself against such hostile criticisms that he appears to have dedicated all his writings to goddess Sarala and passed them as emanating from Her mouth.

Sarala Dasa's egalitarian philosophy developed with the influence of the prevalent socio-religious environment of his times. He protested and sometimes criticized certain social customs and wanted to reorganize the society with the humanitarian principles of morality, tolerance, and good character. Although he was passionately devoted to the goddess Sarala, he was tolerant of and respectful to all other deities and sects. There is hardly an important Hindu deity who has not received homage from Sarala Dasa. The village deities, presiding deities of cities and towns, sacred trees and snakes have not been left out of his purview and have each received homage in course of his writing the epics.[22] Thus, he has sincerely tried to bring out social integration by uniting the godheads.

Sarala Dasa bitterly criticized and protested against the spread of illicit love relation among men and women and its religious justification given by the Buddhist tantrik sahajiyas. He ridiculed the people who were inextricably attached to worldly pleasure and enjoyment and criticized the sahajiya doctrine and its practitioners vehemently. He characterized Sri Krishna as a *Sahaja Siddhacharya*. In spite of the order of Mahavishnu Sri Krishna did not like to leave for *Vaikuntha* because of his thirty-two thousand women, sons, grandsons and worldly pleasure.[23] The poet has condemned this evil trend and tried to preach morality as the essence of society.

Sarala Dasa rescued the spiritual life from the Sahajiya's religious colour of illegal love and propagated the doctrines of *Advait*, *Surya*, *Yoga* and *Sanjam* (self-control). There was a social and ethical need of abolishing the deep-rooted influence of the Sahaja Siddhacharyas and therefore, the poet tried to draw the attention of society by characterizing Sri Krishna as a *Sahaja Siddha* and the evil consequences of the sexual scandal, womanization, and concubinage.[24] The poet has, however, praised the Kshatriya Sri Krishna but not Gopal Sri Krishna. Sarala Dasa has sincerely warned the people not to be unscrupulous, not to be involved in *sahaja* and *parakiya* cult which were scandalous in the name of *nirvana*.[25]

He further criticized the illegal love relations of Parashara, Santanu, Agnika, Brahma, Drona and Vyasa who were respected figures of the Mahabharata era. His criticism of the prevalent Buddhistic Tantrik and sahaja has been concealed in his analysis of the different characters of the *Mahabharata*. He has condemned the *tatvayogic* advocacy of illicit love relations irrespective of caste or colour, Brahmin or Candala, beautiful or ugly, mother, daughter or sister to attain the *siddhi* (perfection) of meditation.[26] His description of illicit love relations of Satyavati, Kunti, Ambika, Ambalika, Nila, Syamala and Ratnavati, the great women of the *Mahabharata* is not the outcome of bad taste and vile environment, but it was the real picture of the later Vedic society.

Having a male child was earnestly desired because of the loss of males in the continuous warfare of Gajapati Kapilendra Dev. However, *niyoga* (to cohabit with a person other than husband for having a male child) was an established tradition in which the people wanted to procure a male child to preserve the line of their family. Sarala Dasa, therefore, advised his readers to adopt the tradition of *niyoga* to produce a male child.[27] But he did not accept the repetition of such traditions with religious justification for worldly enjoyment. He raised his voice against such ugly religious customs and endeavoured to establish an ideal society. His aim was to characterize the women in forms of mother, daughter, sister and wife. So he has very often insisted upon the children to obey their parents and elders failing which there would be a lot of harm to their study, family, age and life.[28] He has thus tried to help mould social network through morality and good conduct.

Sarala Dasa has criticized the discriminative attitude of Acharya Drona towards Ekalavya and Karna. To him, they were the best students of the world, who flourished independently by virtue of their intelligence, sacrifice, perseverance and self-confidence. The poet has condemned the discriminations between man and man on the basis of birth. From his descriptions of the conflict between the Brahmins and the Candalas in the *Adi Parva* of his *Mahabharata*, it is assumed that there was caste-tensions in medieval Orissan society. The poet, however, did neither believe in rituals nor in pilgrimage or *yajnas*. He did neither advocate the rules of Sastras, nor did he compromise with the pundits. He criticized and revolted against the exploitative orthodox traditions. Thus he sang in his *Mahabharata*:

Neither I studied letters
nor I was knowledgeable of Sastras.
Neither I discuss with the Pundits
nor I got of initiation.
Neither I went on pilgrimage
nor did I visit the sacrificial ceremony.
Neither I studied
nor I did know anything,
But the Goddess Hingulakshi
blessed me to write.[29]

SARALA DASA AND THE JAGANNATHA CULT

My discussion will not be complete without assessing an important contribution of Sarala Dasa to revive and preserve the essence and truth of the Jagannatha cult, which faced a serious threat in the process of the Brahmanization of the deity and the shrine in his time. By this time Lord Jagannatha was already Brahminized and the power and status of the non-Brahmin priests had declined. Sarala Dasa protested against the submergence of this tribal deity into the fold of Brahminism and propounded the theory of Jagannatha cult by offering the dignity due to the tribals and lower classes of society.

Lord Jagannatha of Puri has been sung by Sarala Dasa as the source of all incarnations of God. He is the embodiment in one, of Brahma, Vishnu and Mahesh. He is also the great Buddha. Still more interesting and striking in Sarala Dasa's presentation in the *Musali Parva* of his *Mahabharata* is how Jaganatha came to be in his present shape in the *Kali* era. To him, it was Ekalavya, the Sabara boy of the *Dwapara* era, who grew up to become Jara, whose destiny it was to be an instrument for Lord Krishna's departure from the world. After his death, the naval portion of the body remained unburnt and that have served to become the essence of the deities now being worshipped in the temple of Puri.

The rise of Jagannatha from the holy blue mountain of the Sabara tribe to the status of Vishnu, the most popular god of the Hindu pantheon, accumulates a lot of historical explanations. In *Musali Parva* of his *Mahabharata* Sarala Dasa has described Lord Jagannatha as the incarnation of Lord Buddha.[30] He has incorporated the contemporary traditions of society by virtue of his poetic imagination and has strongly established Lord Jagannatha as Sabari Narayana or a tribal deity. This deity was worshipped in the form of a tree and later on in the form of a piece of a blue stone (*Nilamadhav*) by a tribal chief Viswavasu. In *Sabha Parva* the poet has described the *pitha* of Sabari Narayana as a great shrine. *Anna* (rice), the meat of deer and rhinoceros offered to the deity in form of Tantrik worship and there was no discrimination of caste and colour in the shrine. Jara, son of Viswavasu, used to worship the deity after his father. This was the time when the Aryans were expanding towards east and occupied whatever the shrine, regions they came across. Vidyapati, a minister of Galamadhav, the King of Malav, discovered the worship of the Nilamadhav by Jara. Vidyapati wanted to take away the deity, whereas Jara and his tribal soldiers resisted their move with the threat of dire consequences. There was thus a battle between the two groups. The King Galamadhav won the battle by killing 136 tribal commanders and took away the deity. The deity was soon Brahminized and he came to be known as Jagannatha (the Lord of Universe) instead of Nilamadhav. But the great war did not come to an end only with the killing of the Sabaras. The Sabaras also killed all the family members of the King Galamadhava and occupied an indispensable position in ritual hierarchy of the cult as the non-Brahmin priest. It is widely believed that Galamadhav was cursed by the god to be rootless of his family, because he killed the Sabaras, the primary worshippers of the deity.[31] The Daitas or the non-Brahmin priests of the Jagannatha temple of Puri are believed to have been the descendants of Vidyapati, the Brahmin minister of the King Galamadhav and Lalita, the daughter of Sabara chief Jara who got married to each other before the deity that was located in the forest. This is a legendary explanation of the Jagannatha cult embodying a unique cultural synthesis of Aryans and non-Aryans in the land of Orissa. The poet has explained this theory of the Jagannatha cult not only as a form of protest, but has tried to preach egalitarianism by raising dignity and self-respect in the broken heart of the neglected tribals and other depressed classes of society.

WOMEN'S PROGRESS

Sarala Dasa was also a champion of the cultural uplift of women. To bring pride and honour in the heart of the neglected women folks, he made the women characters of his epics more powerful than and superior to their male counterparts. With a remarkable note of dissent he composed his epics almost in opposition to the pattern of writing of the narrators of the patriarchal social order. He endeavoured to elevate the psycho-cultural status of women in society by emphasizing the women character of his epics, i.e. the role of Sita in killing Sahasrasira Ravana in his *Vilanka Ramayana*; the role of Durga in killing Mahisasura (the so-called buffalo-headed demon) in his *Chandi Purana* and the role of Draupadi in killing the Kauravas in his *Mahabharata*.

In his epic, the *Vilanka Ramayana* the story of the battle between Rama and Sahasrasira Ravana (thousand headed demon) of Vilanka has been lucidly described. The poet here also departs from description of the Dasanana (ten headed) Ravana of the original *Ramayana* and gives a new description of Ravana with one thousand heads. The story begins with a conversation between Rama and Sita in which Rama feels proud of having killed Ravana by virtue of his own prowess. Sita did not accept it and retorted by saying that the killing of the terrible demon could not have been possible without her help and assistance. Sita pointed out that there was a thousand-headed Ravana still living in Vilanka. He should try to kill him alone without her help if he is so sure of his own courage and valour. The challenge was intolerable to Rama. Pending the coronation ceremony, he along with his faithful Hanuman set out for Vilanka. He fought with the thousand-headed Ravana hundred times but everytime the battle ended in vain. There was no alternative except bringing Sita to the battlefield. Sita came triumphantly and appeared before the demon with her irresistible beauty and womanly charm. Looking at her the demon was so enamoured of her beauty that he was about to collapse in infatuation. A simple arrow from the bow of Rama could kill the demon easily.[32]

The *Mahabharata* of Sarala Dasa is a significant new creation in Oriya literature. The poet deviates from the Sanskrit original and represents Draupadi as the unseen destructive force working for the death and extinction of all the Kauravas, all the Pandavas excluding Yudhisthira, and all the *Yadavas* including Sri Krishna. This theory of Sarala Dasa which finds a distinct mention in the *Karna Parva* of his *Mahabharata*, is altogether novel, yet it has proceeded from his pen on account of his conviction that female energy is the preserver and destroyer of the world.

Chandi Purana, the third work of the poet, is based on Sanskrit *Durgasaptasati*. Here the story begins with the prayer of the gods to Lord Vishnu for his incarnation on the earth to kill Mahisasura (the buffalo-headed demon) who was causing devastation. And in heaven, the demon had snatched away the power of the gods and had made them his servants. He had also occupied the throne of Indra. Just at the time when the gods were imploring Vishnu, the demon hurled a hillock at them with his horns. All of a sudden a blazing fire sprang from the bodies of exasperated gods and the fire took the shape of a woman of enchancing beauty. The gods named her Durga and prayed her to come to their rescue by killing the terrible demon. They also offered her the best of their weapons. Durga assured them of their protection and went to the mountain Ratnagiri. She lured the generals of the demon with false proposals of her love for them and their master and killed them one by one. At last the mighty Mahisasura came and gave a fierce fight. Durga was about to abandon the fight in despair, but getting a clue from the heaven, she appeared nude before the demon of indomitable strength. The demon was completely overpowered with passion at the sight of her naked body and lost all his strength. At this opportune moment Durga killed him with her trident. When the fight was over, at once she was struck with shame and directed her anger against the gods. But at the end, she was propitiated and she agreed to be the consort of Siva.[33]

However, the narratives related with Sita and Durga of *Vilanka Ramayana* and *Chandi Purana* respectively indeed, establish the importance and superiority of female power in a patriarchal society. But they also remind us of the political conflict between the early Aryans and the pre-Aryans of India to which these stories are related and that in a measure, the narration synchronized with the process of expansion of the Aryan empire, spread of the Vedic culture, Hinduization of the indigenous cults and shrines that appear to have grown less by frontal conquest and more by intrigue and deception.

This great unschooled peasant poet had an intuitive conviction that the quietly pervasive qualities of women are far superior to the activities of the men. His epic characters, namely Durga, Sita and Draupadi, combine in themselves supreme material achievements with supreme feminine charms. They overtake the male characters by their resilient vitality as well as by their irresistible beauty. Sarala Dasa was thus not only a great poet but the most radical of all the poets in old Oriya literature. He may be unique in the whole of Indian vernacular literature from this standpoint. He does not preach in favour of the practice of Sati, rather he has made Sri Krishna to speak to Uttara that self-immolation and killing of unborn infant (foeticide) is a great sin in the world. This in fact, a great message to the modern world. The widow must live for the sake of bringing up her children and by this act she could rescue the *ihaloka* and the *paraloka* of her family.[34] Similarly, Vyasa also persuaded Kunti not to commit Sati because of the death of Pandu. He advised her to live and bring up her little five children. To him it was the most religious work she could do in this world.[35]

Sarala Dasa understood that the role of women was indispensable for family discipline and social integration as well. So they should maintain a good character, be tolerant, peaceful and virtuous. The men are born of mothers who are women. So women are greater than the men and they have more responsibility towards the construction of an ideal society.[36]

EGALITARIAN OUTLOOK

In an unequal agrarian society, Sarala Dasa was the first peasant poet who declared that all men and women were equal. Discrimination between the rich and the poor, the Brahmin and the Candala was a byproduct of the prevailing social order, he believed. He visualized a social order on the basis of the lofty principles of humanism, social equality and brotherhood. The poet had unbounded love and sympathy for all creatures of the world. He was full of remorse when he described the death of numerous birds and wild animals owing to the burning of the Khandava forest.[37] In the *Adi Parva* of his *Mahabharata* he has made Sri Krishna declare that all fifty-six crores of creatures of the universe are equal and that God takes birth in the form of human beings and lives in the body of every man and woman. So there is neither any distinction between man and man nor between man and woman. In the same *Adi Parva,* Sahadeva did not find out a Brahmin to perform the *puja* of Gokarneswar and brought a Tanila Sabara to Yudhisthira. Then Sri Krishna described that all men were equal and there was no harm in the Sabara's performance of *puja* to the deity.[38]

In *Virata Parva* the poet has made Bhima a cook to arrange 'common sitting and common dining' irrespective of Brahmin and Candala. Even Sri Krishna in the guise of Ananta Padhihari welcomed Yudhisthira into the *rajasuya yajna* which is also another example of Sarala's egalitarian outlook. To the poet, humanity is the index of personality and position, but not wealth, power and prosperity.[39]

Sarala Dasa has criticized Sri Krishna characterizing him as an amorous, abductor of women, diplomat and a conspirator. He has hardly used the name of Sri Krishna in his *Mahabharata*. In place of Sri Krishna the poet has used the name of Jagannatha very often.[40] Similarly, his description of Yudhisthira's marriage at his old age with Suhani, the daughter of Hari Sahu, a poor Vaishya gives an ugly picture of society that an old man could also marry a young girl by virtue of his wealth and power. He was opposed to this custom. The poet has also criticized the luxurious life of the king and other feudal nobles, their polygamous tradition and exploitative attitude. He has warned the ruling class that the kingdom will certainly collapse by the rising of the discontented subjects.[41]

POLITICAL THOUGHT

Sarala Dasa's political philosophy was enriched with the influence of the contemporary institutions starting from the durbar of the king to the level of the village political system. The administrative system of medieval Orissa may be characterized as despotism from above and a kind of democracy from below. Each and every village was autonomous and administered by a village headman *gramika*, with the support of a *panchayat* known as *gramasabha* or *janasabha*. Spread of education, cleaning village roads and tanks and redressal of the village disputes were taken care of by the village administration.[42] Sarala Dasa, although he was born and brought up in a village, envisioned a fine picture of an administrative system as is reflected in his *Mahabharata*, by virtue of his experience, vision and imagination.

To the poet, the first and foremost duty of the king is to protect the life and properties of the subjects from the wild animals and the enemies and to work for their welfare.[43] The king has to adopt two policies to accomplish this duty. These are: participation in war and patronage to religious institutions. The poet did not mean the king must adopt the method of warfare to extend his empire, but he may adopt it to protect the frontier of his own empire. Besides this, the king should also patronize the religious institutions oriented towards social welfare. The poet has expressed his deep concern over the situation of anarchy and bloodshed and, therefore, has pleaded for hereditary succession to the throne. The coronation ceremony was an important factor of the royal dignity. It was politically and economically significant to the people as the king used to declare on that occasion his special policies like remittance of certain taxes, tax-free land grants to the temples and Brahmins. The capital also got rejuvenated with gardens, performances of songs and dances, etc. It may be mentioned here that Gajapati Kapilendra Dev, who was contemporary of the poet, had remitted the taxes levied on salt and cowries,[44] and Gajapati Purushottama Dev remitted the *chaukidari* tax from Brahmins, at the time of his coronation to the throne.[45]

The poet was also conscious of the conduct and worthiness of the king. To him, the kingdom would be destroyed if the king was not intelligent and was guided by the evil-minded counsellors.[46] The king should be religious, faithful, wise, conscientious and knower of the Vedas and Shastras (law books on *dharma*).[47] The poet, however, did not believe that the king would be able to keep up the Kshatriya *dharma* only by being a great giver, for that he must be an adept in military and warfare activities.[48] The poet believed that the power of wealth and weapon of a kingdom was not an eternal power; the religious merit of the king was the real and eternal power of the kingdom.[49]

Sarala Dasa has propounded the theory of an ideal kingship.

According to him, the kingdom and the people enjoyed the consequences of the merits and demerits of the king. The poet has made Yudhisthira to explain the theory of kingship to Dhritarashtra in the *Adi Parva* of his *Mahabharata*. To him, it becomes harmful to the kingdom and the people if the king becomes weak and angry. The king should be efficient both in *sastras* (weapons) and shastras (law books on *dharma*). To acquire the territory of other kingdoms by avoiding war is also another element of the ideal kingship. To punish the real culprit is the real *dharma* of the king.[50]

In the *Santi Parva* of his *Mahabharata*, Sarala Dasa has made Bhishma to explain some policies of the State administration which reflects the poet's political thought. Bhishma advised Yudhisthira:

> Oh! Yudhisthira, rule the country according to *dharma*, or else you will lose it. Rule the country in such a way that nobody should be unhappy. Know it for certain that the happiness of the people is the happiness of the king. Indra sends rain, if a king deals justice even handed to all and his subjects become happy. Award punishments to the culprits after due investigation. Ascertain the truths through spies and cut off the heads of the real enemies of the country. Know it for certain that it is not a sin to punish evil doers. Prepare a rod of twenty-five hands in length and with it get the land measured.[51] Know it that twenty-five *gunthas* make up a *mana* (i.e. 100 decimils), and twenty *manas* make up a *vati*. For one *vati* of land take only one *china* of gold from your subjects. The people will then be happy and wish you long life. Through the spies you should gather information from all parts of the country. Send your brothers to punish rebels. Appoint a wise man as your minister and discharge your royal duties in accordance with his advice. Do not offer all the powers to the minister, but entrust certain responsibilities to him. Do not fine the cultivators with money. Supply the right type of horses to the cavalry. Remain vigilant over the activities of other kingdoms. Listen to the Puranas from the learned men. Visit different parts of the country incognito at night to verify the truth of the information received. Do not give up hunting. Do not cast your longing eyes on the property and wives of others. Do not allow the spies of other kingdoms to enter into yours. Do not harass the cultivators. Set apart sufficient pasture lands for cows. Give away your best things at the places of pilgrimage. Station your generals in proper places of your kingdom. Supply sufficient food to horses and elephants. Entrust your cows to best cowherds. Show respect to the learned and do not be niggardly to poets. Do not punish the faultless.[52]

In Sarala Dasa's vision the links between an effective administrative system and espionage are clear. To him the minister is required to be more clever and intelligent than the king. It was an important duty of the king to appoint a wise and faithful minister.[53] The king was supposed to be dependent on aid and advice of the minister. But according to the poet, it was not proper to entrust all administrative power and responsibilities to the ministers. They should be authorized to carry out limited and specified responsibilities.[54] Moreover, if the advice of the minister went against the interest of the citizens or subjects, the poet's advice is to accept the opinion of the many. Sarala Dasa, here upholds democratic values for the State administration. For example, in the *Udyoga Parva* of his *Mahabharata* the Queen Bhanumati advises Duryodhan not to accept the advice of the minister Sakuni; rather she insists that the opinion of many counsellors should be accepted.[55] Besides this, the poet also advises the king to consult the wise men, the pundits and the poets—in the field of State administration.[56]

ECONOMIC THOUGHT

The economic thought of Sarala Dasa has also been reflected in his *Mahabharata*. His economic thought is the shadow reflection of the economic system of medieval Orissa. We know from his writings that the revenue collected from the subjects was the chief source of royal treasury. To him, this treasury should be spent on expeditions, performances of *yajnas* (sacrifices), construction of temples and on various social welfare activities like digging wells, ponds and constructing roads.[57] The kingdom where least possible less poor people live, is a rich and prosperous kingdom. The poet thought it was the foremost duty of the king to remove poverty and elevate the status of the poor. The king should provide one *pauti* (almost 70 kg.) of seeds for sowing one *vati* (20 acres) of land and collect 5 *pauti* of crops as revenue after the production.[58] The field for which the king does not provide seeds is to be cultivated on the basis of *sanja* and the king should collect one *pauti* of revenue from one *vati* of such land. The king should not levy any revenue on the production of fruits and berries from such land.[59] Those who want to pay revenue in cash, they may pay one china gold coin as the revenue of one *vati* of land. The poet was also in favour of assigning land to the officers in lieu of their salaries.[60] The king should also look after animal husbandry by which the elephants, horses, and cattle be properly maintained. He advised the king to keep pasture land for the maintenance of the animals, particularly, the cattle.[61] Land and cattle were the chief resources of the ruling class and the common people as a whole.

The development of industry and spread of commercial activities was essential for the growth of the state economy, the poet believed. The poet does not, however, appreciate if a merchant tells lies for making profit. According to him, the seller should make profit at the rate of one for four, four for twenty and twenty for eighty only.[62] It was not improper on part of a king to involve himself in commercial activities. But he should not be greedy as regards his property or the property of his subjects.[63] The poet puts emphasis on economic stability and on liberal attitude of the king for maintaining a strong and healthy political system.

The political philosophy of the eminent philosophers like Manu, Parashara, Brihaspati, Sukra and Kautilya was directed towards strengthening the sovereign monarchy and protecting the kingdom. But the aim behind the political thought of Sarala Dasa was for people's welfare, development of agriculture and of peasants, protection of hermits and thus reconstruction of a healthy and ideal society.

HISTORICAL AND GEOGRAPHICAL PLACES IN SARALA *MAHABHARATA*

Before I conclude, a word about how important Sarala Dasa's *Mahabharata* could be as a source of the general history of India of his time. Sarala Dasa mentions an unusually large number of historical and geographical names which he incidentally introduces into all his narratives, particularly into those narratives that relate to notable marriages e.g., those of Bhanumati, Draupadi and Uttara, in which the kings of all parts of India are said to have been present. In his *Sava Parva* he presents a historical and geographical picture of India as was known to him and devotes the major portion of thirteen thousand verses to the description of *digvijayas* (conquests) of the Pandavas, in course of which they are taken to different kingdoms passing through numerous temples, shrines and rivers. Arjuna, the third Pandava reached Malwa after coming across Yamuna, Ganga, Gaya, Haridwara, Vaitarani, Narmada, Saraswati, Krishna, Godavari, Kashi, Kaushika, Punyabhadra, Sarvabhadra, Suvarnabhadra, Chandrabhaga, Chitrotpala, Dhauli, and Puskara.[64] The names of the countries and kings that participated in the Mahabharata war, have been given in the *Udyoga Parva*. In the

Asvamedha Parva, the sacred horse has been taken to different parts of India, names of which have been mentioned.

The art of writing history or geography in a direct and systematic manner was not one of the achievements of the ancient Hindu writers. Sarala Dasa could hardly be expected to have been different so far as this feature is concerned. Among the geographical places mentioned, some may be fictitious, but the vast majority of them are identifiable. Evidently the poet did not use any maps. He has left to us certain historical and geographical names which he had heard of, and which he could remember at the time of writing and conveniently incorporate them in his metrical compositions.

Sarala Dasa's knowledge of history and geography constitutes an important and interesting source of information to all classes of readers. After giving a description of each kingdom that participated in the Mahabharata war, the poet puts together the names of the participating kingdoms which practically cover the whole of India. Along with the names of the kingdoms of the Mahabharata age such as Sindhu and Gandhara, occur the names of kingdoms of the historical times such as Garjana (Ghazna or Ghaznì), Tihudi (Tehri in Garhwal), Bhutan, Assam, Bengal, Malwa, Saurastra, Kashi, Kanyakubja, and Maharashtra.[65] The poet also mentions Lohapura (Lahore), Punjab, Haryana, etc. His geographical knowledge extended beyond the north-west frontier of India as is evident from his allusions to place names like Ghazna, Khurswan and Persia.

The geographical names of the central India such as Ajayameru[66] (Ajmer), Ranastambha Pura[67] (Ranthambhor), Amber, Jodhpur, Kalinjar (Kunjara), Chanderi, Bhopal, Seopur, Ujjain[68] and some others of western India have found mention, for example, Baglana[69] (in the Nasik district) and Bhrigukachcha (Bhrigupura), now known as Broach in Gujarat. The sacred cities of the region now known, as Uttara Pradesh have necessarily found mention, but along with them sacred places not traditionally sacred, also occur in his work. Kalpi[70] (in the Jalaun district), Kalanagara (Kara near Allahabad), Suklapura (Sakaldih in the Chandauli tahasil of Bareness), Jaunapur,[71] Delhi and Malwa[72] have been prominently mentioned. Two long narratives of the Sarala *Mahabharata* have been devoted to the wars connected with Kalpi. After the break-up of the Delhi Sultanate on the eve of Muhammad Tughlaq's death, Kalpi became a small independent State and also a bone of contention among the Sultans of Delhi, Malwa and Jaunpur. The tripartite struggle that ensued for its

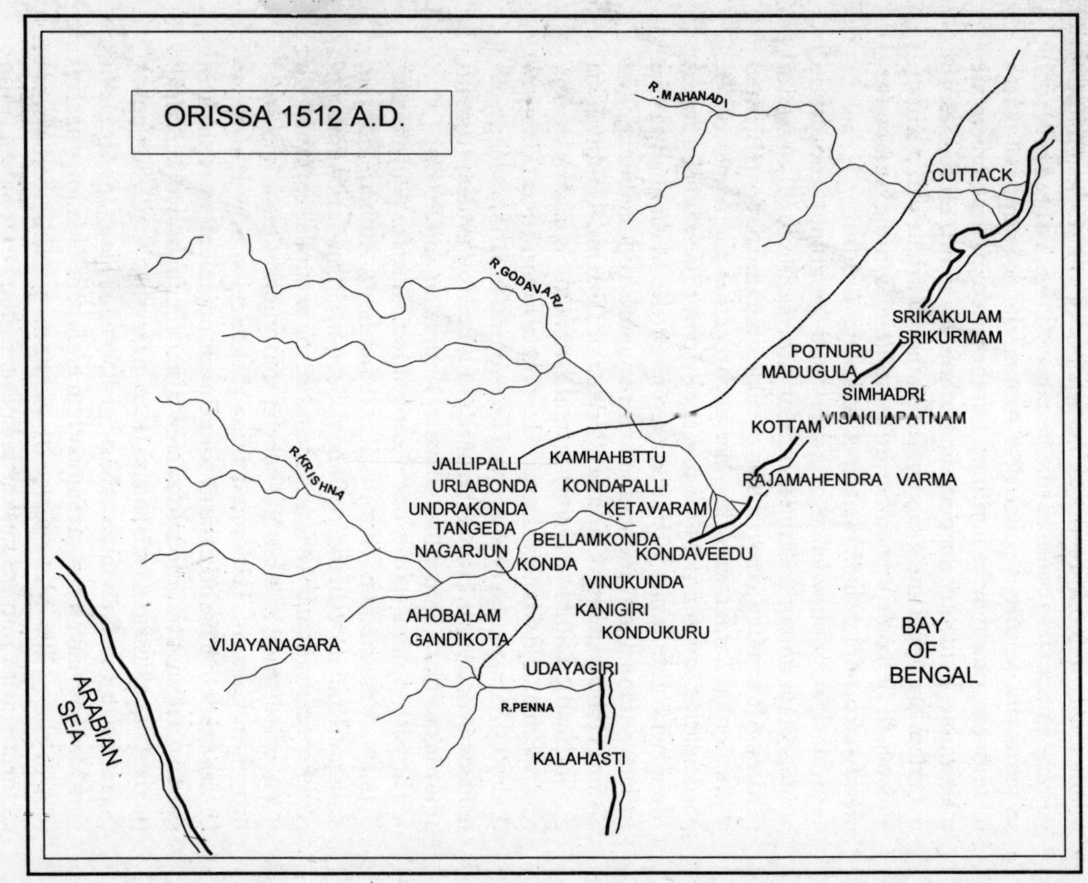
ORISSA 1512 A.D.
R. MAHANADI
CUTTACK
R. GODAVARI
SRIKAKULAM
SRIKURMAM
POTNURU
MADUGULA
SIMHADRI
VISAKHAPATNAM
KOTTAM
RAJAMAHENDRA
VARMA
R. KRISHNA
JALLIPALLI
KAMHAHBTTU
URLABONDA
KONDAPALLI
UNDRAKONDA
KETAVARAM
TANGEDA
BELLAMKONDA
NAGARJUN
KONDA
KONDAVEEDU
VINUKUNDA
KANIGIRI
AHOBALAM
KONDUKURU
GANDIKOTA
VIJAYANAGARA
UDAYAGIRI
R.PENNA
KALAHASTI
BAY
OF
BENGAL
ARABIAN
SEA

possession has become the subject-matter of the narratives, which Sarala Dasa has written in his own way in Puranic settings with changed names of the Sultans, but with the actual names of their territories. Similarly, he has also written a long narrative in the *Sava Parva* echoing the conflict between Orissa and Jaunapur, which he calls Yamunapura or Yamadagnipura.

From the Bihar and Bengal regions, mention has been made of the main political divisions such as Magadha, Mithila, Bhojapura, Anga (Karna-Mandala),[73] Tirabhukti, Varendri (Nilendri), present East-Bengal (Velaladesa, i.e. the country of Ballalasena)[74] and West Bengal (Mandaradesa, i.e. tract where the fort of Mandara existed).[75] Sarala Dasa also refers to a few cities of this region such as Udandapura[76] (Biharsherif), Vaishali (Vrisalanagar), Champapura (the capital of Anga, i.e. the Bhagalpur-Monghyr region), Velav Alipur (i.e. Gaur, the capital of Ballalasena), Jnanapura on the Ganga which he makes the capital of the kings Jnanachandra and Kulachandra, Hari Kalanagara by which he probably means Pattikera, the capital of Harikaladeva, Ranavanka, Malla and Dandapura, perhaps the capital of Dandakabhukti or present-day Midnapore.[77]

The poet knew well the names of the ancient political divisions of Assam such as Kamarupa, Pragjyotisapura, Sonitapura and Kamakshya and also the name of the medieval kingdom Lakshmipura or Lakhipura in the valley of the Brahmaputra, ruled by a tribal people known as Chhutias in the thirteenth century. In the contiguous Himalayan region he places the countries of Nepal, Bhutan, Pasupalaka (probably Sikkim), Khagadesh (the land of birds), Mahatrinadesa (the land of tall grass), the Mahlaradesa (i.e. the land of the wandering tribes) and the Jalatarangadesa (i.e. the land with a very high rainfall).[78]

Sarala Dasa being a poet of Orissa it is natural that a very large number of geographical places of this region have been mentioned by him. He refers to such well-known places as Ekamra (Bhubaneswar), Konark and Puri. He also alludes to the places like Amaravati and Kalakala.

The poet shows a detailed knowledge of south India, particularly of the Andhra region where, probably, he served as a soldier in the army of the Orissan king. He correctly refers to the main political divisions of the south of his time, namely: Coromandala,[79] Vijayamandala or Mallikamandala (which was no doubt the Vijay-nagara empire ruled over by his contemporary Malikarjuna),

Cholamandala, Udayamandala or Kanchimandala (which was no doubt the territory administrated by Saluva Narasimha and in which Udayagiri and Kanchi were situated), Kosalamandala or Brahmasahi by which the poet certainly meant the Bahamani kingdom. Beyond these regions also figure the names of Chitradesa, i.e. Cheradesa or the Kerala country, Kajjaladesa and Khinnadesa which are to be identified with Konkan and its strong fort Khelna.[80]

The poet refers to a very large number of places situated in these broad divisions. Of the places situated in the Andhra region, mention has been made of Mahendranagar (modern Rajahmundry), Kundavedi or Kondavidu situated in the Guntur District, Amarachuda parvata or Devarkonda situated in the Nalagonda District Udayagiri and Chandragiri, the famous forts in the territory of Saluva Narasimha, and Kakatipura which was the old capital of the Kakatiya kings. Many smaller places like Bhadrachalam, Vijayawada (Bezwada), Matanga or Srisailam, Patala-Ganga, etc., have also been referred to.[81] The poet writes connected with the mythological stories about the origins of the shrine of Mallikarjuna situated on the top of the Sri Sailam, by the side of the Patalaganga that flows nearby. He has also written a very long narrative in Puranic form about the battle of Devarakonda fought between the Gajapati King Kapilendra and the Bahamani King Humayun.[82]

The famous places in the present Tamil Nadu region which figure in the Sarala *Mahabharata* are Kanchi, Chandrapura (i.e. Chingleput), Kaveripattna which is perhaps the modern Nagapatam, Udanga which is a shortened form of Urangapura or Urgapura, the ancient name of Trichinopoly, Padmanabha-Parvata (i.e. the temple of Srirangam), Rudra Parvata (i.e. the temple of Tanjore), Pandavanagara (i.e. Madura), Ramesvara, Setuvandha, etc. The names mentioned from the Mysore region are Balaura (i.e. Bellary), Belanagara (i.e. modern Belur in the Hasan District) Suravara-Pattana (i.e. Sriranga Pattanam) and Maulavatinagara which is probably the city of Mysore.[83]

We also come across numerous historical names that have been mentioned by him. He refers in slightly changed forms to such historical royal dynasties as the Chauhanas, Chalukyas, Solankis, Haihayas, Yadavas, and Andhras. Mention has been made of such historical Orissan kings as Yayati of the Somavamsi dynasty and Chudanga (Chodaganga) of the Ganga dynasty. Mallikarjuna and Virupaksha, the emperors of Vijayanagara, who were the contemporaries of the poet, have been referred to more than once. In his *Sava Parva*, Sarala Dasa takes Sahadeva in course of his *digvijaya* to different parts of Bengal, which were said to be ruled by such kings as Kulachandra, Jnanachandra, Belalasena (Ballalasena) and Kesabasena. The poet mentions simultaneously the names Hastikalanagara and Madhu-matangadesa which are probably the corrupt forms of Harikalanagara and *Madhu-mathanadesa*. The existence of the historical kings named Harikaladeva, Ranavanka Malla and Madhumathanadeva ruling in East Bengal, is corroborated by epigraphic records. When Sahadeva went to Mithila on the occasion of the *Rajasuya* sacrifice, Nandasena is said to have been ruling there. It appears that Nandasena is a corrupt version for Nanyasena or Nanyadeva who was a historical king of Mithila.[84]

The above survey of the geographical and historical information obtained from the Sarala *Mahabharata* is a brief one. Sarala Dasa rose above the prejudice of his age and incorporated into his work the mundane matters, which from the orthodox standpoint were not to find place in a sacred book like the *Mahabharata*. He has even given us glimpses of the Muslim history and geography of his time. We have stated earlier that his *Mahabharata* is neither an adoption nor a translation of the Sanskrit original. The story of the original *Mahabharata* has been merely a means to him to portray his own knowledge and experiences, events of the surroundings in which he lived, and above all, the history and geography as were known in his time.

CONCLUSION

Sarala Dasa was the pioneer in writing the sacred texts in Oriya and he was the poet, who laid the foundation stone of the rise and growth of regional literature in eastern India. He was neither a court poet, nor did he receive any political patronage. He was very much of the village to which he owed all his nurture. It was the deity of the village who offered him the qualities and sensibility of a poet and it was in the same village that he composed the three major works, namely, the *Mahabharata*, the *Vilanka Ramayana* and the *Chandi Purana*. It must have been a difficult job for him to write these epics in Oriya and to get them recognized by the readers of the contemporary literary taste, so far away from the king and his court, and assume, in climax, the designation of *Sudramuni*. It is not true that the poet called himself so, because he belonged to the Sudra or non-Brahmin class. It was a time when all pundits were invariably Brahmins, and they looked down upon all those who wrote and belonged to the other caste groups as nothing but Sudras. As a challenge to this situation and for repudiation of this prejudice of the pundits, Sarala Dasa called himself *Sudramuni* and wrote in his epics that he had been conferred upon the title '*Sudramuni*' by the great mother goddess Sarala. He was the first in Oriya literature to challenge and prove that a Sudra can also be a *muni* (the writer and analyst of epics and worshipper of deities) and was successful in disproving the elitist superstition and social prejudice. He deviated from the set tradition through his philosophy and action which was never tolerated by the orthodox sections of society. The poet had to face a lot of criticism and humiliation, because he was a Sudra and dared to compose Puranas and Shastras in the language of the common people. To protect himself from the anger and criticisms of the learned pundits, he described himself as uneducated, unknowledgeable of Shastras, and whatever he wrote was due to the grace of the goddess Sarala.[85]

The first regional epic literature that was composed in eastern India was Sarala Dasa's Oriya *Mahabharata*. It was then widely read in Orissa and Bengal as well. Sarala Dasa composed his *Mahabharata* in the late fifteenth century and his *Mahabharata* after being delineated in Bengali script, was widely read in Bengal till the Bengali *Mahabharata* came to be written by Kasirama Dasa.[86] Kasirama Dasa's *Mahabharata* was heavily influenced by the Sarala's *Mahabharata*. The legends of 'Jarasandha killing' (*Sava Parva*), the story of 'True Mango' (*Vana Parva*), 'Draupadi-Hidimbika quarrel' (*Madhya Parva*) were borrowed by Kasirama Dasa, from Sarala's *Mahabharata*. Kasirama Dasa had a close relation with Orissa and he lived in south-western Bengal (Radha Desa) which was a part of the Gajapati empire of Orissa during fifteenth and sixteenth centuries. This region was deeply influenced by Oriya culture and literature during the time of Kasirama Dasa.[87]

Adikabi Krittibasa, who wrote the *Ramayana* in Bengali, after half a century of Sarala Dasa, also faced similar kind of opposition and criticisms from the orthodox sections of society. The orthodox pundits systematically propagated an idea that those who would listen to the *Ramayana*, the *Mahabharata* and other eighteen Puranas written in the regional languages would go to hell after their death.

To give a justification for their propaganda they composed the following *sloka* in Sanskrit :

Ashtadasha puranani ramasya charitani cha
Bhashayah manavah srutwa rourabam narakam brajet.[88]

They also created a Bengali proverb characterizing three peoples' poets: Krittibasa, Kasi Dasa, and Bamun Ghosh as the symbols of destruction. The proverb is as follows.

Kruttibese, Kasi dase aar Bamun gheshen,
Ei tini sarbanese.[89]

One may well imagine the nature and contents of criticism faced by the poet Sarala Dasa who wrote his *Mahabharata* half a century before Krittibasa wrote his *Ramayana*. In spite of the bitter criticisms and opposition of the orthodox sections of society, the epics of Sarala Dasa earned tremendous popularity in Orissa and Bengal as well. His language was simple and expressive. His *Mahabharata* was a national epic from many standpoints. Although written in medieval Oriya, the book contains a lot of significant information as regards the history and geography of India. The epic has been extremely popular in Orissa, because it is a portrayal of Oriya social life that in several respects is true even today. To make his motherland important in the eyes of his compatriots with the holiness of Puranic sanctity, he not only linked Sri Krishna's death in Saurastra to the rise of Jagannatha at Puri, but he brought the Pandavas to visit all the holy places of Orissa and made them to live like common Oriya people.

The *Mahabharata* of Sarala Dasa was written two centuries before the *Mahabharata* came into existence in Bengali. The *Mahabharata* in Telugu was written by three successive court poets and was completed in the eighteenth century.[90] Perhaps in no other modern Indian language was a *Mahabharata* produced so early (fifteenth century AD) and by so gifted a poet as Sarala Dasa, a semi-educated Sudra. And no other vernacular *Mahabharata* had the same hold on the common people as the Oriya *Mahabharata* of Sarala Dasa. The stories, characters, episodes and lines from Sarala's *Mahabharata* have gone deep into the life of the people of Orissa and Bengal. In the eyes of the people of Orissa, this epic assumed the sanctity and the sanctifying power of a scripture. Many an Oriya peasant ceremonially starts its recital in order to bring about the birth of a son. The popularity of this *Mahabharata* caused it to be translated into old Bengali and according to B.C. Mazumdar it was translated in the early sixteenth century.[91] There was also a considerable impact of Sarala *Mahabharata* on the Bengali *Mahabharata* of Kasi Dasa, written in the early seventeenth century.[92]

The growing importance of Sarala *Mahabharata* and the custom of listening to its recital with love and devotion, in order to get a male child, assume the very Brahminical notion of sanctity of a religious scripture which the poet sought to present as a feature that was contested. Although in a measure the creation of epics in the regional language was considered a way of challenge to the Brahminical order, it was not successful in wiping out the very Brahminical concept of the sanctifying power of the scriptures from the mindset of the people of medieval Orissa. The sanctifying value of the scripture or religious literature continued to exist whatever language it might have been put in.

Besides this, one praiseworthy effort of Sarala Dasa was to have advised the people in the *Adi Parva* of his *Mahabharata* that they should plant trees on roadsides as a last resort of begetting a male child. The ancient kings planted trees and dug wells on roadsides as a matter of their welfare measures, which was of course, in a limited manner; but the peasant-poet in Sarala Dasa could spread the message of planting trees as an act of earning religious merit would have been more effective. In one way, he may not have been fully successful in erasing the Brahminical notion from the mindset of the people, but associating religious fervour with the plantation of trees his message would have been quite successful as a measure of the welfare of society. By this Sarala Dasa achieved two things with one stroke. First, his own *Mahabharata* became popular when it was widely read out and listened to by the people. Second, the people were also encouraged to plant trees on roadsides which was certainly a contribution to community benefit.

The works of Sarala Dasa were the literature of protest. They were a protest against the poets and writers of the court at a time literature was possible to flourish when the king was there to patronize it. It was a protest against the empty religiousities of the time with the king as the protagonist and also against all writings in Sanskrit which were patronized by the king. The real life was then lived far away from the king and his court. The beliefs and superstitions that had evolved in the shape of worship and inspiration of several religious traditions which had their sway over the land, there had been almost no outlet to give an expression to true feelings and aspirations of the people. It was Sarala Dasa who took to the pen to bring in all that to literature and filled in the gap. More than anything else, he so brilliantly proved that Oriya language could make really many things possible and that as regards its potential and competence as a medium of expression, Oriya would in no way fall behind Sanskrit. It was, in fact, Sarala Dasa who gave new vitality and ability to Oriya as a language.

In the subsequent time three other important poets were there who contributed to the growth of Oriya literature by following the tradition set-up by Sarala Dasa. They were Arjuna Dasa, Markanda Dasa and Chaitanya Dasa who composed the *Ramabibaha*, the *Keshav Koili* and the *Nirguna Mahatmya* respectively.

The *Ramabibaha*, composed by Arjuna Dasa was a popular poem of medieval times. It is believed to have been written in a manner following the stories narrated by Sarala Dasa. The poet's description of the events of birth of Bali, Sugriva and Hanuman is almost identical to the narration style in the *Vilanka Ramayana* of Sarala Dasa. Poet Arjuna Dasa has lucidly described from the beginning of Biswamitra's invitation the episodes of killing of Tadaka, liberation of Ahalya, birth of Bali, Sugriva and Hanuman, Sita's marriage with Rama and defeat of Parashurama by Rama. This work has been divided into twelve *chhandas* and is composed of different lyrics. It was widely popular among the people of all classes of village society.[93]

Markanda Dasa's *Keshava Koili* is earliest of the Oriya *Koili* literature. Pundit Suryanarayan Dash has placed Markanda Dasa as a poet of pre-sixteenth century. But there is no evidence to regard him as a contemporary of Sarala Dasa, nor can he be placed in pre-Sarala Dasa period. Markanda Dasa composed his *Keshava Koili* before the period of Jagannatha Dasa (sixteenth century) and because of the popularity of *Keshava Koili*, Jagannatha Dasa composed his *Artha Koili* being influenced by the earlier. *Keshava Koili* was included in the school syllabus of medieval Orissa since the time of its composition and thus it came to be extremely popular. Similarly Dinakrushna Dasa's *Gunasagar*, Hari Dasa's '*Ka-Ka Kalindi tire, Kha-Kha Khelanti dhire*', etc., *chautishas* were taught and recited in every medieval Oriya village.[94]

Chaitanya Dasa in his *Nirguna Mahatmya* openly declared the superiority of the Buddha to Krishna as an incarnation of Vishnu. He said, 'Krishna not only abducted many women and enjoyed princesses as well as cowherd girls, he even committed incest with his own aunt and sister. He killed cows and he killed his own uncle.' But Chaitanya says of the Buddha,

> He condemned sacrifices and preached the knowledge of 'Brahman'. He repudiated the knowledge of 'Brahman' alongside performance of rituals such as pilgrimages, sacrifices, and fasting. He extolled the superiority of Brahmajnana to mere ritualistic outward performances. The Buddha-Narayan thus discarded all superficial tenets and emphasized on self-culture.[95]

Chaitanya Dasa propagated the philosophy of *nirguna* and tried to establish the superiority of Buddhism to the tenent of Hinduism propounded by Krishna.

The subsequent developments in Oriya literature owe a great deal to Sudramuni Sarala Dasa. He influenced as we will see, not only Arjuna Dasa, Markanda Dasa and Chaitanya Dasa, but also the Panchasakhas of the sixteenth-seventeenth centuries and later several other poets down to the modern times. Many a poet including Utkalamani Gopabandhu Das, the Western-educated Radhanatha and Madhusudan of modern times (twentieth century) drew heavily on Sarala Dasa's storehouse of poetic creativity for their own literary creations. Sarala Dasa's writing in Oriya educated the common peasant folks and brought about an awareness against injustice and exploitation. Besides contributing enormously to the growth of Oriya language and literature, Sarala Dasa also tried to pave the way for the construction of an egalitarian social order.

As a poet and reformer Sarala Dasa was profoundly sensitive to the great socio-political and religious upheavals through which he li[illegible]ed. His poetic achievement was not something which transcended [illegible]nvironment but was directly enlarged by his social conscious-[illegible] and his critical relations to a changing social fabric. His phase of literary activity coincides with the first challenges to the institutions of the ruling class and traditional social structure with its caste base and gender biases. He shows how far-reaching transformations in the social hierarchy which simultaneously began to take place in medieval eastern India are crucial to an understanding of the complicated contemporary social systems.

NOTES

1. R.S. Sharma, 'Problem of Transition from Ancient to Medieval in Indian History', *The Indian Historical Review*, vol. I, no. 1, March 1974 p. 7.
2. Idem.
3. Ibid., p. 8.
4. Chittaranjan Das, *A Glimpse into Oriya Literature*, Orissa Sahitya Akademi, Bhubaneswar, 1982a, p. 12.
5. *JASB*, vol. XXIII, 1907, p. 282.
6. *JBORS*, vol. VII, 1931, p. 175.
7. K.N. Mohapatra (ed.), *Charya-Gitika*, Cuttack, 1976, p. 8.
8. K.C. Panigrahi, *Sarala Dasa*, Sahitya Akademi, New Delhi, 1975, p. 12. See for detail K.C. Panigrahi, *Sarala Sahityare Aitihasika Chitra*, Prajatantra Prachar Samiti, Cuttack, 1989 pp. 93ff.
9. P. Mukherjee, *The History of the Gajapati Kings of Orissa*, Kitab Mahal, Cuttack 1981, p. 1, vide H.K. Mahatab, *History of Orissa*, vol. I, Cuttack, 1959, p. 263, and Panigrahi, op. cit., 1975, p. 13.
10. *Paika Kheda*, Jagannatha Gabeshana Samiti, Emar Math, Puri, 1953, Chap. 1.
11. The Puri Plates of Narasimhadev IV dated AD 1384 and 1385 refer to four persons who had the title of *mahasenapati* but, in fact, they were *srikaranas* (chief accountants). These copper-plates refer to seven persons who had the title of *sandhivigrahika*.

    So the military titles are observed with many castes in Orissa, such as: senapati, chhamupati, champati, champtiray, rauta, rautaraya, dandapata, dandasena, dakshina kabata, uttara kabata, samanta, samantaray, patra, mahapatra, samantasimhar, singha, manasingha, paharasingha, baliyarsingha, ray, raysingha, rayamohapatra, nayaka, pattnayaka, dandanayaka, gadanayaka, padhihari, pradhan, khuntia, behera, dalabehera, jena, badajena, samal, sasmal, parija, parichha, jagaddeva, mardaraja, harichandan, majhi, bhramarabara, vahinipati, parikarnaya and bahubalendra.
12. Surendra Mohanty, *Oriya Sahitya Adiparva,* Cuttack Students Store, Cuttack, 1963, p. 121.
13. Ibid., p. 125.
14. Quated in B.C. Mazumdar (ed.), *Typical Selections from Oriya Literature*, vol. I, Calcutta University, Calcutta, 1928, p. xxvii.
15. Sarala's *Mahabharata* (*Madhya Parva*).
16. '*Na padhili akshara mu nuhen Sastrabadi,*
    Panditanka Sange basi na kali samadi,
    Kusthane basili na basili bipra gosthi,
    Sishubuddhi mohara, bayasa alpati'.
17. Sarala's *Mahabharata* (*Madhya Parva*).
18. Sarala's *Mahabharata* (*Drona Parva*), Radharaman Pustakalaya (R.P.), Cuttack, n.d., p. 2.
19. K.C. Panigrahi, op. cit., 1975, pp. 16–17.
20. Sarala's *Mahabharata* (*Sava Parva*), R.P., Cuttack, n.d., p. 390.
21. D.D. Kosambi, *Myth and Reality*, Popular Prakashan, Bombay, 1962, pp. 14–18.

22. K.C. Panigrahi, op. cit., 1975, p. 36.
23. Surendra Mohanty, op. cit., 1963, pp. 162–3.
24. Ibid., p. 170.
25. Ibid., p. 177.
26. '*Prajoopaya vinischayah Siddhih*', two Vajrajana works of Oriental Institute, Baroda, quoted in Surendra Mohanty, op. cit., 1963, p. 269.
27. A.B. Mohanty (ed.), Sarala's *Mahabharata* (*Adi Parva*), Directorate of Culture (D.C), Orissa, Bhubaneswar, 1968, pp. 284–5.
28. Ibid., *Adi Parva*, p. 29.
29. Sarala's *Mahabharata* (*Bhishma Parva*), Radharaman Pustakalaya, Cuttack, n.d., pp. 2, 3, 142.
30. Ibid., *Mushali Parva*, R.P., p. 38.
31. Ibid., pp. 28–9.
32. Sarala Dasa, *Vilanka Ramayana* (*Lanka Kanda*); see also Banamali Rath, 'Development of Oriya Literature (AD 1434–1803)', in P.K. Mishra and J.K. Samal (eds.), *Comprehensive History and Culture of Orissa*, vol. 2, pt. II, Kaveri Books, New Delhi, 1997, p. 533.
33. Ibid., p. 534; K.C. Panigrahi, op. cit., 1975, pp. 10–11.
34. Sarala's *Mahabharata* (*Drona Parva*), R.P., p. 54.
35. A.B. Mohanty (ed.), Sarala *Mahabharata* (*Adi Parva*), D.C., Orissa, Bhubaneswar, 1968, pp. 70–2.
36. Sarala's *Mahabharata*, R.P., *Adi Parva*, pp. 22, 26; *Madhya Parva*, pp. 52, 120, *Drona Parva*, p. 57; *Vana Parva*, p. 241; *Udyoga Parva*, p. 3.
37. Ibid., *Madhya Parva*, pp. 28–9.
38. Ibid., *Adi Parva*, p. 634.
39. Ibid., *Sava Parva*, p. 240.
40. Ibid., *Sava Parva*, pp. 425–80.
41. Ibid., *Santi Parva*, pp. 11–12.
42. N.K. Sahu, *Oriya Jatira Itihasa*, Orissa State Text Book Publications Bureau, Bhubaneswar, 1974, p. 37, 1st edn.
43. Sarala's *Mahabharata, Adi Parva*, p. 164; *Vana Parva*, p. 136; *Santi Parva*, p. 12; *Asramika Parva*, p. 46.
44. *South Indian Inscriptions* (*S II*), vol. V, no. 1035.
45. *Jagannatha Temple Inscriptions*, dated AD 1470.
46. Sarala's, *Mahabharata*, *Adi Parva*, p. 131.
47. Ibid., *Sava Parva*, p.138.
48. Ibid., *Adi Parva*, pp. 65 and 100.
49. Ibid., p. 160.
50. Ibid., pp. 88–9.
51. Idem.
52. Ibid., *Santi Parva*, p. 89.
53. Ibid., *Madhya Parva*, p. 105.
54. Ibid., *Santi Parva*, p. 12.
55. Ibid., *Udyoga Parva*, p. 56.
56. Ibid., *Gada Parva*, pp. 29–30.
57. Ibid., *Santi Parva*, p. 12, *Aswamedha Parva*, p. 18.
58. Ibid., *Asramika Parva*, p. 46.
59. Ibid., *Santi Parva*, p. 11; *Swargarohan Parva*, p. 2.

60. Ibid., *Santi Parva*, p. 12.
61. Idem.
62. Ibid., *Svargarohana Parva*, p. 6.
63. Ibid., *Sava Parva*, p. 32; *Virata Parava*, p. 29.
64. Ibid., *Sava Parva*'s, pp. 332 and 558–9.
65. Ibid., *Udyoga Parva*, p. 88.
66. Ibid., *Adi Parva*, p. 116.
67. Ibid., *Vana Parva*, p. 287.
68. Ibid., *Sava Parva*, p. 131.
69. Ibid., *Virata Parva*, p. 88.
70. Ibid., p. 162.
71. Ibid., p. 87.
72. Ibid., *Madhya Parva*, p. 76.
73. Ibid., *Śava Parva*, p. 206.
74. Ibid., *Adi Parva*, p. 116; *Virata Parava*, p. 29.
75. Ibid., *Madhya Parva*, p. 257.
76. Ibid., *Virata Parva*, p. 87.
77. K.C. Panigrahi, op. cit., 1975, p. 61.
78. Ibid., p. 62.
79. Sarala's, *Mahabharata* (*Madhya Parva*), R.P., p. 293.
80. Ibid., *Virata Parva*, p. 86.
81. Ibid., *Adi Parva*, p. 116.
82. K.C. Panigrahi, op. cit., 1975, pp. 62–3.
83. Sarala's *Mahabharata* (*Virata Parva*), R.P., p. 87.
84. K.C. Panigrahi, op. cit., 1975, pp. 63–4.
85. Ibid., pp. 17, 18 and 23; quoted from *Vilanka Ramayana*, *Chandi Purana* and *Mahabharata* (*Kainshika Parva*), in Pathani Pattnaik, *Sarala Dasa*, Orissa Sahitya Akademi, Bhubaneswar, 1995, pp. 14, 15, 21 and 54; and see also Surendra Mohanty, *Oriya Sahityara Madhyaparva O Uttara Madhyaparva* (Oriya), 6th edn., Cuttack Students Store, Cuttack, 1995, pp. 240–1.
86. B.C. Mazumdar (ed.), 'Introduction', in *Typical Selections from Oriya Literature*, vol. I, Calcutta University, Calcutta, 1928.
87. Sukumar Sen, *History of Bengali Literature*, Sahitya Akademi, New Delhi, 1960, pp. 132–3; see also Surendra Mohanty, *Oriya Sahityara Adiparva*, Cuttack Students Store, Cuttack, 1963 pp. 196–202.
88. Quoted in D.C. Sen, *Bengali Language and Literature*, Calcutta University, Calcutta, 1911, p. 7.
89. Idem. See also Pathani Pattnaik, op. cit., 1995, pp. 14–15.
90 M. Mansingh, *History of Oriya Literature*, Sahitya Akademi, New Delhi, 1962, p. 67.
91. B.C. Mazumdar (ed.), op. cit., 'Introduction', 1928.
92. Sukumar Sen, op. cit., 1960, pp. 132-3.
93. S.N. Dash, *Oriya Sahityara Itihasa*, Grantha Mandir, Cuttack, 1963, p. 417.
94. Ibid., p. 412.
95. Chaitanya Dasa, *Nirguna Mahatmya*, edited by A.B. Mohanty, Prachi Samiti, Bhubaneswar, 1927, Chap. XVI.

CHAPTER 3

The Social Resurgence: Role of the *Sudramunis* and other Reformers

SARALA DASA in his version of the legendary origin of Lord Jagannatha gave primacy to the Sabaras (hunters) or the non-Brahminic priests of the Lord. His radical attempt to shape the Oriya language and literature inspired the later generations. In the sixteenth century, five *bhakta-kavis* (devotee-poets), popularly known as the *panchasakhas*,[1] who came from generally the downtrodden background followed the tradition created by Sarala Dasa and contributed to the growth and efflorescence of Oriya literature. They challenged the legitimacy of the prevailing social order and even suffered on that account at the hands of the dominant vested interests.

The *panchasakhas* represented a movement of protest against all authoritarian interference and imposition. They could not accept everything as genuine and sincere that succeeded in securing the king's approval and patronage. They refused to be swayed by the stream of Gaudiya Vaishnavism even if such refusal lost them the protection of the king and his courtiers. They had to face the authority's anger, many trials and much humiliation. Despite all obstacles on their path they raised their voice against caste hierarchy and discrimination against the Sudras, low status of women, against all exploitative institutions including the king's authority, Brahminical ritual and priesthood and the sanctified hegemony of Sanskrit language. Their protest was also against all authoritarian Shastras and even against all authoritarian *guruvada*. They were well versed in Shastras and took great pains to translate important Shastras to bring their essential contents within the reach of the common men. They were themselves the gurus, but did not approve of the dogmatic pretensions of the gurus. They sang the glory of Lord Jagannatha and the great values He symbolized, but they were all against any institution that tended to become static and insensitive.

The *panchasakhas* ascertained the right and dignity of mankind. They struggled hard and endeavoured to establish justice and equality in a caste-ridden medieval society. Four of these *bhakta-kavis* were non-Brahmins and, of course, all of them identified themselves as Sudras, the exploited class of society; they worked for their spiritual liberation. Their movement, however, should not be characterized as a non-Brahmin movement against the Brahmins as a class. It was launched against Brahminism, a concept which signified claim of a privileged position by a narrow group based on prescriptive rights and upholding a society based on exploitation, domination and discrimination. It is also noteworthy that Jagannatha Dasa, the author of Oriya *Bhagavata* being a Brahmin joined this movement. The common tenor of their assertion was that one could be high or low according to one's quality or merit, but never on the basis of birth or social origin.

BALARAMA DASA

Of the *panchasakhas* who flourished in the first quarter of the sixteenth century, the eldest and the most radical was Balarama Dasa. He was born in AD 1473, at Puri.[2] It is said that his father Somanatha Mohapatra was one of the ministers of the Gajapati kings and his mother was Manamaya. Gopinatha Mohapatra was a minister of Kapilendra Dev and according to Pundit Binayak Mishra, Gopinatha Mohapatra was an ancestor of Somanatha Mohapatra.[3] On the other hand, according to Nagendranath Vasu, Somanatha was a minister of the Bauri caste. The Bauris who are now living in Mayurbhanj District believe that their ancestors bearing the title of Mohapatra used to be ministers at the Gajapati courts. They were deprived of this position from the period of Prataprudra Dev.[4] This may be a personal reason which led to Balarama Dasa to go for *samnyas* and raise his voice against this discrimination. Despite being the son of a former minister of the Gajapati court Balarama Dasa's social status was considered ignominious because of his birth in a lower non-Brahmin community. He was called the *Sudramuni* by the Brahmin priests of Puri and he had also unhesitantly identified himself as *Sudramuni* in his writings.

However, Balarama Dasa lived in Puri and he had already completed his *Jagamohan Ramayana* in Oriya before the coming of Sri Chaitanya to Orissa. According to *Jagamohan Ramayana*, he was uneducated but he completed this epic at the age of thirty, (i.e. in AD 1503).[5] He himself also acknowledged in his *Ramayana* that he was born in a Sudra family at the command of God. Thus he sang,

I Balarama Dasa was during the time of
the incarnation of Rama,
And I saw everything holding
a light in my hand.
My Lord instructed me to come to this world
and appear in this Kali era
as a Sudramuni.[6]

From the *Brahmanda Bhugol* and the *Vedantasara Gupta Gita* of Balarama Dasa it is known that he was a contemporary of the king Prataprudra Dev (AD 1497–1540). In the seventeenth *anka* (i.e. AD 1509–10) of Gajapati Prataprudra Dev, it is mentioned that, *Vedantasara Gupta Gita* was written by Balarama Dasa. Thus he writes,

There is a King Gajapati Prataprudra
in the line of Solar dynasty
during his seventeenth regnal year,
in the lunar fortnight of the month of Makar.[7]

He championed the cause of the Sudras at the *muktimandap*, challenged the orthodox Brahmins and proved that the Sudras were in no way inferior to them in *jnana* or knowledge. Once there was a debate in *muktimandap* between Balabhadra Rajguru and Purandar on a metaphysical problem. The debate became fierce and nobody could give a proper answer. Balarama Dasa who was present there, dressed as a Brahmin, stood up and solved the issue. But his real identity was soon revealed and he was taken to task by the pundits for participation in the debate. The Brahmins rebuked him in harsh language and said that he, being a Sudra, had no right to listen to and participate in Vedanta discussion. The writings of Balarama Dasa clearly reflect on discrimination of Sudras by the Brahmins and their deprivation of knowledge in the sixteenth-century Orissa. Thus he writes in his *Vedantasara Gupta Gita*:

The Brahmins disputed after
listening to my answer,
rebuked me in harsh language
that you are son of a Sudra,
And speaking of Vedanta?
You are a stupid, the lowly man
And speaking of Vedanta?[8]

The king imprisoned Balarama Dasa following the appeal of the priests. Balarama Dasa declared then that Lord Vishnu was nobody's exclusive possession: 'He is his who is a good and pious man—be he a Brahmin or Candala by birth. Nobody has monopoly with the kind and merciful Lord Jagannatha.' But he finally passed the test by performing a miracle. The following morning he put his hands on the head of Haridasa, an unlettered 'dumb', who with his blessings recited the Vedanta instantly to the great astonishment of the king and the priests.[9] Balarama Dasa was then freed. The incident suggests the extent to which Balarama Dasa had worked to spread education among the masses. A result of his contribution in this respect was that Haridasa who was taken by the Brahmins and the ruling elite virtually as a dumb could now discuss the high Vedanta philosophy.

Balarama Dasa's keenness to make knowledge accessible to all is further illustrated from another incident. Once he tried to listen to the *Brahmavidya* discussion by the pundits in the premises of the Jagannatha temple. He was caught and again rebuked by the orthodox Brahmins. They said he being a *Sudramuni* had no right to listen to *Brahmavidya*. They also referred to him as a dog that had ventured to eat fine rice. Balarama Dasa has thus described this sorrowful incident in his *Gita Abakasa:*

Seeing me the Brahmins rebuked
and told me, 'you lowly man'
listened to the knowledge of the 'Brahman'?
What the God told earlier to Aditya
that you listened to
being a Sudramuni?

That you ate the fine fried rice
being a dog?
Catch hold of him,
We will inform to the king.[10]

Balarama was taken to the king and the latter also reprimanded him by saying that it was not within his rights to have entered into the assembly of scholars. Balarama, however, was undeterred. In a bold and open challenging tone he declared before the king that 'all have the right to acquire knowledge and that only the Brahmins cannot monopolize it'.[11] That was taken as an act of insubordination and was not to be tolerated by the king. Balarama was again thrown into prison and it was ordered that to prove his claim, he should now make an untouchable recite the sacred *Gita*. Balarama spent the night alone praying to Lord Jagannatha so that he get out of the sad situation. In the morning when the king was in the temple to have the test played through, Balarama submitted before him that as no untouchable would be allowed to enter into the temple, he was ready to recite the *Gita* in the form of Oriya *chhandas* as he had composed them the night before. He did as he said and surprised the whole assembly including the king. The poet established that, with the grace of God, any ignoramus was competent enough to speak and express what the right knowledge of God really was. The incident indicates simultaneous smashing of two myths. One, that only Brahmins were able to interpret the scriptures and the second, that the scriptures could be only in the Sanskrit language. Projecting himself as an untouchable Balarama interpreted the *Gita*, and at the same time, he rendered the holy scripture into the language of the people. The king and pundits were surprised and Balarama was freed.

The devotional and poetic part of Balarama's personality is best revealed in his book *Bhava-Samudra* (Sea of Emotion). Once there was a car festival in Puri and *bhakta* Balarama Dasa was madly rushing over to climb up the chariot and to have a *darshan* of Lord Jagannatha. But it was not simply that he was not allowed *darshan*; he was, instead, beaten and thrown out in the presence of the king and the vast crowd that had gathered for the festival. In desperation Balarama then retired to the solitude of the Puri sea-beach and poured out his heart in shame, anger and defiance. He made three chariots of sand on the sea-beach and worshipped them. On the other hand, to everyone's surprise, the three original chariots of Lord Jagannatha,

Lord Balabhadra, and goddess Subhadra mysteriously stopped. Nobody could know the reason. King Prataprudra Dev then saw in a dream that night that the Lord had shifted to the sand chariot of the *bhakta* Balarama Dasa, and that the original chariot would move only if the king invited to Balarama Dasa. Further, the Lord told the king, 'I will go wherever my devotee does go and it will be ever true in the world.'[12]

In his *Bhava-Samudra*, the poet's heart-deep love and unbound devotion to Lord Jagannatha is very much revealing. Thus he sang in his *Bhava-Samudra*:

My Lord, you drove me out
of the Nandighosha car,
who will pull the ropes of your car ?
My lord, you will make a move
taking me with you
or else, you will be there.
My Lord, I have held you up in my heart,
How could you make a move ?
My Lord, you are the only shelter
of this slave Balarama.[13]

But the sublime, all-forgiving, self-forgetting love and devotion of a pious soul comes out at innumerable places as follows :

You made me a prisoner
at the hands of the king,
But I have made you prisoner,
in the secrecy of my heart
Tell me, my Lord, that you are my prisoner
And that gives me blessed happiness.[14]

Desperately the poet has appealed to Lord Jagannatha and wants to know to whom he should tell his worries if 'He' will not look at those. In the same work *Bhava-Samudra* he says:

'Oh Hari', I stayed at Kshetra (*Puri*) *as your refugee,*
I got the result of your shelter,
Oh Hari, you betrayed me,
Balia Dasa does not believe that
you made me a prisoner at the hands of the king,
Oh Hari, I believed you so strongly,

And I got the punishment now
why did you do like this?
You did not tolerate me once
if I committed a mistake?[15]

Besides his magnum opus *Ramayana*, Balarama Dasa has left behind a very large number of smaller works like *Bhava-Samudra*, *Mriguni Stuti* (the Hind's prayer) and the *Lakshmi Purana* which are socially significant and noteworthy in many respects. Almost all of them are still popular, but the most universally read and enjoyed of all his small pieces are the *Mriguni Stuti* and *Lakshmi Purana*. The poet has tried to establish through the *Mriguni Stuti* that a devotee can save his life from danger if he could really pray to God with devotion. The deer's prayer propagates the *bhakti* and Vishnu cults through the sad predicament of a deer being caught between a hunter in front and forest fire behind. She is saved from this situation through prayers to the Lord who sent clouds to quench the fire and a snake to bite the hunter.

REFORM THROUGH *LAKSHMI PURANA*

Lakshmi Purana is a unique literary product, which transgressed the gender boundaries of the Brahminical Hinduism. Even today, after four centuries of its creation, this book provides one of the finest, highly edifying and intensely entertaining folk-plays in Orissa. Moreover, it is socially remarkable, as a crusade against untouchability and caste hierarchy. It preaches the triumph of love and devotion. The *Lakshmi Purana* describes the visit of goddess Lakshmi to the house of Sriya, a Candala woman, who worships her with *bhakti* and inner purity. According to Balarama Dasa, humility is the essence of the *bhakti* that is expressed through Sriya. Thus he writes in his *Lakshmi Purana*,

I salute mother, thou art the wife of God Vishnu,
I am a lowly woman of lower caste,
do not know how to worship,
And I stay in the slum of Candals,
Kindly accept my devoted prayer,
The chief queen of Vishnu was moving on the road,
She could not tolerate the humility
of Sriya and appeared in front of her.[16]

The poet has tried to bring out social reform through Goddess Lakshmi, who is the most popular deity in the agrarian society of Orissa. Thus he begins his story. Goddess Lakshmi visited the house of her devotees irrespective of their caste and granted them boons for their prosperity. But it was not tolerated by Lord Jagannatha and Baladeva, who were supposedly the upholders of caste hierarchy. Consequently Lord Jagannatha did not allow Goddess Lakshmi to enter into the temple at the instance of Lord Baladeva, and therefore, she lived alone at the sea-beach of Puri. Lord Jagannatha and Baladeva became pauper at the departure of Lakshmi. They did not get alms, although they wandered from door to door with a begging bowl. They spent days after days without food and in the end they unknowingly reached the house of goddess Lakshmi and asked for some food. Goddess Lakshmi came to know this and she sent a message through her maid that it was the house of a Candala woman and food would be served if they were ready to accept. Lord Jagannatha and Baladeva gave their consent to take food from the Candala house. Thereupon food was immediately served. Lord Jagannatha, however, could guess from the taste of the food that it was cooked by Goddess Lakshmi and everything was disclosed very soon. Lord Jagannatha and Baladeva then requested Goddess Lakshmi to forget all things of past and to come back to the temple. At last Goddess Lakshmi agreed to come to the temple if her principles of social equality were to be accepted by Lord Jagannatha and Baladeva. Goddess Lakshmi wanted that the people of all denominations, from Candala to Brahmin, had to take food together in the premises of the temple. Even the Brahmins would snatch away food from the hands of Hadi (untouchables) and they would wipe unwashed hands on the heads of each other. Lord Jagannatha and Baladeva accepted the ideology of Goddess Lakshmi and permitted her to visit the houses of her devotees, Candala or Brahmin.[17] In the end, victory came to the untouchables and the women class through Goddess Lakshmi. Balarama Dasa endeavoured to reconstruct society with the principles of 'equality' not only between man and man but also between man and woman and symbolized women as the cornerstone of social change, that is what he really wanted to convey through the story of Goddess Lakshmi. Installing dignity to womanhood and simultaneously fighting against caste, untouchability and the custom of divorce and bringing a reform were the aims behind the story.

REFORM THROUGH *RAMAYANA*

The *Jagamohan Ramayana* of Balarama Dasa is one of the three most important epics in Orissa, the other two being Sarala's *Mahabharata* and Jagannatha Dasa's *Bhagavata*. What makes it unique is its portrayal of character, making the heroes and heroines of the epic much more human and natural. Above all, it is purely an Oriya composition. Though *Jagamohan Ramayana* is the title in the colophon, the work subsequently acquired the name *Dandi Ramayana*, as it became a popular work and the contents were being recited or sung by the *danda* or the roadside (i.e. before the crowded public). Sanskrit *Ramayana* was read out by the pundits on a high *mandap* (altar) of the temple or of a village where the king, zamindars, and Brahmins of high class came to listen to the sacred text. When Balarama Dasa wrote the *Ramayana* in Oriya and it became popular and began to be sung and recited outside the humble house in the *danda* (common street between two rows of houses) the high priests of Sanskrit and opponents of the text ridiculed it as *Dandi Ramayana*.

Balarama Dasa condemned the priests who were responsible for degrading religion to mere means of making a livelihood. In his *Ramayana* he exposed the greedy and exploitative attitude of the priests. When Rama, Lakshman and Sita had been to Gaya to offer *pinda*, the priests also did not spare them from collecting *dakshina*.[18] Sugriva, Hanuman and Bibhishan were the ideals of the poet because of their honesty, sincerity and helpful attitude. When the city of Ayodhya was reconstructed, Rama himself invited these three persons to the ceremony celebrating the inauguration of the city. The poet expressed his view through the story of Rama that the persons who help selflessly at the time of danger, their footprints are more important than the greatest religious activity like *yajna*.[19] The poet did not surrender to the traditional view of superiority of Brahmins, on the basis of merely their birth in the Brahmin families, and if they were ignorant of true dharma, i.e. social equality. He believed that only those were the real Brahmins who knew the religion of the Vedas, and were engaged in right deeds and recognized the sanctity of the selfhood of others. Those who lived only in the shrines and exploited people in the name of religion were not, according to Balarama, true Brahmins.[20]

To Balarama Dasa all human-beings are of the same blood and

flesh. To prove this he went on describing the close friendship between Purushottam Rama and Guhaka, a tribal chief of the forest. Both of them were so close that Rama delivered the message of killing Ravana first to Guhaka. Secondly, the poet also made Rama eat the berries already tasted by a Sabari (tribal woman) while he was in exile in the forest.[21] The poet has tried to establish the significance of *bhakti* here. The God accepts anything when the devotee offers it with love and devotion. Particularly here Rama being represented as God and his acceptance of half-eaten berries from a tribal woman proves the system of high and low to be a myth. The poet's description of the incident of the meditation of the Sudramuni Sambuka in his *Ramayana* symbolizes his deep concern for the development of status of the Sudras. To him, Sambuka attained *nirvana*, being killed by Rama, on the day of *Sukla-Panchami* of the month of Bhadra. This day has been regarded as the *Rishi-Panchami* and according to a popular belief, those who worship the Sudra saints on this day get fortune and propserity.[22] It is not only an instance of the poet's concern for the Sudra community but also of his vision and objective of building an egalitarian social order.

CONDEMNED PRIESTHOOD AND RITUALS

Balarama Dasa protested against the tradition of begging mercy and sympathy of the king. To him, the ideal amongst the people or subjects are not to beg before the king, rather they should beg before God. His message to his readers was to assert their right before the king, not to seek his mercy.[23] In a measure thus he upheld a revolutionary idea that would lead to equality between the king and the people of his kingdom. As a social reformer he condemned the oppressive features of the Brahminical religion and was critical of the classes who exploited the people, subsisted on their toil without giving them anything in return. The class of Brahmin pundits, well-versed in the Puranas, Dharmasastras, Smritis but unsympathetic towards social problems was the exploiting class. Besides, there was another class of fraud *samnyasis* who only grew beard, wore beads, put *tilak* on the forehead, ashes over the body and remained social parasites.[24] In his *Ramayana*, Balarama Dasa preached that there was no difference between the rich and poor, strong and weak, ignorant and knowledgeable in the eyes of Lord Jagannatha. The Lord treated equally everybody, be he a Brahmin or from an ordinary lowly insect.[25]

When Balarama repeatedly asserted that he was 'son of Lord Jagannatha', it was not that he thought of himself. He identified himself with the entire humanity and meant that the whole mankind irrespective of caste, creed and colour were the children of Lord Jagannatha. To him, an ordinary man lost his caste when he became a *bhakta*. All *bhaktas* identified themselves as *dasas* or servants of God. In *Bhava-Samudra* he described that a person of higher varna could not ordinarily be compared with a Candala if the latter worshipped Vishnu.[26] Balarama also criticized rituals. He did not believe in ritualistic fast or meditation. He also did not worship any god other than Lord Jagannatha, who for him symbolized the monotheistic ideal of his religious life. Thus he sang in his *Bhava-Samudra*,

That neither I did fast
nor I did meditate,
Neither I worshipped the idols
nor the image of any deity,
My Lord, I have no existence without you
then whom should I tell my worries.[27]

The literature of Balarama Dasa was a source of inspiration for social revolution in the medieval times. The potentiality of social revolution which is embedded in his writings is, in fact, very much rare in the Oriya literature. It was an intellectual adventure on the part of a *Sudramuni* to snatch away the hidden and sacred *Brahma-vidya* from the clutches of the Brahminical culture and the orthodox varna system and to introduce it to the untouchable sections in the sixteenth-century Orissa. The long-ranging foresight that was behind his endeavour to advance the progress of humanitarian principles in medieval times is beyond description. Faced with the wrath of the king and harassed by the orthodox priests, Balarama made a lofty declaration of social equality in the land of Lord Jagannatha that knowledge cannot be monopolized by a particular section of the society nor be expressed in a particular language. The poet's *prajna* and potent thoughts have ever widened the horizon of the liberation of the human community.

JAGANNATHA DASA AND ORIYA *BHAGAVATA*

Jagannatha Dasa, the second of the celebrated *panchasakhas*, is popularly remembered for his unique contribution to the Oriya literature through his *Bhagavata*. The Oriya *Bhagavata* like Balarama's poetic creations helped in checking the pride and traditional outlook of the orthodox pundits. Jagannatha Dasa himself was a Brahmin and an erudite scholar in Sanskrit. He was many years junior to Balarama Dasa and almost of the same age as Chaitanya. He had already completed his *Bhagavata* before the coming of Chaitanya to Orissa in AD 1510. Chaitanya first met him under the *Kalpa-bata* (eternal banyan tree) within the precincts of Jagannatha temple, reciting there his recently composed *Bhagavata* to the common folk from the rural areas. Chaitanya, like the common folk, was charmed to listen to the episodes of Krishna's life described in such lucid, sonorous, rhythmic and mellifluous couplets. These are some outstanding characteristics of Jagannatha's popular Oriya *Bhagavata*. Chaitanya intuitively saw in the poet Jagannatha a spiritual kinship that developed into a warm, lifelong friendship between them. He was deeply impressed by Jagannatha Dasa's work and his intellectual discourses on metaphysical matters. Therefore, Sri Chaitanya called him *Atibadi* or the 'Very Great'.[28] The Bengali Vaishnavas were enraged at the title of *Atibadi* given to Jagannatha Dasa. Chaitanya very calmly replied:

> The sand, stone, wood and trees of this land are equal to gods. Comparatively the dignity of man is so high that it is beyond imagination and therefore it is correct to address Jagannatha Dasa '*Atibada*'. . . . Be small like grass and tolerate all like trees. Be pleased when held in respect and don't be sorry over disregard. Then you will be a pure Vaishnav. And remember, the devotion is destroyed in discrimination.[29]

Atibadi Jagannatha Dasa was born in AD 1487 at Kapileswarpur Sasana, Puri. His father was Bhagawan Dasa a *Purana panda* by profession. His mother was Padmavati.[30] Padmavati was a pious lady with a deep religious instinct. It is said that because of her keen interest in listening to the stories of glory of Krishna that Jagannatha Dasa made up his mind to render the Sanskrit *Bhagavata* into Oriya. She could not understand the Sanskrit *Bhagavata*. So the noble son, to fulfil his mother's pious desire, started writing the Oriya *Bhagavata* chapter by chapter, which grew into a scriptural composition in course of time. Jagannatha Dasa had acquired enough knowledge in his early age in philosophy, Vedas, Vedantas, and in Oriya and Sanskrit literatures. According to Dibakara Dasa, the author of the *Jagannatha Charitamrita* (seventeenth century) Jagannatha Dasa composed Oriya *Bhagavata* at the age of eighteen only,[31] which was an outstanding achievement, surprising everyone.

Balarama Dasa had already established himself as a revolutionary poet, a *bhakta* and a *sadhaka* as well. He had already maintained a distinct character of Utkaliya stream of Vaishnavism, quite different from the Gaudiya stream. When the Gaudiya Vaishnavas took exception to the fact of Jagannatha not being technically a Vaishnava, the latter wanted to be initiated into it, even though Chaitanya had argued with his followers that a person like Jagannatha Dasa was in spirit a true Vaishnava whether technically he had embraced the faith or not. However, the poet Jagannatha Dasa was initiated into Vaishnavism by Balarama Dasa at the instance of Chaitanya himself.[32] The very act of initiation of Jagannatha Dasa by Balarama Dasa, who was considered to be a *Sudramuni* by the Brahmins, was certainly a revolutionary step taken by Chaitanya and Jagannatha Dasa as well. It shows their egalitarian attitude and perception of social equality. Poet Jagannatha did not give importance to varna in the worship of Radha and Krishna. To him, any person irrespective of his or her caste or sex, Brahmin, Sudra or a woman, could be taken as a guru, if he/she worshipped Radha and Krishna with twelve lettered *mantras*.[33]

Jagannatha Dasa was a great believer in *bhakti* and he particularly emphasized a harmonious and balanced relationship among *jnana, bhakti* and *yoga*. His immense popularity among the masses cannot ordinarily be estimated. His Oriya rendering of the original Sanskrit *Bhagavata* recited in his own sweet voice had incomparable impact on the people. In fact this was an event of great significance in the history and development of Oriya literature. The Prakrit form of Oriya language received a great thrust of development from such renderings of a major work of Sanskrit. With this came a mass upsurge for regional literature, along with Jagannatha's growing eminence as a poet, scholar and thinker. There were naturally some envious people who tried to run down his achievements and even paint him as a man of low morals. He had created enemies among the *Purana pandas* by his recitations as they had lost the *dakshina* which they used to receive from the devotee-listeners. As for himself, even though hundreds gathered at his recitations of the Oriya *Bhagavata*, he never even asked for a penny. There were others too who considered his Prakrit rendering of *Bhagavata*, a rich source material of classical Sanskrit learning, as an assault on that tradition and an affront to scholarship. Needless to mention that Sanskrit pundits had a rather poor opinion of regional literature and languages. Sarala Dasa and Balarama Dasa, the authors of Oriya *Mahabharata* and *Ramayana*, had encountered severe wrath from the classicists. Jagannatha Dasa, however, became the focal point of all envy, resentment and anger due to the added reason of the envy of the followers of Chaitanya. We notice the instances of how the Oriya *Bhagavata* of Jagannatha Dasa was called in derogatory terms *Teli Bhagavata* or the oilman's Bhagavata by the Brahmins of *Muktimandap mahasabha*.[34] There are legends which describe how even King Prataprudra Dev was misled into believing in some of these evil rumours circulated by Jagannatha Dasa's envious enemies concerning his morals. The pundits, deadly jealous of Jagannatha Dasa lodged a complaint against him with a charge of abducting women. The pundits alleged that Jagannatha Dasa was a magician and by virtue of his *mantras* he was attracting a large number of women than men. The time would come when all women would be running after him leaving their own husbands.[35] This complaint against Jagannatha Dasa led to his imprisonment by King Prataprudra Dev. It is a fact that a large number of his women devotees caused trouble for him. Finally he was released when he proved that he had half the body of a woman. Jagannatha Dasa made it possible through the yogic practice of *Kaya-sadhana*, which was also another characteristic of the *panchasakhas*.

Jagannatha Charitamrita of Dibakara Dasa (seventeenth century) and *Dardhyata Bhaktirasamrita* of Rama Dasa (late seventeenth century) give varying versions of the above legends. Some of these also attribute extrasensory and almost supernatural, spiritual powers to Jagannatha. Once an affluent merchant from Kasi presented a piece of very valuable sandalwood to King Prataprudra Dev who in turn handed it over to Jagannatha Dasa to prepare paste and anoint Lord Jagannatha. He made the paste but applied it to the walls of his own monastery. When news of this reached the king he was naturally furious and wanted an explanation for this preposterous behaviour. Jagannatha's cool reply was that he had applied sandal paste on the Lord with perfect devotion. The king wanted the *sevaka* to verify and report to him. And to their utter surprise they found that the Lord had actually been anointed with this special aromatic sandal paste. At this the king realized his own mistake and the greatness of poet Jagannatha and he promptly apologized to him.

Jagannatha Dasa did not travel to various places of pilgrimage in India like other religious personalities and saints. He considered it adequate to stay at Srikshetra (Puri) all his life. And instead of putting overriding emphasis on knowledge or observation of rituals, he put a high premium on right living, right action, simplicity of lifestyle and on devotion or *bhakti*.

From several episodes in the Oriya *Bhagavata* one can get vivid and realistic pictures of the contemporaneous Oriya society, its value-systems, organizational structure, its royal courts and their splendour, social mores and taboos, hopes and aspirations, religious faith, and ethical attitudes. It is eminently clear from the Oriya *Bhagavata* that to its poet Krishna was only another name for Lord Jagannatha, and Srikshetra, the seat of the Lord of the Universe, was the focal point of Orissa's social life and culture. It is Jagannatha consciousness that fully permeates the Oriya *Bhagavata*. It is observed that the religion of the *Bhagavata* is the religion of Jagannatha, unique for its cultural synthesis, universal brotherhood, assertion of the uniqueness of man in the entire creation and the equality of all before the Lord.[36]

Jagannatha Dasa composed a new poetic language which was balanced, effective and creative. Its general aroma of sanctity, its soft fluency, its quiet dignity and the sublime air of high moral and spiritual life it breathes, go straight into the hearts of the listeners and readers. He thus sang in his *Bhagavata* in his mellifluous voice:

Born on this earth
  even the gods die.
In everything embodied Narayana resides
  as the cause without beginning.
In all embodied beings
Narahari inheres as the atman.
The fire consumes everything
Unconcerned with the good and the bad.
Wealth acquired is for religious deeds,
  and through that you attain to the Lord.
With humble words like nectar.

You should please men's minds.
This human body is a rare gift
meant only to aspire for salvation.
Wherever a crowd gathers,
there is bound to be a quarrel.
In food there should be no choosiness
Whatever, wherever is available.
With the soul's well-being everything is achieved,
and you cross the ocean of Samsar.
The savings acquired through pain
are of no avail for happiness.
Karma is your own guru
What else do you inquire O Uddhava?
What can the powerful do to one
Whom the Lord protects.
The mind is the giver of pleasure and pain
the author of sin and guilt.
He who has the power to punish
also sometimes forgives.
All the places of pilgrimage are at your feet.
Why then should I go to Badrika?
The good and bad of a Being
You know only at the time of death.
Son and off-springs, wives and servants
they are only flashes of lightening.
God is the eternal, the one without blemish
He is above attributes, the true and the eternal.
The sky totally vacant,
be detached like it.
In whom desirelessness is born
he saves his own soul.
Ever engrossed in material pursuits
they don't notice the erosion of life.
The soul, like the sky
extends everywhere without bonds;
dwells within the body
and yet remains fully detached
like the sky reflected in a jar of water.
See all these rivers, rivulets
they flow on and join the sea.

Mingling with saline water
they forget their name and identity.
Likewise the cowherd maidens
have merged their life and mind in me.
They forget the body, the Samsar
and were delivered over
from birth and death.[37]

Poet Jagannatha not only rendered emphasis on spiritual liberation of man irrespective of caste, he also contributed to the cultural and spiritual uplift of the women by accepting them as disciples.[38] The poet looked upon Buddha as another incarnation of Lord Jagannatha. In Orissa Krishna was also worshipped as Madhava and Gopinatha. In Jagannatha Dasa's *Bhagavata* these two names are used very frequently.

Apart from Chaitanya, Jagannatha had close relations with Balarama, Achyuta, Jasovanta and Sishu Ananta, all of whom contributed to the growth of Oriya literature, religion and philosophy. They had their disciples and followers. Sishu Ananta mentions that Jagannatha had around three thousand and six hundred disciples of whom twelve were quite prominent. Quite a few of these also became important figures in Oriya literature in their own right. Dibakara Dasa, the biographer of Jagannatha Dasa, was one of his prominent disciples. Jagannatha breathed his last on seventh day in the bright fortnight of the month of Magha in AD 1550. Thus ended a life of a dedication that had ushered in significant religious, literary and linguistic transformations in Orissa.

POPULARITY OF THE ORIYA *BHAGAVATA*

It is reasonably certain that Jagannatha Dasa's translation of the great classic into Oriya was one of the earliest translations in a regional language. Jagannatha was born in AD 1487 and as we have pointed out according to *Jagannatha Charitamrita* of Dibakara Dasa (seventeenth century) he composed Oriya *Bhagavata* at the age of eighteen only. Upon this calculation we may ascertain that he composed Oriya *Bhagavata* in AD 1504 or AD 1505. The Bengali translation of Sanatana Goswami is believed to have been done in the seventeenth century. The translation of the tenth *skandha* by Suradas was incorporated in his *Sursagar* around the middle of sixteenth century. Jagannatha's eleven volumes or *skandhas* in Oriya contain 329 chapters whereas the original Sanskrit *Bhagavata* contains the 322 chapters. The additional seven chapters are in the tenth and eleventh volumes, six in the former and one in the latter.

The poet has also sometimes felt it necessary to give the theme more of a local context, social credibility and pictorial quality. At other times he seems to have been driven by his religious fervour to emphasize and expand those portions dealing with the *leela* or activities of Lord Krishna. It should, however, be remembered that these expansions or dilations of the theme rarely detract from the poetic quality of the original or make them little more than verbose transcreation of it. In fact, the most important of the Oriya work is its essential originality of language and idiom, of a profound philosophical attitude to life fused with passion and intensity of poetic fervour. It is, indeed, a unique poetic creation. Basically a translation, it looks and reads more like an original than perhaps any work of similar dimension. With a philosophical backdrop, it never degenerates into arid, obscure or abstruse, philosophical debates and discussions. On the other hand, the most difficult philosophical propositions are delineated through simple stories narrated in the traditional manner of story-telling. A work which, among other elements, had a gentle religious or spiritual motivation never degenerates into a mere listing of litanies or observances of rituals or ceremonies. This explains why the Oriya *Bhagavata* remains the most intimate expression of the Oriya soul as well as the culture and social ethics of the Oriya-speaking people. Among the masses of Orissa, lines from this book are widely quoted, as are appropriate to various situations. The spirit of liberal humanism, tolerance, sacrifice and humility, so characteristic of traditional Oriya social life, is, in many ways, the gift of this epic.

Jagannatha Dasa is remembered not only as an author of the Oriya *Bhagavata*, but also as the innovator of the *nabakshari brutta* (nine-lettered-rhyme) in which he composed his epic. Although, the *dandi brutta* introduced by Sarala Dasa, was in use in the Puranas, he felt that a new form of rhyming had become necessary to give poetic lines internal rhythm and to induce proper development of moods or *rasas* as a new dimension. His new *nabakshari brutta* enjoyed immense popularity as it combined flexibility of recitation with the facility of easily remembering the rhymed lines and singing them in varying patterns and methods. Even though five + four was the normal break-up of the nine-letter line, it was capable of being broken up into various other permutations. This also opened up immense possibilities of reciting the lines into two + three + four or three + three + three the lines which could be read slower, more mellifluously if the occasion so demanded. In fact, in medieval poetry the rhythm and sound-patterning introduced by the *nabakshari brutta* was a unique development.

Jagannatha Dasa accepted and used *tatsam* words in ample measure. He also adopted the generally accepted terms and frequently used local *tadbhab* words and blended them marvellously with the *tatsam* words to create a new poetic language. The excessive use of Sanskrit words with their complex meanings and word-joining and an over-dependence on the uneven local folk-idiom had not gained wider currency. Jagannatha Dasa thus created a poetic revolution in his Oriya *Bhagavata*. Later poets took his practice of blending *tatsam*, and *tadbhab* words in right proportions as an objective of poetic craft. Upendra Bhanja said, 'The poet's job was to please the mind with divine and non-divine lines' (*Dibya-adivya padare mannas mohiba*). These two words broadly refer to words derived from Sanskrit which was looked upon as the divine language and the local Prakrit. Abhimanyu Samantasimhar also said the same thing, 'the lines will attain perfection in language both divine and non-divine.' (*Divya-adibya bhashare pada heba siddhi*). Evidently, these two great poets of the eighteenth century were influenced by the language created by Jagannatha Dasa. His language transcended all barriers and acquired universal appeal and significance. This explains why Jagannatha Dasa's language was not just a local regional language, uneven and colloquial, and which almost fully rejected the Sanskrit vocabulary. He wanted to speak as much to the unlettered common man, as to the learned and the elite. This is a measure of his greatness and it explains the difference as regards the use of language between him on the one hand and Sarala Dasa, Balarama Dasa and Achyutananda on the other. The language of Jagannatha Dasa inspired and made possible the later *chhanda sahitya* in Oriya.

Jagannatha Dasa's *Bhagavata* became extensively popular in eastern India as a whole. Sanatana Vidyavagisha, the author of the *Bhasabandha Bhagavata* has acknowledged to have borrowed the Oriya language and style of Jagannatha Dasa for completing the tenth volume (*dasham skandha*) of his *Bhagavata*.[39] Besides this, the *Tulabhina* and the *Dhrubacharita* of Jagannatha Dasa and the Oriya

Rasalila and the Oriya *Garuda Purana* were printed in Bengali scripts with Oriya language and were extensively read in Bengal,[40] which suggests the impact and popularity of the Oriya poets spread across the neighbourly political boundaries. There were several Oriya poets who contributed to the growth of medieval Bengali literature. In this regard, particularly the writing of Rai Ramananda (sixteenth century) in Bengali on the theme *Krishna Lila*; *Ganga Mangal* composed by Jagannatha Dasa (sixteenth century) in Bengali and *Manasa Mangal*' written by Dwaraka Dasa (seventeenth century) in Bengali have enriched the Bengali language and literature, that was possible following the regional cultural interaction in medieval times.[41] In the light of the *Bhagavata* of Jagannatha Dasa, Janaki Ballabha Karasarma of Bhogarai in north Orissa, composed another *Bhagavata* in the seventeenth century. Besides, Dwaraka Dasa, Mahadeva Dasa and another Jagannatha Dasa (who wrote *Gupta Bhagavata*); Ghateswara Das wrote *Bhagavata Bala Charita*, Padmanabha Dasa wrote *Bhagavata Mahatmya*, Krishna Dasa and Ananta Dasa wrote *Bhagavata Ratnamala*, Sadhu Charan wrote *Bhakti Bibhava Bhagavata*, Bipra Uddhava wrote *Lilamrita Bhagavata* and Dasia Bauri wrote *Baligan Dasa Bhagavata* under the influence of *Atibadi* Jagannatha Dasa.[42]

Besides the *Bhagavata*, Jagannatha also composed a number of minor philosophical and devotional treatises in the language of the people. *Arthakoili*, *Gajastuti*, *Daru Brahma Gita*, *Gundicha Vijay Dutibandha*, *Radhamanjari*, *Sola Chaupadi Manasiksha* and *Dhruba Charita* are just a few of them. These works, however, do not come near the *Bhagavata's* level of excellence in combining the religion of *bhakti* with great poetic excellence. They are smaller and limited reflections of the great classic whose appeal remains universal and timeless.

ACHYUTANANDA DASA: POET AND REFORMER

Achyutananda Dasa was also one of the distinguished figures of the Panchasakha movement. He was born in AD 1498 in the village Tilakana, on the river bank of the Mahanadi in Cuttack district.[43] From the *Janma Bibarana* of Achyutananda Dasa we come to know that he was born in a Sudra family and he had a house in the village Nemala.[44] The poet, therefore, is believed to have been born in the village Tilakana and to have set up his monastery at Nemal, one mile away from Tilakana. His father was Dinabandhu Khuntia and mother was Padmavati. It is known from his own description that he was a contemporary of King Prataprudra Dev. His grandfather Gopinath Mohanty was one of the private secretaries (*chhamukaran*) of the king. His father Dinabandhu was honoured with the title 'Khuntia' by the king and he lived in Puri for his livelihood.[45] However the poet's grandfather was a Mohanty (Karana), father was a Khuntia and he identified himself was a *Sudra*.[46]

Achyutananda Dasa was not simply a devotee, a meditator and a poet, but a critic of the contemporary society, and using his imaginativeness and foresight he also predicted what the future would turn out to be. He composed a lot of prophetic poems called *malikas,* which reflected his extraordinary vision of future. The contemporary social condition is reflected in his writings although he has written about future. A general note which runs through all these *malikas* appears to be rather striking. It states, that in the times to come, (i) the Brahmins will deteriorate to the level of Sudras; (ii) there shall be no castes, all being equal in status; and (iii) after many catastrophes there shall be a revival of spirituality under the guidance of a new prophet.

Of all the five comrades, Achyutananda, the youngest was the most active social reformer. His contribution to uplift different neglected and deprived communities of Orissa shall long be cherished. He was the spiritual-patron of millions of Kaivartas (fishermen), Gopalas (cowherds) and Kamaras (blacksmiths). He actually lived among them and for the first time in their social history imparted to them the *mantras* and *sastras*. To explain the esoteric truth in their own terms he wrote in Oriya, the *Kaivarta Gita* for the benefit of the fishermen, the *Gopalanka Ogal* (riddles for the cowherds) for the cowherds and socially uplifted the blacksmiths. This sort of social sensitiveness in an author was remarkable at that time and we have not really many instances of it, at least in Oriya literature.

The *Harivamsa* of Achyutananda, like the *Mahabharata* of Sarala Dasa and the *Ramayana* of Balarama Dasa, is an original work, retaining only the framework of the Sanskrit model. This book describes the life-story of Krishna, the Lord of the Gopal class, probably to bolster up the social status and social consciousness of the milkmen communities in Orissa, of whom Achyutananda still remains the spiritual patron. This book is held in esteem next to the *Bhagavata* of Jagannatha Dasa among the Oriya masses as a sacred book. Pious rural folk arrange the full recitation of all its seven volumes as fulfilment of vows to gods and goddesses, after their prayers have been granted.

In *Kaivarta Gita*, Achyutananda has narrated the life-story of Dasaraja, the mythical king of the Kaivartas through the conversation between Krishna and Arjuna. To bring pride and honour to the broken heart of the Kaivartas, he narrated that Dasaraja was born from the ear of Krishna and Krishna himself had offered him a boat and a horse for his livelihood through trade.[47] The poet clearly has got everything described by Lord Krishna to elevate the status of the fishermen in society. As a whole, the *Kaivarta Gita* is considered to be a remarkable social document which represents the social resurgence of the Sudras in medieval Orissa. It not only links the age-old tradition, customs, occupation and festivals of the Kaivarta community with religious justification but also propagates *bhakti* to Lord Jagannatha, goddess Vasuli and also to Ananta Vasuki (Naga cult). It gives, besides the message of the eradication of untouchability, a description of the naval and maritime trade activities of the Kaivartas and the commercial relations between Kalinga and Sri Lanka.[48] In *Gopalanka Ogala*, the poet has described the heroic activities of Krishna at Gopa in a lyrical form, which has been a source of entertainment and consolation for the Gopal communities.[49]

Achyutananda witnessed the socio-political instability and peaceless condition during his lifetime (sixteenth century) which led him to compose his own prophetic poems. His writings allude to the major Muslim invasions of Orissa during the period of Gajapati Prataprudra Dev (AD 1510) and Mukunda Dev (AD 1568). In AD 1510 Hussain Saha, Sultan of Bengal, attacked the temple of Lord Jagannatha at Puri and destroyed some idols. But the idol of Lord Jagannatha was safely protected. In AD 1568 Kalapahada, a commander of Sulaiman Karrani of Bengal, attacked the Jagannatha temple of Puri. He burnt the idol of Lord Jagannatha on the sea-beach of Puri which terrorized the people of Orissa and made the contemporary *bhakta-kàvis* like Achyutananda Dasa to give warnings to the people through their devotional songs. Thus he sang in his *Varan Charita Gita*,

From the King Prataprudra to Mukundadev,
the people will enjoy half of their happiness.
The world will be stormed from the period of Mukundadev
Oh brother, you will not get a scarce of peace,

Since then till the three successive reigns,
Kali will appear and happiness
will evaporate from the world.[50]

The poet describes the deplorable condition of the people caused by famine and flood during the period *of* Mukunda Dev. Thus he sings in his *bhajan*,

The king Mukundadeva,
Look at his fifth regnal year,
Oh devotees,
alms will not be given to the beggars.
The seeds will be washed away
and many fields will remain uncultivated,
Oh devotees,
Some will not open their seed-packets.[51]

Achyutananda travelled over many parts of Orissa for the propagation of his faith and outlook. Because of his profound experience of the wretched plight of the poor and the exploitation of the subjects by the State machinery, he criticized authoritarianism. His writings protest against injustice and exploitation. He compared the subjects with dead bodies and the kings with vultures. To him it was a curse for the subjects to undergo such suffering. Again he postulated that the king would snatch away the properties of the subjects and the subjects would flee away to the forest. He also desired not to live to see the sorrowful condition of the people.[52] His writings were based on his social experiences and his insights and outlook had been shaped by his own experience. A strong anti-feudal feeling has been clearly expressed in his writings.

Achyutananda also travelled outside of Orissa to a number of pilgrim centres like Gaya, Ayodhya, Mathura, Mayapuri, Kasi, Brindaban, Magadh, Mithila, Dwaraka, Dhanuskoti, Madurai and Kamaksha. He came into contact with some fraudulent *samnyasis* and criticizing them he said that nobody could be a meditator only because he had a beard and long hair. To him determination, meditation, honesty and truthfulness were the essential characteristics of a *samnyasi*. He protested against the exploitative nature of priesthood and vehemently challenged the validity of the authority of Brahmins and the philosophical basis of *godan* (taking of cows in donation) by them. He asked a number of metaphysical questions relating to cow, the mother goddess and wanted to know from the priests whether they were Brahmins or Sudras? How did they emerge? Which god did they worship everyday and whether *dharma* is a result of *karma* or *karma* is a result of *dharma*?[53] The king and the Brahmins of the Jagannatha temple, Puri, were, in fact, surprised and had to perforce acknowledge his greatness.

The poet did not forget to present the contemporary social picture in his discussion of *pinda* (body) and *brahmanda* (world) philosophy. He predicted revolution and change. He believed that first there would be a hole in the west and the four commanders would be killed. The *nayakas* of the fort would be flogged and the people would be frightened and run away. To him the forts were constructed by torture and exploitation of the toiling masses, they would be seized by killing the *nayakas* (the fort commanders). There would then be a large crowd in eighteen drains, and it would be a fighting between archers and gunmen.[54] The poet visualized a revolution and he believed that there would be end of exploitation and suffering of the people, if the sufferers unitedly fought against oppression.

The complete treatise titled *Baran Charita Gita* is a conversation between Achyutananda and his disciple Ramachandra Dasa. From an analysis of this *Gita* it is observed that there were points of a difference between Achyutananda and Sri Chaitanya. Chaitanya was a protagonist of the *Nadiya Kirtan* but Achyutananda started the *Rahas Kirtan* in Jhankar. Chaitanya propagated the *Krishna Lila* of the *Sarat Rasa* of autumn, whereas Achyuta introduced the *Basanta Rasa* of the spring. Chaitanya described the association of Krishna with the *gopis*, but Achyuta wrote of the heroic deeds of Krishna in association with the *gopalas* (young milkmen of Gopa).[55] In spite of these differences Achyutananda had a profound respect for Sri Chaitanya and was one of his distinguished associates.

CONDEMNED RITUALS AND ORTHODOX TEXTS

Achyutananda believed in *jnana, bhakti* and *yoga*. To him, the pundits did not understand the hidden meaning of the *Gita* and *brahma-jnana*. They understood only the literal meaning of it. He believed that *bhakti* was essential to understand the inner meaning of the *Gita*.[56] Giving emphasis on realization of self the poet thus sang in his *Sunya Samhita*,

Fast, pilgrimage, reading Puranas and Sastras
All are futile without knowing thy self,

As rainlessness harms the product
Ignorance of the self harms the knowledge.
Anxiety is destroyed
with kind and forgiveness
And if heart remains
at the feet of Lord Krishna
from life to life.[57]

Achyutananda was critical of the rituals and pilgrimage, idol-worship, caste, and authority of the Vedas. In his *Charikhani* or *Sabdabrahma Samhita* he has bitterly criticized the traditional social structure and has aimed at a new social order. He sang that fasting, pilgrimage and rituals were nothing, but the ways of inflicting pain to one's body in a different manner. Thus he sang,

Fasting, rituals and pilgrimage
nothing but accepting physical pains,
Vedas and puranas are woven round it
And if there is punya or (religious merit)
Why then people die at all?[58]

The poet protested against idol-worship and criticized different rituals which were material arrangements performed before the deity only for personal enjoyment and nothing else. Thus he sings,

Again we will tell about ourselves,
your tale bears many shapes.
World is endless and there is nothing
without your existence.
They make idols, images or pictures
of wood, stone, eight metals and soil.
This mind installs the idol
and worships by chanting his name.
prasad, flowers, sandal, scents and many presentations
are only performed before the deity,
then they eat it just giving water
as a final offer.
They take so much care of the deity,
and by His blessing they are redeemed.
This living God does not understand the self
and unknowingly worship the lifeless idol.[59]

Achyutananda has been bitterly critical of the notion of superiority of the Brahmins in the caste system. He compares the Brahmins and goats and explains the significance of the life of the goat as eater of grass and links it to the practice of Brahmins as the eater of meats. His satire can be seen in his *Charikhani* in passages like the following:

Brahmins are polluted
just touching a dead body,
But they eat meat of goats
after they are killed !
This animal is so great because
he reads Vedas and mantras
And that animal is so much low
because he eats grass.[60]

Achyutananda did not accept the Vedas to be infallible. He emphasized the freedom of thought of the individual and established superiority of knowledge earned by one's own feeling, experience and reason. Thus he sings,

It is not the Vedas are 'the beginning',
And it cannot be compared.
Again whatever the epics we read
are nothing but the poetic works.[61]

The significance of human life is not justified on the basis of birth, but by virtue of *karma* or the noble deeds, Achyutananda believed. He sang in his *Charikhani*,

The noble deeds are eternal
and lasts for ever,
The man believes in karma
reaches in the highest of glory.[62]

ANTI-CASTE PRONOUNCEMENTS

Giving emphasis on realization of one's own self and the selfhood of others, the poet advocated for an egalitarian social order. He believed that Hari (i.e. God) existed everywhere and in everything starting from lifeless matters and insects to the body of human being of all castes and classes.[63] In another context, the poet predicted there would be equality among all with the instructions of God Nirakara and there would be no discrimination between the Brahmins and Candalas, which clearly signified social equality that the poet advocated for. He sang in this context,

There will be no varna or (caste),
from Untouchable to Brahmin
and from the preceptor to disciples;
This is the instruction of the Nirakara
that there will be no discrimination
and all-being will be one.[64]

Achyutananda accepted disciples from all castes. Among his disciples Ramadasa was a potter, another Rama was a blacksmith while Nanda and Naran were blacksmiths.[65] There were 12 prominent disciples who came from the Gopal community.[66] Dwijabar Sharma of Anantapur Sasan near Panchakroshi and Dasa Mohapatra of the Prachi river bank were devotees of Achyutananda Dasa. Another group of 140 followers of his lived in the village of Kasi Muktiswar *grama*. There were also 110 devotee-followers at Chitrangatota.[67] Ganesh Pati, the *ganaka* (astrologer), Kanhu and his son Parikshita, Saranga, Upananda, and 300 followers from Jajanagar (Jajpur) including Bandhu Mohanty of Jajpur were Sri Krishna devotees at the time of Achyutananda.[68]

Dismissing the notion of sacredness of rituals, Achyutananda argued that there was no need of *asana*, *suddhi* and *anganyasa* (decoration of body by use of sandal, etc.), in performance of worship. Recitation of the name of void (*sunya*) with deep love and devotion was the method of worship that he preached. King Prataprudra was pleased to see the method of *sunya* worship of Achyutananda and granted him a place at Banki Muhan, for his *math*.[69]

DASAS JASOVANTA AND ANANTA

Of the remaining Dasas of the *panchasakha* group, Dasas Jasovanta and Ananta have the glory of contributing to *tantra* and *yoga* as well as the miracles of *bhakti*. Jasovanta Dasa is now remembered only through his ballad *Govinda Chandra* sung by Natha cult mendicant singers. This is a story, of a prince named Govinda Chandra who renounced royal comforts for an ascetic life, strangely enough on the advice and persistent persuasion of his own mother Mukta Dei. The Prince's Yogic guide was Hadipa, an untouchable *siddha*.

All this fitted very well into the ascetic and cosmopolitan aspirations of the 'five comrades' and was therefore taken up by one of them for popularization among the masses. It must be said to the credit of Jasovanta Dasa that his literary venture has been quite successful. The story casts a spell of mystic melancholy over women in rural areas.

Jasovanta was born in the Adhanga village near the Jagatsinghpur District of Orissa. It is known from the *Udaya Kahani* of Achyutananda that Jagannatha Dasa and Jasovanta Dasa were born in the same year. If we were to believe *Udaya Kahani*, Jasovanta Dasa was born in AD 1487. His father was Jagu Mallick and mother, Rekha Devi.[70] Jasovanta became indifferent towards the world while he was twelve years of age. He was determined to be a *samnyasi*. Since his early age Jasovanta used to travel over many parts of India and lastly returned to Puri. Before his return to Puri, Sri Chaitanya had already arrived in Orissa.

Jasovanta Dasa composed many devotional songs among which *Premabhakti Brahmagita*, *Govinda Chandra Gita*, *Siva Svaraday*, *Chaurashi Ajna*, and *Rasa*, etc., were important. He has deciphered a number of methods of *yoga* in his *Siva Svaraday*. His language was very simple and intelligible to all. He also propagated the knowledge-cum-devotion ideology among the people and discussed the philosophy, ethics and principles of *nirakara, anakara* and *omkar Brahma*. The relation between the soul and the great soul (*paramatma*) was also investigated by him. The philosophical aspects of the Universe, Sun, Moon, Stars, Wind and the Sky have been described by him; and he says that there are eight flutes of the Nityaloka, i.e. God of Gods. He loved Orissa; to him *Neelachal Purushottam Kshetra* was a rare place in the Universe, and the shrines like Gopa, Mathura, Vrindaban, Dwaraka and Kashi were prevalent there.[71]

The picture of the contemporary society, family and the eternal love between mother and son are to be found in his book *Govindachandra Gita*. It deals with the tradition of social behaviour in the human world. Mother Mukta Devi taught her son, prince Govind Chandra, the requirements of social behaviour, at the time of his departure to practise the ascetic order. Sacrifice was given a higher position than enjoyment. Another important thing the treatise preaches is that the gurus should be accepted irrespective of caste, creed and colour, if they possessed real knowledge. Prince Govinda Chandra had worshipped his guru Hadipa, who was a sweeper by caste.[72] The poet also propagates the necessity of determination to control one's desire. Besides, Jasovanta Dasa also protested against the existing norms of socio-economic domination and discrimination. According to him, meditation and devotion to God can never be monopolized by a particular caste or community, they are open to all mankind.

Jasovanta believed in *premabhakti* and propagated worship of god with the *gopibhava*. In his *Premabhakti Brahmagita* he has made Sri Krishna speak to his devotees that He comes to closer to them who worship Him with *premabhakti*. He writes,

Gopi is my own body,
Those who worship her with me
Sit in the eternal abode.
There is no better devotion
than love-based devotion,
And I am always closer to the
love-based devotion.[73]

ANANTA DASA

Sishu Ananta Dasa was another distinguished member of the Panchasakha movement. He was born in the *Karana* community in AD 1486, at the Balipatna village, near Bhubaneswar of Puri district. His father was Kapila Mohanty and mother Gouri Devi.[74]

He was a contemporary of King Prataprudra Dev and was an associate of Sri Chaitanya. He composed a number of treatises, namely, the *Garuda-Keshav Sambad*, *Thikabahar*, *Agat-Bhabishya Malika, Arthatareni*, *Chumbak Malika*, *Bhakti-juktidayak Gita*, *Anakar Sabad*, *Dibi Dibi Dhola*, *Pinda Brahmanda Gita* and *Hetu Uday Bhagavata*. The *Hetu Uday Bhagavata* was the most important work in which he described the implications of the *gurumahima* (significance of the religious guides), *panchamana* (five stages of the mind) and *pachis prakriti* (twenty-five natures of human being) and also defined the philosophy of the creation of the Universe: *Chauda Brahmanda* (Fourteen Worlds), *Gayatri Tattva*, *Pinda Brahmanda Tattva* and *Abdhut Charita,* etc. His predictions regarding the future of society were simple and were understood in the poet's narration in Oriya by the common men.

Ananta Dasa, like his other comrades, was also one of the exponents of the *bhakti* cult. He asked his devotees to submit their mind and soul to God as a wife submits herself to her husband.[75] This was the way of *bhakti* and the method to achieve the relation of the supreme God, Vishnu. Apart from this, he propagated that God has no colour. He is *avarna*.[76] According to him, everything depends on *mana* (mind or motive) and God is inside one's heart and not in the temple. The control of mind is real meditation. The poet did not attribute the worship of God via the priests. He personified the system of worship which, according to him, is mental and is in the realm of thought.[77]

THE *PANCHASAKHA* IDEOLOGY

The religious philosophy of the *bhaktas* of medieval Orissa is distinguished in many respects. The *panchasakhas* were in search of the metaphysical theory of creation of the Universe. Not only the *panchasakhas* of medieval Orissa, but also the *rishis* of the Vedic period were in quest of knowledge regarding the creation of the world. What was created first in the Great Void? Achyutananda observes:

> All these forms are only creations of the one formless and all manifestations of form will ultimately realize themselves in the formless. Thus one, ought to be able to look at the two as one. Only by looking at the seemingly opposites with an attitude of equanimity, one can realize the whole range of truth.[78]

The *panchasakhas* were in quest of the metaphysical matters such as *pinda* and *brahmanda*, the individual microcosm and the universal macrocosm. Balarama Dasa in his *Amarakosha Gita*,[79] Jagannatha Dasa in his *Arthakoili*, Achyutananda in his *Kaivarta Gita*,[80] have stated that whatever we see in this world also exists in one's body.

God is omnipresent and exists in everybody, said Balarama, Jagannatha, and Achyutananda as well. They compare the water inside the pot with soul and the pot with the body or *pinda*. When the pot breaks down or the body dies, the water-like soul evaporates with the *sunya*, i.e. the great soul.

The *panchasakhas* made a happy synthesis between *Saguna* and *Nirguna* schools of *bhakti* by rising up to a height from which one could see both of these and also see beyond. Achyutananda compared *Saguna* and *Nirguna* with two wings of a bird and two eyes of a person, and to him it was not possible to meditate perfectly with the loss of one school of thought.[81] The *panchasakhas* also had gone beyond the areas of mere *bhakti* or mere *jnana* and could look at both as one. To speak by using their metaphor, 'As a bird must have both its wing to be able to fly, the *sadhaka* must have *jnana* and *bhakti* in his schedule if he has to make any real advance in his *sadhana*.'[82]

The *panchasakhas* did neither believe in idol-worship, nor in fasting, pilgrimage and celebrating the sacred days. According to Balarama, the people worship idols, because they do not know that Basudeva (God) is imageless. The poet wonders how the people worship the God who does not even speak a word. The traditions of idol-worship, pilgrimage, fasting, sacrifice, rituals and even existence of gods and goddesses are superfluous, he firmly believed.[83] The poet wondered how the people did not understand the reality although they were guided by the *panchsakhas* to think that all religious externalities were meaningless and means of exploitation. According to Achyutananda, the innocent people were deceived to worship spirits and gods. They did not know that the *mantras*, *japas*, fasting, pilgrimages and meditations were not for the welfare of society.[84] The *panchsakhas* advised the people not to believe in idol-worship or in fasting, pilgrimage or rituals, etc., because they wanted to protect people from the clutches of priesthood and Brahminism as well. They wanted to keep direct relations between the God and the devotees through *bhakti* and therefore, there was no need of the intermediary priestly class, the *panchasakhas* believed.

The *panchasakha* philosophy cannot be categorized and limited to a particular sect or religious community. The five poets were above any sectarian zealotry. They did not as such condemn any particular way of *sadhana* and plead in favour of their own way; but they were against narrow and rigid adherence to any particular way. Their attitude behind all what they spoke and wrote was one of an all accepting inner-integrity and purity. They accepted the noble principles of many contemporary religious strands but never fell into any of the sectarian lines. The *panchasakhas* were Vaishnavas, yet they were much more than those who close themselves into a sect called Vaishnava. They spoke and wrote about the necessity of *kayasadhana*, but they were not only *kayasadhakas*. They were Buddhists in much of their avowals, yet not Buddhists as far as to be Buddhists meant following a particular sect and nothing else. They sang of and adored the supreme Brahma, yet were much more than the doctrinaire Advaitins. They made a synthesis between *Nirguna* and *Saguna* and between *jnana* and *bhakti*. They were *bhaktas* and *jnanis* at the same time, because the real *bhakta* and real *jnani* do combine the two in the process of his becoming. They proclaimed that to remain engrossed with the transitory worldly living was to live buried in *maya*, but they were not *mayabadins*. They were on the side of life, its enhancement and in its excellence in the full spiritual liberation of the term. They were inextricably attached with the human situations, and they were true *bhaktas*, *sadhaka*s, and social reformers.

The *panchasakhas* endeavoured so much to elevate the status of the lowly-placed in society and wrote special books to make them feel equal to others and also indispensable for the total functioning of the society. It is not surprising that these poets who proclaimed the presence of God in everybody did not find much justice in the contemporary caste society. So they had their own way of dealing with the problem in order to solve it. Traditionally when the caste structure has been looked upon as a divine dispensation and its whole ethics was built with clever insularity, the *panchasakhas* declared themselves to be Sudras.[85] In fact, they belonged by birth to different castes in society; at least one of them was a Brahmin but became Sudra by choice. They had their own way of explaining the origins of caste as a system. Achyutananda, for example, did not acknowledge the definition of the origin of the varnas, given in the *Purusha-sukta,* i.e. Brahmins from the mouth, the Kshatriyas from the arms, Vaishyas from the thighs and Sudras from the feet of the God. He provided an alternative in his *Gupta Gita* that Vaishyas were the eyes, Kshatriyas the ears, Brahmins the breaths of the nose and the Sudras the face as a whole. These four varnas were created from a flame. With this analysis the poet has tried to explain the different components of society and their interdependence. At the height of feeling of high and low, caste and untouchability, his struggle thus was successful in raising the spirit of egalitarianism.

Achyutananda has referred to the four stages of *bhakti* following one another in an ascending order. He explains: first, the attribute of a *bhakta's* evolution is that of a Kshatriya's attribute. At this stage, he destroys his lower nature and puts an end to many hostile elements within him that keep him stuck and staggering. At the second stage of evolution, the *bhakta* goes out for commerce with the further stages of his development as a Vaishya with the name of Krishna, the lord, as his capital. As the second stage becomes stable, the *bhakta* takes to the propensities of a Brahmin and acquires all knowledge and thus comes to realize what the path of a knower of *Brahma* is ordained to be. Realizing the *Brahma* or self and thus knowing him in his real essence, he becomes a servant at his feet. This is the fourth and the last stage, the stage of the Sudra, which ultimately makes the aspirant stable and sure in following the path of *bhakti.*

Thus in terms of experience and fulfilment, the *sudrabhakti* is the *bhakti* at its summit, *bhakti* that can sustain itself without faltering and also sustain the adherent *bhakta* on his onward path. It may also be pointed out that, during the first three stages, *bhakti* remains at the religious level and makes allowances for the necessary religiousities, but at the last level of *sudrabhakti*, it is elevated to the spiritual plane and the *brahmadarshin* fulfils himself by becoming a *dasa* of the Lord. He does His work in whatever way he does and thus dwells constantly in Him. The course of his evolutionary *sadhana* touches all the areas of his life, saturates it completely and becomes transformed into an act of total consecration and service.

Propounding the social connotation of the theory of the *bhakti* Achyutananda and other *panchasakhas* have openly moved against all caste considerations and attributes of high and low in society. With no qualm in their conscience they had voluntarily declared themselves to be the lowest in society. They had declared that they had the Sudra propensity as the determining propensity and thus they were nothing but Sudras. Doing this, the *panchasakhas* gave a new connotation to the very concept of Sudra as a symbol of the *sudrabhava* and suggested that every aspirant after God-realization pursuing the highest attainment had also to be a possessor of this *sudrabhava*. Through this kind of the philosophical exposition Brahminism was certainly challenged, and as a result of the resurgence of the consciousness of the dignity of the common men, the Brahminical order underwent significant modification.

The *panchasakhas* have warned that without the guru coming to help, one cannot know the real truth in the world. But as in everything else, the *panchasakhas* revolted against the idea of hero-worship i.e. making an idol of the guru. A guru, who encourages helpless dependence and makes an idol of himself will be more of a hindrance than a help. The *panchasakhas* were determined to start a mass movement in society for a change in outlook and attitude. Having personified the system of worship, they said that one could not see God only in the temple, one could feel Him inside one's heart also. In this regard said Achyutananda, 'The knowledge you seek for is stored in your heart. You have to find it there and realize it. The knowledge of the *Brahma*, *Brahma-jnana*, is never far from you, it is inseparably contained in your own temple'.

Orissan society, culture and religion have developed and conglomerated together mainly concentrating with Lord Jagannatha. Lord Jagannatha became the nucleus of the Orissan polity and culture. In medieval times and particularly during sixteenth century the cult of Jagannatha reached its climax. It was completely by then Brahminized and had become an integral part of high Hinduism. But the striking feature of the period is that in course of the resurgence of the *sudramunis'* movement Lord Jagannatha found a remarkable position in their literature and the contemporary *bhaktas* and *kavis* tried to reform the society by creating the regional literature woven round the name and cult of Lord Jagannatha. In course of time of the Brahminization/Hinduization of the deity Lord Jagannatha was considered an elite deity at least up to the period of Sarala Dasa (late fifteenth century) and since then from Sarala Dasa to the *panchsakhas* all *bhakta-kavis* have challenged the high Hinduism and endeavoured to retrieve Lord Jagannatha with a view to reviving their submerged glorious past. They have however been, successful in establishing Lord Jagannatha as the *Patita-pavan* (the redeemer of the fallen or depressed) and a peoples' deity. Thus Lord Jagannatha, His cult, His temple and His *kshetra* found admiring expressions in the devotional songs and other writings of those *bhaktas*, the *sudramunis*, considered to be the people's poets of Orissa. The holy town of Puri was exalted in the writings of the *panchasakhas* and other poets. It was believed to be the replica of the eternal Gokul. Yashovanta Dasa described in his *Premabhakti Brahma-Gita* that Nilachal (Puri) is greater than the religious places like Dwaraka, Mathura and Brindavan. Balarama Dasa composed and dedicated his *Jagamohan Ramayan* in honour of Lord Jagannatha. Jagannatha Dasa in his *Daru Brahma Gita* has lucidly described and reinforced the viewpoint of Sarala Dasa that the image of Lord Jagannatha was carved out of the dead body of Krishna which became the sacred log. Ray Ramananda composed his drama *Jagannatha-Ballav Natakam* in order to narrate the eternal dalliance of Radha and Krishna. He conceives of the idea that Ekanamsa alias Subhadra as no other than Radha. Again in Balarama Dasa's *Vedantsara Gupta Gita* and in Achyutananda's *Sunya Samhita* Jagannatha has been described as the embodiment of all the incarnations of Lord Vishnu. By this time, in Orissan Vaishnavism Jagannatha was conceived to be an *avatari* (source of all incarnations) and all other manifestations were his *avatara* (incarnations).

The features of social protest and the peoples version of their glorious past and heritage are conspicuous in the writings of the *sudramunis* and other like-minded poet reformers who spearheaded the social movement during fifteenth and sixteenth centuries. Sudramuni Sarala Dasa laid the foundation stone of this movement by opposing all sorts of formalities of life and religion. The poet had a deep sense of sympathy for the down-trodden classes like tribals, Sudras, women and other commoners. In his *Mahabharata*, Jara Sabara who was offended and debarred from military training by the Kauravas, emerges later as the victor. Again he (Jara) kills Krishna, conceals his body and becomes the first worshipper of Lord Jagannatha, in the form of Nilamadhava. Sarala Dasa was the pioneer for propounding the theory of the tribal origin of the Jagannatha cult. The primary analysis of the very fact of Sarala *Mahabharata* bears bright testimony to the poet's onslaught on the Brahminical super-structure. The Brahminical monopoly placing them as the custodians of religion and religious texts received a great challenge. Not that the poet merely challenged the prevailing social norms for the sake of opposition. His works prominently breathe an air of freedom in the process of social regeneration of the lower classes, women and other neglected groups. His *Vilanka Ramayana* and *Chandi Purana* present the benign aspects of womanhood. He presented through literature the view that women were not weak, but equal and powerful along with the menfolks of society.

The social movement inaugurated by Sarala Dasa was carried forward to its logical end by the *panchasakhas*. The *panchasakhas* launched the movement at a time when the Brahminical pretentions were at their apex. The *panchasakhas*, four of whom were *sudramunis*, were all opposed to the Brahminical supremacy. They followed Lord Buddha in their definition of Brahminhood that a Brahmin was a Brahmin by character and not by birth. Two outspoken revolutionary *sudramunis*—Balarama Dasa and Achyutananda Dasa—challenged the Brahminical hegemony at the *muktimandap* of Puri. Balarama Dasa, in his *Ramayana*, shows his appreciation of Sugriva, Hanuman and Bibhishan for their honesty, sincerity and truly helpful attitude to Rama, and has also established friendship between the King Rama and a tribal chief Guhak. In a critical tone, Achyutananda, in his *Sabdabrahma Samhita* satires, the supposed sacredness of Brahmins in that a Brahmin considered himself polluted if he touched a dead body. But how come the same Brahmin could take meat of goats after they were killed and dead? Achyutananda questions this paradoxical hypocrisy.[86] In his *Kaivarta Gita* he emphasizes that a Candala is no other than the Brahman (Almighty) itself.[87] As regards the varna system, Balarama Dasa even says that the four orders like Brahmin, Kshatriya, Vaishya and Sudra originated from a single flame of light and therefore all belonged to one caste in this world.[88] Achyutananda stipulates in his *Gurubhakti Gita* that before one gets blessings from the guru (preceptor) one has to invite four persons from four different varnas and entertain them equally as honoured guests,[89] which shows his attempt not only to blow the caste distinction but also to assist the process of social equality, stability and integration.

The *panchasakhas* protested against the authoritarian activities of both the priests and the king. Achyutananda wrote his *Harivamsa*, *Gopalanka Ogal* and *Kaivarta Gita* to glorify the milkmen and fishermen communities who had hitherto shrunk to the position of Sudras. Jagannatha Dasa translated the Sanskrit *Bhagavata* into Oriya for the people especially for the common men and women, who had no access to learning and education in the Brahmin dominated society. In the *Vedantasara Gupta Gita*, Sudramuni Balarama Dasa openly declared before the king and the assembly of the learned Brahmins that access to the *Sastras* was not the exclusive privilege of the Brahmins alone. He invited the wrath of the Gajapati and the Brahmin priests. He offered his *Brahmavidya* test in the royal court as revealed from his *Gita Avakasha*.

In course of the social movement launched by the *sudramunis* it is observed that they developed a protest ideology and departed from the religious orthodoxy of the Brahminical order. The *panchasakhas* maintained their distinction as the followers of the concept of void or *sunya*. They were regarded as concealed Buddhists (*Prachhanna Buddha*) by the Brahmins and thus the situation led to inflicting of the political torture upon them. The dominant vested interests created certain situations in which the *panchasakhas* were made to go through different humiliating tests. Sometimes they were imprisoned and were exiled from Puri (the religious headquarter of Orissa and then the centre of *sahajiya premabhakti*) to different isolated places: Balarama Dasa to Samagara pata, Jagannatha Dasa to Balibantara sea beach, Achyutananda to Banki Muhan and the followers of the *panchasakhas* to the Dandakaranya forest region of Orissa.[90] It is true that although the *panchasakhas* had in some ways compromised with the established order and accepted the theory of *premabhakti* concentrating on Radha and Krishna, internally in their heart of hearts they believed in the worship of *sunya*.

I have already discussed how Lord Jagannatha was the linchpin of society and also how the *panchasakhas* struck against the different props of the said society. The question that arises is: Why did they spare Jagannatha? Most of them had prayed to Jagannatha at the initial stages of their writings. Very often they also claimed to have been born by the grace of Lord Jagannatha. Besides, a large number of devotees renounced their affiliation with different minor religious sects and they worshipped Lord Jagannatha as the supreme deity. Here we should not forget that originally Lord Jagannatha was a tribal deity and it was only from the twelfth century onwards that he underwent the process of Brahminization. This must surely have been disliked by the Sudras or non-Brahmins who often tried to project Him as a God of the Little Tradition. It was proved by the version of Sarala Dasa in his *Mahabharata* that Jagannatha was being worshipped by the Sabara Jara in the form of Nilamadhab.[91] Balarama Dasa and his other comrades have also characterized Lord Jagannatha as a deity of the Little Tradition.[92] *Lakshmi Purana* of Balarama Dasa is another evidence in which Lakshmi got a declaration of social equality and a casteless society by Lord Jagannatha himself. So it appears that the tirade was not so much against Jagannatha as it was against the metamorphosis that they (the *panchasakhas*) experienced in course of time. Apart from this, when Lord Jagannatha had been so popular, and was already considered to be the Lord of the Universe, it was wise on the part of the *panchasakhas* to use His name to mould the rest of the society. One could well argue that had Jagannatha continued as a deity of the Great Tradition, the majority of the people in Oriya society, who were no doubt Sudras, would have been alienated from Him and possibly might have set-up a deity of their own. But it is not so in case of Orissa and its people. The cleavage thus ended in cohesion. Jagannatha, the central pivot in Oriya socio-religious life, who was considered to be a deity of the king and the priests, now occupied a place in mass consciousness because of the lofty efforts of the *panchasakhas*.[93]

The *panchasakhas*, through their numerous writings, widened the scope and dimensions of social protest. Their protest was never a negative one. They were not merely iconoclasts. They had a more enduring commitment to society. Whatever they did was prompted by a vision, the vision of a new egalitarian society based on common humanism. The most striking aspect of the Oriya literature created by the *panchasakhas* was born, developed and thrived because of the masses of unknown, secluded and marginalized people. Their feelings, dreams and aspirations found expression through literature. There is no praise of the sovereigns; no glorification of their deeds finds a place in these literary works. The literature of this period remained a world by itself with its indigenous style and rhythm. It therefore fulfilled the psychological need of the people. It also met their mythological, religious, aesthetic norms and expectations. The *panchasakhas* brought the spiritual lore that was as yet a sealed book in Sanskrit to the doorsteps of the peasant's cottage. Through their *Ramayana*, *Bhagavata* and *Harivamsa* they made all the esoteric teaching accessible to the common Oriya, unschooled in Sanskrit. They wrote ballads to carry their messages of ideal living and desirable attitudes to life even to the unlettered womenfolk in the inner courtyards. Even now Balarama's *Baula Gai*, *Lakshmi Purana Suanga*, or Jagannatha's *Mriguni Stuti*, Jasovanta Dasa's *Govinda Chandra* constitute the main stack-in-trade of the wandering minstrels of Orissa. Their recitals of these ballads from door to door to the accompaniment of the monostring *kendra*, draw children and womenfolk to the doors, windows and streets as though by magic. Their appeal is undying because they were written by devout souls with their eyes fixed on the common man's spiritual benefit. All that is moral and cultural in rural Orissa, even today, is most certainly due to the sincere endeavour of those *sudramunis*.

NOTES

1. A.B. Mohanty (ed.), *Madalapanji*, Prachi Samiti, Bhubaneswar, 1940, pp. 54–5; also vide Achyutananda Dasa, *Sunya Samhita*, Arunodaya Press, Cuttack, 1914, Chap. 1.
2. Chittaranjan Das, *Achyutananda O Panchasakha Dharma*, Visva Bharati, Santiniketan, 1951, p. 8.
3. B. Mishra, *Prachina Utkal*, Orissa Sahitya Akademi, Bhubaneswar, 1990, p. 91.
4. N. Vasu, *Archaeological Survey of Mayurbhanja*, vol. I, Calcutta University, Calcutta, 1911, pp. clxvii–clxx.

5. Balarama Dasa, *Jagamohan Ramayana* (*Uttara Khanda*), Dharmagrantha Store, Cuttack, n.d.
6. Ibid. (*Lanka Kanda*).
7. Balarama Dasa, *Vedantasara Gupta Gita*, Union Printing Works, Cuttack, 1910, p. 1.
8. Ibid., p. 2.
9. Ibid., p. 12 also vide his *Pranab Gita*, Chap. 1, quoted in N. Vasu, op. cit., pp. clxvii–clxv and Surendra Mohanty, *Oriya Sahityara Madhyaparva* (Oriya), Cuttack Students' Store, Cuttack, 1973, pp. 245–7.
10. Balarama Dasa, *Pranab Gita*, quoted in N. Vasu, op. cit., pp. clxviii–clxx.
11. Idem. See also Surendra Mohanty, op. cit., p. 247.
12. Rama Dasa, *Dardhyata Bhakti*, vol. I, Radharaman Press, Cuttack, n.d., Chap. XIV, pp. 107–17.
13. Balarama Dasa, *Bhava Samudra*, Dharmagrantha Store, Cuttack, 1972, Canto 12.
14. Ibid., Canto 182.
15. Ibid., Canto 94–5.
16. Balarama Dasa, *Lakshmi Purana*, Sanyasi Pustakalaya, Berhampur, n.d., p. 7.
17. Ibid., pp. 23-4.
18. M. Mansingh, *History of Oriya Literature*, Sahitya Akademi, New Delhi, 1962, p. 95.
19. K.C. Sahoo, *Kavi Balarama Dasa*, Orissa Sahitya Akademi, Bhubaneswar, 1988, p. 51.
20. Ibid., p. 54.
21. Ibid., p. 55.
22. Idem.
23. Ibid., p. 58.
24. Ibid., pp. 60–1.
25. Ibid., p. 62.
26. Balarama Dasa, *Bhava Samudra*, Dharmagrantha Store, Cuttack, 1972, Canto 96.
27. Ibid., Canto 99.
28. Dibakara Dasa, *Jagannatha Charitamruta*, Bada Oriya Math, Puri, 1963, Chap. XIII.
29. Ibid., p. 42.
30. Ibid., pp. 12–13.
31. Ibid., p. 13.
32. Ibid., Chap. II, p. 31.
33. Ibid., Chap. II, p. 21.
34. Nilakantha Das, *Atma Jeevani*, Cuttack Students Store, Cuttack, 1973, p. 20; See also B.B. Shukla, *Bhagabata Ghara and Village Panchayat in Medieval Orissa* (AD *1510–1803*), Bharati Publications, Cuttack, 1986, p. 29.
35. Dibakara Dasa, op. cit. p. 113.
36 'In everything embodied Narayan resides
As the cause without beginning,
In all embodied beings
Narahari lives as the *Atman*,' *Bhagavata*, vol. X, Chap. 2.

37. Sitakanta Mahapatra, *Jagannatha Dasa*, Sahitya Akademi, New Delhi, 1989, pp. 37–59.
38. Dibakara Dasa, op. cit., p. 112.
39. Orissa State Museum Manuscripts, B/10; also vide Nilamani Mishra, 'Orissan Palm-Leaf Manuscripts', in M.N. Das (ed.), *Sidelights on History and Culture of Orissa*, Vidyapuri, Cuttack, 1977, p. 660.
40. Surendra Mohanty, *Oriya Sahityara Madhyaparva*, op. cit., pp. 291–5.
41. B.P. Panda, 'Contribution of Oriya Poets to Medieval Bengali Literature', in H.K. Mahatab et al. (eds.), *Glimpses of Orissan Art and Culture,* Orissa State Museum, Bhubaneswar, 1984, pp. 306–7.
42. N. Mishra in M.N. Das (ed.), op. cit., p. 662.
43. Achyutananda Dasa, *Sunya Samhita*, Arunodaya Press, Cuttack, 1914, Chap. XVIII.
44. Achyutananda Dasa, *Janmabibarana.*
45. Achyutananda Dasa, *Varnatika*, see R.K. Chaini (ed.), *Achyutananda Rachanavali* (*Kavita Khanda*), Achyutananda Smruti Samsad, Cuttack, 1989, pp. 50–8.
46. Achyutananda Dasa, *Varna Samhita*, R.K. Chaini (ed.), op. cit., 1989, p. 93. See also his *Harivamsa* (*Patal Khanda* and Seventh *Khanda*).
47. Achyutananda Dasa, *Kaivarta Gita*, Chap. 1, p. 3.
48. A.N. Parida, 'Kaivarta Gita: Eka Samkshipta Adhyayan', in K.S. Behera (ed.), *Sagar O Sahitya* (Oriya), Dasarathi Pustakalaya, Cuttack, 1993, pp. 196–208.
49. Achyutananda Dasa, *Gopalanka Ogala*, Orissa Jagannatha Company, Cuttack, 1990.
50. Achyutananda Dasa, *Varna Charita Gita*, vide R.K. Chaini (ed.), op. cit., 1989, pp. 1022–4.
51. Achyutananda Dasa, *Thike hua sabadhan*, vide R.K. Chaini (ed.), op. cit., 1989, pp. 6, 13, and 55.
52. Achyutananda Dasa, *Varna Charita Gita*, vide R.K. Chaini (ed.), op. cit., 1989, pp. 1025–6.
53. Achyutananda Dasa, *Bipra Chalaka*, quoted by K. Pathisharma in B. Mohanty (ed.), *Konark* (Panchasakha Special), Orissa Sahitya Akademi, Bhubaneswar, 1971, p. 148.
54. Achyutananda Dasa, *Tane Bhaja Rama Nama*, R.K. Chaini (ed.), op. cit., p. 123.
55. R.K. Chaini (ed.), *Achyutananda Gitavali*, Achyutananda Smruti Samsad, Nemal, Cuttack, 1983, p. 11.
56. Achyutananda Dasa, *Sunya Samhita*, p. 17.
57. Ibid., p. 19.
58. K.C. Sahoo (ed.), *Charikhani ba Sabdabrahma Samhita of Achyutananda Dasa*, Books and Books, Cuttack, 1979, p. 9.
59. Ibid., pp. 4–12.
60. Ibid., p. 15.
61. Ibid., p. 17.
62. Ibid., p. 28.
63. Achyutananda Dasa, *Sunya Samhita*, Chap. IV, p. 44.
64. Ibid., Chap. XXIII, p. 121.

65. Achyutananda Dasa, *Sri Gurubhakti Gita*, pt. II, Prachi Samiti, Bhubaneswar, 1970 (Preface).
66. Achyutananda Dasa, *Sunya Samhita*, Chap. III, p. 23.
67. Ibid., pp. 102–3.
68. Ibid., p. 105.
69. Ibid., p. 60.
70. B.M. Mohanty, 'Mahapurusha Jasovanta Dasa', in B. Mohanty (ed.), op. cit., p. 130, vide S.N. Das, op. cit., pp. 492–3.
71. Jashovanta Dasa, *Premabhakti Brahma Gita*, Prachi Samiti, Bhubaneswar, 1st edn., n.d., Chap. V, p. 40.
72. B. Mohanty (ed.), op. cit., pp. 130–3.
73. Jashovanta Dasa, *Premabhakti Brahma Gita*, op. cit., Chap. III, p. 20.
74. B. Sahu, 'Hetu Udaya Bhagavata', in B. Mohanty (ed.), op. cit., p. 429.
75. Ibid., p. 430.
76. Ibid., p. 431.
77. Idem.
78. Achyutananda Dasa, *Chhayalispatal* (Fourth Patal), in R.K. Chaini (ed.), op. cit., p. 128.
79. Achyutananda Dasa, *Amarkosha Gita*, Chap. II, in R.K. Chaini (ed.), op. cit., p. 153.
80. Achyutananda Dasa, *Kaivarta Gita*, Chap. III.
81. Achyutananda Dasa, *Sri Gurubhakti Gita*, vol. II, Prachi Samiti, Bhubaneswar, 1970, p. 44.
82. Ibid., vol. III, p. 183.
83. Balarama Dasa, *Chhatis Gupta Gita*, Dasarathi Pustakalaya, Cuttack, n.d.
84. Achyutananda Dasa, *Brahmasankuli* (*Prathama Kalpa*), ed. A.B. Mohanty, Mukur Press, Cuttack, 1926.
85. Quoted by K. Pathisharma, 'Mahapurusha Achyutananda', in B. Mohanty (ed.), op. cit., p. 459.
86. K.C. Sahoo (ed.), *Charikhani Ba Sabdabrahma Samhita of Achyutananda Dasa* (Introduction), Books and Books, Cuttack, 1979.
87. Achyutananda Dasa, *Kaivarta Gita*, Chap. XXIII.
88. Balarama Dasa, *Chhatis Gupta Gita*, Chap. VI.
89. Chittaranjan Das, op. cit., p. 187.
90. Surendra Mohanty, op. cit., 6th edn., 1995, pp. 215, 231, 240–7 and 269.
91. A.B. Mohanty (ed.), *Sarala Mahabharata*, Directorate of Culture, Bhubaneswar, 1968, pp. 208–27.
92. Nilambara Dasa, *Deula Tola Suanga*, quoted by B.M. Padhi, '*Panchasakha Sahityare Sri Jagannatha*', in B. Mohanty (ed.), op. cit., pp. 85–93.
93. R.K. Das, 'Social Protest in Medieval Orissa', in *Proceedings of Indian History Congress*, 41st Session, Bombay, 1980, p. 345.

CHAPTER 4

Samkirtan and Assimilation: The Regional Cultural Interaction between Orissa, Bengal and Assam

THE MESSAGE of the *panchasakhas* was for deliverance of the individual soul and for its relationship with the universal soul which they conveyed through a number of generally comprehended images and metaphors. In their literature, the psychic conditions and the emotional states which were associated with the craving to attain to the personal God were explored in depth. *Moksha* to them, was the union of the soul through devotion or *bhakti* with the over-soul. It was achieved not through any external rites or pilgrimages but through an intense meditative way, through a cleansing of the doors of perception. Their notion of *bhakti* was similar to, if not identical with, the concept of *bhakti* of Sri Chaitanya, with whom they also had close association. It is therefore necessary for us briefly to elucidate the ideology and the practice of Sri Chaitanya.

The *panchasakhas* practised meditation as a way of *bhakti* and at the same time they also believed in the *premabhakti* and joined the *samkirtan* movement of Sri Chaitanya. Chaitanya propagated a new religion which disowned caste and *Varnashrama Dharma* and treated Candala to Brahmin as equal if they had *bhakti* for Lord Krishna. The present chapter is an attempt to illustrate the religious outlook of Sri Chaitanya and to show how it developed after his religious tour to Puri, particularly after his meeting with Ray Ramananda, one of the remarkable exponents of the *bhakti* cult of Orissa. I shall also take a look at Chaitanya's vision of society and the measures of social reform that he carried out through his *samkirtan*.

The advent of Sri Chaitanya in Orissa signified a remarkable change in the socio-religious life of its inhabitants. His philosophy successfully spread over coastal Orissa and had a remarkable influence upon the prevailing religious ethos. He arrived in AD 1510 and stayed for eighteen years in Puri. His propagation of the new faith, based on egalitarianism and brotherhood, was cherished with great reverence by millions of followers. In every important village his name was chanted and the sacred Vaishnava literature were read out and explained to the masses in a spirit of fervent devotion. In Bengal it could not attain equally widespread popularity owing to the opposition by the people of the Sakta cult.[1] Apart from this, the rule of Sultan Hussain Shah did not offer a congenial atmosphere for its propagation.[2]

It was not that the cult of *bhakti* and Radha-Krishna worship were quite unknown in Orissa before the arrival of Sri Chaitanya. There were several instances of Krishna worship and pre-Chaitanya Vaishnavism in Orissa. In the twelfth century, Chodaganga Dev turned out to be a patron of Vaishnavism and Jaideva, the most celebrated poet of the period who composed *Gita Govindam* in Sanskrit, which was widely considered as a perennial source of the Radha-Krishna cult. Gajapati Purushottamdev, the father of the King Prataprudra Dev, was credited with the composition of several hymns, which clearly indicate the worship of Krishna and his sportive pranks with the *gopis*. That Krishna worship was quite extensive can be ascertained from the existence of the Gopinatha temple at Remuna, the main centre for Krishna worship.[3] Although, Krishna worship had reached its apex, the image of Krishna and popularity of his cult declined in the late fifteenth century due to bitter criticism of the cult by Sarala Dasa in his *Mahabharata* and Chaitanya Dasa in his *Nirguna Mahatmya*. Sri Chaitanya did a great service to the Krishna cult by regenerating the Lord's image and popularizing his worship in Orissa, Bengal and Assam. The cult of Radha-Krishna and propagation of *bhakti* gained momentum and received mass support by the *samkirtan* movement of Sri Chaitanya.

Great has been the influence exercised by Vaishnavism on the minds of the people—so much so that it even penetrated into the innermost recesses of the country. To be able to understand this we should begin by giving a brief account of the life and teachings of Sri Chaitanya, who founded Vaishnavism on an altogether new basis. His association with the *panchasakhas* and the patronage of Gajapati Prataprudra

Dev stimulated the faith and confidence of the people and accelerated the progress of his teachings.

On 27 February 1486, corresponding to the *Phalguna Purnima, Saka* 1407, Sri Chaitanya was born at Navadvipa or Nadia.[4] The Bengal Vaishnavas reckon the commencement of the Chaitanya era to this date. There was a lunar eclipse at the time and pious men and women of the locality were taking bath in the Ganges, and chanting hymns, as they often do on such occasions. Chaitanya's earlier name was Vishwambar. His father, Jagannatha Mishra, was a pious Vaishnav given to scholarly pursuits. His mother, Sachi Devi, was also deeply religious. They were a family of modest means.

It is stated in the old records that Chaitanya's ancestors were formerly residents of Jajpur (Orissa) from where they migrated to Sylhet in Bangladesh (then in Assam) owing to the oppression of Raja Bhramaravara. Raja Bhramaravara has been identified with Kapilendra Dev who is called Bhramaravara in an inscription at Gopinathapur in the Cuttack District.[5] Bhramaravara is a title and also used as a name. According to Jayananda, the author of *Chaitanya Mangal*, Madhukar Mishra, a Vedic Brahmin, left Jajpur and migrated to Sylhet. His grandson Jagannatha Mishra was forced to leave Sylhet because of drought and lawlessness there. He settled at Navadvipa which was a great seat of Sanskrit learning.[6]

During his youth Chaitanya led a householder's life and set-up a Sanskrit school for his livelihood. His wife Lakshmi died while he was on tour in Bengal to earn money. To please his mother Sachi, Chaitanya married again. But Vishnupriya, the second wife, could not fill the void of his heart, made by the sudden death of Lakshmi. It appears that Chaitanya sought solace from religious discussion with Isvar Puri, when he went to Gaya. Up to the age of twenty, he evinced little interest in religion. It seemed that he would spend his life as a householder and a school teacher. But suddenly, a great change took place in his life which completely changed its course.

In the year 1510, when he was in his twenty-fourth year, Chaitanya renounced the world and entered the holy order of *samnyasin*. From that day he came to be known in history as Sri Krishna Chaitanya or simply Sri Chaitanya. On taking the vow of an ascetic his first act was to visit Vrindavan, the place richly associated with Sri Krishna. Returning from Vrindavan, in the same year, he set out for Orissa with a view to having *darshan* of Lord Jagannatha of Puri. After he had taken the vow of *samnyasin* he lived for twenty-four years, of which he spent six years in visiting shrines in northern and southern India, and the remaining eighteen years in Orissa. His fervent devotion and religious ecstasy had a magnetic influence which drew thousands of admiring followers wherever he visited. His appearance was sober and gentle; besides, he was a great scholar.

RAY RAMANANDA, SRI CHAITANYA AND *PREMA-BHAKTI*

After an extensive tour of the different shrines of India and subsequent contact with different scholars, Chaitanya formulated his own ideas of *bhakti*, which bore distinct marks of Orissan *bhakti* ideology. In Puri he met numerous Vaishnavas and came to know about Ray Ramananda from Sarvabhauma, who was an illustrious scholar of Radha-Krishna cult and exponent of the *prema-bhakti*. Ray Ramananda was then the Governor of Rajhmuhendry, under Gajapati Prataprudra Dev. Chaitanya went Rajhmuhendry to meet Ray Ramananda and the latter thus explained to him lucidly the cult of Radha-Krishna and *prema-bhakti*:

Told Raya, then listen to the glory of 'love', that 'Radha-love' has no comparison in these three worlds, when Krishna escaped from the circular dance of the Gopis, Radha moved waiting for Krishna in the forest.[7]

He further explained:

Radha-Krishna love is really enchanting. And it is not so visible if you take Him to be your Master or your child; Their sport is not fine without the female companions (*sakhis*); So one should have a feeling of a female companion to get his grace, His worship has no other way but for one's feeling to be a female companion.

Therefore, bearing the mood of a *gopi*, thinking of their sport day and night who perfectly worship in this method, obtains, instead, the feet of Radha and Krishna.[8]

The Master further added:

I came here after hearing about you,
to fulfil my desire that listening to the stories of Krishna
I saw your glory exactly
What I had heard earlier,
that is your boundless knowledge of the love-cult of
Radha and Krishna.
Let us stay together at Neelachal (Puri).
And pass the days by discussing the colourful stories of Krishna.[9]

Chaitanya stayed for ten days at Rajhmuhendry and had discussions with Ray Ramananda on the subject of Krishna *bhakti*. This was an important dialogue which shaped and enriched his religious philosophy. He identified Lord Jagannatha to be Krishna, propagated as such, and sought to obtain his grace through emotional *prema-bhakti*. In addition to the concept of *sakhibhava*, the *hladini-sakti* of the Brahman (the almighty) and the identification of *hladini-sakti* with Radha was also Ramananda's contribution to Gaudiya Vaishnavism.[10] Chaitanya gratefully acknowledged that he learnt from Ray Ramananda *prema-bhakti*, the prime of the *purusharthas*, including the emotional feelings of 'servant', 'friend', 'child', 'teacher' and 'wife' to the personal God. In the words of Krishnadas Kabiraja Chaitanya observed:

> Ramananda Raya, the famous Vaishnava, taught me that Krishna was God Himself. I learnt from him the ways of '*Raga*' and '*prema*', and the *prema-bhakti*, the prime of the emotional feelings of servant, friend, child, teacher and wife; Ramananda taught me all these who was an eloquent of the theme of the love-based-devotion.[11]

The Gaudiya School of Vaishnavism took shape as a result of the neo-Vaishnava movement initiated by Chaitanya in Bengal and Orissa. His ideas later served as the foundation of the Vaishnava system of philosophy, namely, the *Achintya-vedaveda-vaba*, associated with the Chaitanya school. This new Vaishnava school was an addition to the already existing similar schools, earlier founded by Ramanuja (eleventh-twelfth century), Nimbark (late twelfth century), Madhavacharya (AD 1197–1276) and Vallabhacharya (born around AD 1481). He completely differed with the ideology of Madhavacharya, who emphasized upon the observance of *Varnashram Dharma*, for following the Vaishnava religion.[12] But Chaitanya relaxed the observance of *Varnashrama Dharma* in his new gospel of Vaishnavism, which was certainly a blow to the orthodox Brahminical social order.[13] His disagreement with Shankara's *Advaitavada* and *Mayavada*,[14] also helped consolidate the philosophy of neo-Vaishnavism. Thus, Chaitanya propagated an egalitarian social gospel amidst the caste-ridden societies of Bengal and Orissa.

ESSENCE OF THE CHAITANYA DHARMA

Chaitanya's religious message was simple and clear. It was liberal and broad-based. It was that of *bhakti* for Lord Krishna and Krishna alone. He advocated Krishna *bhakti* as a total form of religion which could be followed to the exclusion of everything else. However, no formal exposition of this religion was offered by him. There is no religious text which he believed in and preached. His spiritual message can be known through his biographies and the philosophical writings of the Vrindavan *goswamis* whom he had himself asked to write in support of his faith.

In the writings of the Vrindavana *goswamis*, Krishna *bhakti* is delineated as a religious path, self-sufficient and complete in itself. According to them, if one follows this path, there remains no need for performing the duties prescribed in the *sastras*. Those, it is said, can bear no fruit if not accompanied by *bhakti*. Salvation can be attained only through Krishna *bhakti* and not by following what is laid down in the Gaudiya Vaishnava thought. Krishna *bahkti* is placed above all other religious injunctions, and is set apart as a religion unto itself. The path of *bhakti*, it is said, is easy to follow. Whereas other religious modes may prove subtle and difficult, one can please Lord Krishna even by making small offerings to him such as leaves, flowers, fruits, water, etc. One must, therefore, turn to Krishna as the only support. One must work and think in a manner agreeable to Him with the faith that He would protect his devotees. One must dedicate all one's actions to Him and confess to Him all one's imperfections. The devotee must consider himself as totally dependent on Krishna and wait for His grace to attain salvation. All sins are washed away by reciting and listening to His name and glory.[15] Kabiraj Krishnadasa, therefore, states in his *Chaitanya Charitamrita* that man can attain salvation just by chanting and singing the name of Krishna. Identifying *nama-kirtan* with *bhakti*, he describes it as the *dharma* most suitable to *Kali-yuga*. He goes on to explain that this *dharma* is most efficacious for the householders or the common men who remain tied throughout their life to worldly affairs. For them the only way to salvation is to hear Krishna's *lila-katha* or the story of Krishna's divine sport.[16]

Bhakti is also described as the highest form of religious obligation. Placing it in line with the four obligations (*purusharthas*) accepted by the Hindus' namely, *dharma, artha, kama* and *moksha*, the Gaudiya Vaishnavas called *bhakti*, the fifth *purushartha*. Besides, *bhakti* is described by them as the highest of *purusharthas*, and the other four as its subordinates. In the Gaudiya Vaishnava tradition, *bhakti* is placed higher than even *moksha* (salvation), which was always understood as the highest and the ultimate goal of all religious pursuits. It is not regarded as a means to *mukti* (liberation), but as *mukti* itself. In short, Krishna *bhakti* is explained in the Gaudiya Vaishnava thought, as the ultimate end.[17]

Belief in a highly personalized god served as the very core of Chaitanya's conception of *bhakti*. Total dedication to a personal god was the essence of the realm of his religious thought. Chanting the name of Krishna (his personal god), singing and dancing in praise and remembrance of his glorification and satisfaction and bearing constant love and emotional attachment to him was what Chaitanya had enjoined upon his followers. Besides this, he wanted them to hold everything connected with the life and exploits of Krishna as most sacred. Here was worship advocated of a personal god in the ultimate sense. That is to say, not of god as personality in a conceptual sense only, but a personal god accepted in his human incarnation. Chaitanya's Krishna is the Krishna of Mathura who performed the *rasa-lila* with the *gopis* in Vrindavana—Krishna, who was beloved of Radha. Chaitanya is believed to have said Krishna is at his best when he plays the role of a man. His form is essentially human as a cowherd boy with the 'flute' in his hands—young and gay'.[18]

To establish the ultimate supremacy of Lord Krishna and the importance of Krishna worship, the Gaudiya Vaishnavas minimise the importance of the Vedas and Upanishads and relegate them to the background in order to uphold their faith in the personal deity Krishna. The argument they offer is that since the Vedas are difficult to understand and can be interpreted differently, greater validity should be attached to the Itihasa and Puranas. They refer to the latter as the fifth Veda and go to the extent of suggesting that it is these which should be regarded as the true Veda. The reason for making such suggestions is quite obvious. The personality of Krishna figures essentially in Itihasa (i.e. various Vaishnava Puranas) and not in the Vedas and Upanishads. Among the Puranas, they regarded the Vaishnava Puranas as higher than all others and out of all Vaishnava Puranas, it is the *Bhagavata Purana* which is considered as the most sacred by them.[19] That is why Chaitanya conferred the title *Atibadi* on Jagannatha Dasa for his translation of the *Bhagavata* into Oriya.

Chaitanya's *bhakti* was definitely pitched against the *Advaitavada* of Sankaracharya. In the biographies of Chaitanya, a number of references can be found of his getting into argument with the advocates of the *Advaitavedanta*, and also of his attempts to convert them to his path of Krishna *bhakti*. An instance may be cited here in this connection. It is said that a prolonged discussion went on at Puri, and that Chaitanya lectured for full seven days trying to convince Sarvabhauma of falsity of *Advaitavada* and the *Mayavada* of Sankaracharya.[20] Sarvabhauma, who later turned out to be one of the most illustrious disciples of Chaitanya was an *advaitavadin* to begin with. The popularity of Chaitanya spread over all the religious centres of Orissa, when Sarvabhauma accepted the ideology of the *bhakti* of Chaitanya. He was acknowledged not only as a great *bhakta* but also an erudite scholar.

Chaitanya preached what has been called the *Dvaitadvaitavada* or 'non-dualism within dualism'. *Advaitavada* of Sankar advocates the theory that the Universe is identical with the deity. The line of demarcation between the human soul and the Great soul embracing all, is more fancied than real—the origin of imagined reality being the phenomenal world denominated *maya* in the midst of which we live. The moment we attain *jnana*, or true knowledge, the phenomenal world, which is a mere illusion, passes away, and the little soul becomes merged in the Great soul; so that all that has created the differences ceases to be exist.[21]

The *Dvaitavada* or dualism is, of course, the common theory accepted by most people, which propagates that God and man are eternally different, the latter having to rely constantly on His mercy, help and compassionate grace.

The *Dvaitadvaitavada* of Chaitanya advocates dualism in religious speculation, but lays emphasis on the devotional aspects, implying that when faith has reached the state of perfection, the human being forgets its own self, the eyes see nothing but Him—the sight of all sights, the ear hears nothing but the sound of His flute, which fills all space and every touch of Him. The sense, in fact, instead of leading to the consciousness of *maya* makes the devotee aware of the presence of Him only, so absolutely that he forgets his own existence. That is Chaitanya's non-dualism within dualism—only a refined form of dualism in the highest stage of devotion.[22]

There were three principal centres for the propagation of Vaishnavism, inspired by Chaitanya. They were Nabadvipa in Bengal, Puri in Orissa and Vrindavan in Uttar Pradesh. Of the three, Orissa occupies an important position in the history of the Chaitanya cult. In assessing the role of Chaitanya in the history of Vaishnavism in Orissa, it should be borne in mind that Vaishnavism was prevalent in Orissa even before Chaitanya's arrival at Puri. It is interesting to note that there were two trends in the pre-Chaitanya Vaishnavism of Orissa. One was the purely devotional religion based on Krishna worship. The other was devotion, mixed with knowledge of Lord Jagannatha, who was considered as Buddha. When Chaitanya began to propagate his faith, based on the cult of Radha-Krishna, the earlier previous Vaishnava trend was gradually absorbed into the mainstream of the neo-Vaishnavism preached by him. But the second one, nevertheless, maintained its separate existence for a considerable period of time even after Chaitanya.

Gajapati Prataprudra Dev was deeply impressed by Sri Chaitanya and he gladly invited him to his court. He arranged accommodation for him in the Vakul *math* and patronized the propagation of his *bhakti* cult. It may be reiterated that the king was upset with the prevailing religious ethos, and to check the growing power of the priests of the Jagannatha temple he extended his patronage to an unorthodox devotee Sri Chaitanya and to his Gaudiya followers. It may be asked, therefore, that if the king was looking for an opportunity to curb the growing power of the Brahmin priests, why then he did not welcome the local radical *bhaktas*? The reason may be that the king was the protector of the Hindu *dharma* and he had to maintain the social system. Therefore, he was not in a position to replace the orthodox Brahmin priests by the local radical *Sudramunis*. So he welcomed Chaitanya, an unorthodox Brahmin *bhakta* to Puri and extended to him royal patronage. With the growth of the king's special support and patronage to the new faith of Sri Chaitanya, the other varieties of Vaishnavism came to be somewhat looked down upon and discriminated against. The smaller vassal chiefs also took to the same line by following the motive of the Gajapati king. This new faith, however, did not try to complement what was already there in local Vaishnava tradition in Orissa; it came as a megastructure, as it were, and took the day as a conqueror.

SRI CHAITANYA AND THE *PANCHASAKHA* IN ORISSA

Sri Chaitanya was closely associated with the *panchasakhas* and other Oriya followers during his long stay in Puri. It is evident from the *Madalapanji*[23] and different writings of Achyutananda Dasa[24] and Sudarshan Dasa[25] that the *panchasakhas* participated in the *samkirtan* of Sri Chaitanya. They were the people who carried *samkirtan,* i.e. chanting the name of Krishna and Hari to the doorsteps of the common men of Orissa. We have earlier discussed that major literary works of Balarama Dasa, Jagannatha Dasa and Achyutananda Dasa were completed by the time of the arrival of Chaitanya at Puri. The Orissan school of Vaishnavism under the leadership of the *panchasakhas* was proceeding in its own way. Although the *panchasakhas* accepted Chaitanya's *Bhaktidharma* and Krishna cult, they did not sacrifice their own system of worship. It is known from the *Jagannatha Charitamrita* of Divakara Dasa (seventeenth century) that there was a sort of rift between the Gaudiya and Orissan stream of Vaishnavas. The Gaudiya Vaishnavas protested against Chaitanya's conferment of the title *Atibadi* to Jagannatha Dasa for his translation of the *Srimad Bhagavata* into Oriya. Suspecting that Chaitanya was showing special favour and affection towards the Oriya Vaishnavas, the Gaudiya camp became intolerant. They gave vent to their hurt feelings before Chaitanya who would not go by them.[26] Chaitanya tried to pacify the Gaudiya Vaishnavas and explained that even the insects, stones, sands and wood of this land (Puri) are greater than anybody of other places and therefore, the title *Atibadi* (very great) given to Jagannatha Dasa was not over-estimation.[27] But the Gaudiya Vaishnavas were not convinced with such explanation. The whole thing seems to have reached a climax when the Gaudiya followers left Puri first for Jajpur and ultimately for Vrindaban, leaving back Sri Chaitanya to be at Puri till his death.[28] But Chaitanya did not leave Puri because of many reasons. Besides political patronage, Chaitanya found the echoes of his own beliefs and teachings in those of the *panchasakhas* and the ruling class and the people of Orissa responded to his philosophy so enthusiastically that nowhere else such a movement was seen.

It must, however, be said here that similarity apart, there was an unmistakable difference between Chaitanya *bhakti* and Orissan Vaishnavism. The *panchasakhas* maintained their distinctive characteristics in spite of their close association with Chaitanya and the Gaudiya Vaishnavas.

In Orissa, Krishna did not receive exclusive devotion of the Vaishnavas before the advent of Chaitanya. To them, He was an epic god with his failings and virtues. But according to Chaitanya faith, Krishna or Bhagavat constitutes the complete manifestation of personal God-head in its perfect form. Chaitanya is believed to be the dual incarnation of Radha and Krishna.

Chaitanya propounded the cult of *prema-bhakti* giving emphasis on complete surrender of the self before the personal God. Devotion with emotional fervour was inextricably attached to his expressions of *bhakti*. The *panchasakha*, however, gave a new connotation to the concept of Sudra and had declared the highest form of *bhakti* to be *Sudrabhakti*. They explained the Sudra as an embodiment of *Sudrabhava* (humility) and suggested that every aspirant of God-realization had to be a possessor of *Sudrabhava*. Achyutananda said that he did neither aspire for achieving the status of Brahmins nor depend on the varnas of Kshatriyas and Vaishyas. To him, someone of lowest rank possessed modest and the simplest attitude to life. The Sudras are not proud, the feeling of service to God by humility is only realized with the Sudras. The *panchasakhas*, declared that they had the Sudra propensity and they were nothing but Sudras.[29] Chaitanya also cherished the value of humility but with a difference, i.e. as an essential charac-teristic of *bhakti*. He once advised his followers to be 'modest like grasses and tolerant like trees'. He further advised them 'to respect everybody without expecting honour in return'; according to him, 'those who will do it will obtain the grace of Hari'.[30]

Further, the Gaudiya Vaishnavas regarded Radha next to Krishna, the divine consort of Krishna. The Orissan stream of Vaishnavas deviate from such thinking of the Gaudiya Vaishnavas. Bhima Dhibara the author of *Kapatapasha*, a near contemporary of the *panchasakhas*, has placed Rukmini and Satyabhama by the side of Sri Krishna, instead of Radha. In the Oriya *Bhagavata* of Jagannatha Dasa, Vrindabati and not Radha, has been acclaimed as the Gopi nearest to him. Achyutananda had the conception of Anadi Krishna as a step beyond Nitya Radha.[31]

Chaitanya succeeded in making a large number of disciples, including Oriyas and non-Oriyas. Nityananda, Damodar Pundit, Mukunda Dutta, and Jagadananda were predominant Bengali disciples who had accompanied him on his journey to Puri.[32] In Orissa, many prominent persons also became his followers. Ramananda Ray and Gopinath Badajena, the governors of Rajmuhendry and Midnapur respectively, had been ardent followers of the love cult of Radha and Krishna.[33] Sikhi Mohanty and his sister Madhavi Dasi (being a woman she could not meet Chaitanya) were considered to be the chosen followers. Other prominent Oriya Vaishnavas of the Gaudiya school were Ramananda's brothers and father, Bhavananda Patnaik, Kanai Khuntia, Janardan Mohanty, Tulasi Parichha, Kesi Mishra, Pradyumna

Mishra and Krishnadasa. It is to be noted that except for the families of Ramananda and Pradyumna Mishra, the rest were priests or scribes of the Jagannatha temple.[34] Besides, there were a large number of followers of the Chaitanya sect specially drawn from the common mass of the society. Initially, the activities of Sahajiya Vaishnavas had degraded Krishna and Radha to the position of a lover and beloved in the estimation of the common people. But due to the efforts of the Gaudiya Vaishnavas the peasant folk began to entertain the idea of worshipping the dual image of Krishna and Radha as the Supreme God and His consort.[35] Besides this, the Radha-Krishna cult also became popular among the common people because of the birth of Lord Krishna in the house of Nanda, the chief of the milkmen community. The people, therefore, embraced this cult without any second thought. It was popularized by many vassal chiefs and zamindars when they worshipped the images of Radha and Krishna during the festival of Holi, with great pomp and grandeur. This tradition is still current in Orissa.

REFORMS IN BENGAL

In eastern India, the powerful movement organized by Chaitanya spread from Bengal to Orissa and Assam and went beyond, to the other parts of northern India and Deccan. The essence of Chaitanyaism is given in two sentences by Kaviraj Krishnadasa, 'If a creature adores Krishna and sings His name, he is released from the meshes of illusion and attains to Krishna's feet.' To him, 'the theory of *jnana* and *karma* could not be effective without *bhakti* to Krishna. *Jnana* without *bhakti* cannot give salvation. But Krishna *bhakti* without *jnana*, of course, brings salvation to the devotee.'[36]

According to him, worship consisted in love and devotion, song and dance, producing a state of ecstasy in which His presence is realized. All men were competent to perform this worship, irrespective of caste and creed.[37] Chaitanya also condemned priestly rituals and caste segregation, and is said to have admitted many Muslims and Hindu lower castes to membership and to have regarded all devotees of Krishna as equal.[38] Also worth noting is the fact that several distinguished disciples of Chaitanya were traders by caste. Rupa and Sanatana, two high-rank officials of Hussain Shah of Bengal were also ardent disciples of Sri Chaitanya.[39]

One of the most ardent and sincere of Chaitanya's companions who showed great devotion and adhered to his spiritual convictions was Haridasa, popularly known as Yavan Haridasa, the Muslim. We have not come across his Muslim name. He was given the Hindu name, 'Haridasa' after his conversion to Vaishnavism. His father, Malae Kazi, was the owner of considerable property in the District of Ambua. Haridasa was born in Budan near Bangraam in the District of Jessore about the year AD 1464. He came to Santipur as a youngman and was converted to the Vaishnava faith by Advaita. Nityananda and Haridasa became close friends and both preached the Chaitanya cult in the city and its suburbs.[40]

As early as AD 1509 (during his preaching at Katwa in Bengal), Chaitanya declared in public that he was endeavouring to build up a neo-Vaishnava society based on the principles of social equality. Subsequently after his south Indian tour he began to preach socially egalitarian thoughts. Chaitanya declared that need to give up *Varnashrama Dharma* formed an essential prerequisite for worshipping Krishna. To him, all the people from Candala to Brahmin, irrespective of gender, could worship Lord Hari or Krishna.[41] It may be observed that the social objectives of Chaitanya being different, he could not agree with the ideas of the Madhava school. Krishna devotion is possible, according to Madhava, only after fulfilling the obligations of the *Varnashrama Dharma*, whereas Chaitanya considered *Varnashrama Dharma* as an obstacle to attain Krishna. Further the attainment of the five minds of *mukti* has been declared as the ultimate goal by Madhava, whereas Chaitanya considered love for Krishna as the only supreme value of life and considered *mukti* relatively insignificant. To him, a true Vaishnava should shun evil company, female companions and agnostics; he should give up *Varnashrama Dharma* and humbly take refuge in Krishna.[42] He further elaborated that the moment you say that you love God, all human beings will be your brethren; there will be no Brahmin and no Sudra. Chaitanya proclaimed this in unqualified language. He said, 'He that eats a meal cooked by a Dom (an untouchable community) becomes pre-eminently entitled to the grace of God.' The motto of the Vaishnavas was 'even a Chandal should be held higher than Brahmin if he has devotion for God', and this is a well-known text of the *Naradiya Purana*. As Chaitanya remarked:

> If a *muchi* (cobbler) prays to God with devotion, I bow a hundred times to his feet.[43]

Sri Chaitanya had entrusted the charge of social reform to Nityananda. This saintly man, though a Brahmin, ate the food cooked by Udharan Dutt of the Savarna banik caste (one of the unclean castes) and he spent his time mainly in the houses of low-class men. Nityananda and Advaita opened their portals of brotherhood to all men irrespective of their castes. The fallen Buddhists, mainly represented by the mercantile classes of Bengal with a few exceptions had lived as out-castes. No Brahmin would formerly do any religious function in their houses. The Vaishnavas accepted them as disciples, ate at their houses and performed the priestly functions in their temples. Nityananda and his son Birabhadra raised the social status of 1200 *Neras* (Buddhist monks) and 1300 *Neris* (Buddhist nuns) by admitting them into the Vaishnava order, which was a great achievement in terms of social regeneration.[44]

Numerous complaints were made against Nityananda for violating the caste rules. Sribasa was ridiculed with the term *Jatinasha*, a violator of the caste rules, because he had allowed Nityananda to live with him. But the Vaishnavas repudiated caste in an uncompromising way. In later times Narottam Dasa, a Kayastha, was raised to the status of a Brahmin by the unanimous voice of the Vaishnavas gathered at a meeting held at Khetri in the District of Rajshastri. The religious leaders proclaimed that one who had realized himself and the selfhood of others was a true Brahmin and one who merely wore the sacred thread was so only in name. Another incident may be cited which stirred the orthodox section of society to a large extent. Narahari Sarkar of Srikhanda, the famous poet and friend of Chaitanya, and Narottama Dasa of Khetri who lived in the sixteenth century—one a Vaidya and the other a Kayastha received the Brahmin disciples for initiation. Narahari Sarkar was not an ascetic but a householder. The nature of disciple in medieval society was to take the left-over from the plate of one's *guru* and to drink water touched by his feet. The revolution brought about in the world of caste by these acts, raised a tempest of opposition among the orthodox sections of society.[45] Earlier we have discussed that Jagannatha Dasa, a Brahmin and author of Oriya *Bhagavata* was initiated by *Sudramuni* Balarama Dasa and he accepted the latter as guru. The inspiration of this great revolution came of course, from Chaitanya himself.

In Puri, Chaitanya upheld the act of Kalidasa's (a *bhakta* of Kayastha caste) eating of a mango already tasted by Kanai (a *bhakta* belonging to sweeper caste).[46] He paid regular visits to Yavan Haridasa who stayed outside of the Jagannatha temple premises and observed that he was purified by touching him (Haridasa). And when Haridasa died, he made all the good Brahmins drink water touched by his foot.[47] His conduct towards Sanatan also showed the same catholicity and affection. Sanatan, though originally a Brahmin, had adopted the ways of Muslim life and had consequently been socially boycotted. But Chaitanya accepted him as a disciple by offering a respectable position in his Vaishnava order.[48]

Chaitanya faced a lot of opposition and criticism. Of course, he gained strong political support, but he could not win over a considerable orthodox section of society. An influential section led by the orthodox and proud pundits of Orissa remained in opposition to the neo-Vaishnavism and social reform carried out by him. In their intellectual pride, they not only scorned and ridiculed the emotional Krishna devotion, but also tried to obstruct its growth. According to Mayadhar Mansingh:

> The Brahmins are as a class intensely hostile to Chaitanyaism and some of its ceremonies even today. We find a bitter diatribe against the Chaitanya *bhakti* cult. It is typical of the general attitude of the Orissa intelligentsia. Many Brahmins in Orissa are hostile to the Chaitanyaian *bhakti* cult because it makes no discrimination between the Brahmins and non-Brahmins.[49]

On the other hand, Chaitanya wanted to effect a change of heart in them and to win them over to his faith of universal love and tolerance. His advice to regulate one's life before one can reach the higher plane of mystic bliss is all comprehensive. He said:

> Song in praise of Sri Krishna cleanses the mirror of mind, towards extinguishes the great conflagration of worldliness, diffuses like moonlight towards all that is good among the people. It (*samkirtan* of Sri Krishna) is the life of bride-like education by which theology and emotional devotion i.e. *bhakti* are roused and kept in the heart. It increases the ocean of joy. Full nectar is tasted in every step of it (all sentiments could be experienced). It satisfies all the senses.[50]

On another occasion he advised the religious preceptors in the following terms:

> Do not take too many disciples, do not abuse God worshipped by other people and their scriptures, do not read too many books and do not pose as a teacher continuously criticizing and elucidating religious views. Take profit and loss in the same light. Do not stay there where a Vaishnava is abused. Do not listen to village tales. Do not by your speech or thought cause pain to a living being. Listen to the recitation of God's name. Recollect His kindness; bow to Him and worship Him. Do what He wills as a servant ; believe Him to be a friend and then dedicate yourself to Him.[51]

It is evident from the views of Chaitanya that he underlined one's freedom of thought. He advised people not to rely completely on traditional scriptures but to do some noble deeds which may bring joy, happiness and peace for the people of all denominations. He wanted a change in society with moral uplift and spiritual progress of the people.

NEO-VAISHNAVISM IN ASSAM

The neo-Vaishnavite movement was initiated in Assam by the son of the soil Sankardev (AD 1449–1569). He popularized the use of the Assamese for the spread of the *bhakti* literature in the fifteenth century. He composed a number of short one-act plays, of the nature of morality plays, incorporating themes from the Puranas.[52] He propagated the Vaishnavism, that was quite different from Gaudiya Vaishnavism. It is said that although Sankar came to Puri twice only to see Lord Jagannath, no meeting could take place between him and Sri Chaitanya.[53] His religious philosophy was enriched by the prevailing situation of Assam and the influence of the ongoing religious movements in Orissa and Bengal. It appears that two streams of Vaishnava movement like that of Orissa, developed in Assam, i.e. one under the leadership of Sankardev and the other with the influence of Gaudiya Vaishnavaism under the propagation of Sri Chaitanya. The neo-Vaishnavism of Sankar was an egalitarian movement of the commoners of the society. Like Chaitanya's *samkirtan* party, in the *samkirtan* of Sankar, all enjoyed social and religious equality. There were a large number of followers of Sankardev of whom Madhava and Damodar were two prominent disciples. Gradually, Assamese Vaishnavism was influenced by Buddhist ideas and rituals, in which the Brahminic influence played a remarkable role which led to the worship of Buddha widely as an incarnation of Hari.[54] There was also another religious current associated with the long travel of the *bhakti* cult started by Ramanuj in the eleventh century from south India to Assam and other parts of India through Orissa. Since Jagannath Puri in Orissa enjoyed the status of the nucleus of the religious and cultural life of Hindus, it played the role of a link line of the *bhakti* cult between the south and the north.[55]

Besides, the contribution of Sankardev, the spread of Chaitanya movement in Assam was also noteworthy. The neo-Vaishnavism of Sankar and its two sub-sects, *Mahapurushia* and *Damodaria* or

Bamunia (it is probably called *Bamunia* since *Damodar* belonged to Brahmin caste) were the real Kamrupa Vaishnavism. Besides these two sects, an independent sect belonging to the Gaudiya Sampradaya of Bengal is found in Kamrupa. It is said that two brothers, Rama Chandra and Rama Bhadra, descendants of Nityananda, came to Assam with a few followers about the end of the sixteenth century. They were given land and property by the Ahom King Lakshmi Singh, and these two brothers with their followers settled in Kamrupa about the year AD 1775 and propagated the philosophy of Sri Chaitanya.[56] In the *Charit Puthis* of sixteenth century there are some references to Bengal Vaishnavism in the western part of Assam. The medieval biographies of the Vaishnava saints contain a few references to Chaitanya from which it is known that the cult of Chaitanya silently entered into the western part of Assam towards the middle of the sixteenth century through the propagation of some Chaitanya followers. One of the biographers even wrote that Chaitanya, the saint of Bengal remained sometimes as an ascetic in a cave near Hajo, a place situated at a distance of fifteen miles from Gauhati. Jayananda wrote that Chaitanya stayed some days at Hajo and there is a cave called Chaitanya Gumpha or Chaitanya Cave.[57] In this way, Chaitanyaism had a stronghold in Assam.

BHAKTI AND *SAMKIRTAN*

Sri Chaitanya found a medium of externalizing his devotional fervour through *samkirtans* invoking or praying to the deity through group-singing. These *samkirtans* became very popular since the people could worship God directly without help of the priests. Groups participating in them became larger and larger with each passing day and soon they developed into *nagar-samkirtans*—mass singing in streets. These *nagar-samkirtans*, the singing orgies in which Chaitanya poured out his whole being, became a very effective vehicle for the propagation of his newly acquired faith. His worship of God in the form of Krishna found expression in his preaching of universal love. This was Chaitanya's message and mission. The social context of Vaishnavism, as pronounced by Chaitanya, was the idea of the oneness of man in the eyes of God. The manifestation of *bhakti* in service, love and devotion broke the barriers of caste which, at least theoretically, lost all significance. The call of Chaitanya for universal, unmotivated love found expression in his sweet and enchanting

Krishna songs in which multitudes of people avidly joined. *Nama-samkirtan* introduced by Chaitanya, went a long way in popularizing the Vaishnava faith among the masses of Orissa. Iswar Dasa, a poet of the seventeenth-century Orissa writes in his *Sri Chaitanya Bhagavata* that there were sixty-four *sampradayas* of *kirtan* music during the time of Chaitanya, who once performed *Samkirtan* for thirteen days by singing the name of Krishna and playing numerous *veenas*, flutes and four hundred conches.[58]

The element of *bhakti* and the Radha-Krishna cult emerged found expression in literary form in the Sanskritic *padavalis* of Jayadeva. In the verses of his *Gita Govindam*, both the *madhurya* and *aishvarya* aspects of Krishna worship were expressed in the exaltation of Radha. Those devotional verses of Jayadeva had a deep appeal to Chaitanya himself. He was a great admirer of Jayadeva's *Gita Govindam* and very much liked to listen to those songs. We have earlier discussed that *Gita Govindam* used to be recited everyday in the Jagannatha temple of Puri as a part of ritual. Compositions of Jayadeva not only appealed to Chaitanya greatly but were also considered as a source of living inspiration to the Gaudiya Vaishnava movement. Though expressed in terms of human longings, the songs of Jayadeva contained fervent devotional cravings for realization of the divinity.

After Jayadeva, the most famous musical composition belonging to the Vaishnava faith or Radha-Krishna cult was the *Sri Krishna Kirtana* by Vadu Chandidasa. Unlike the former *Gita Govindam* in Sanskrit, the *Sri Krishna Kirtan* was composed in Bengali language. Chandidasa composed this *kirtan* about a century before the advent of Chaitanya.[59]

Chaitanya introduced the *nama-samkirtan* in the first quarter of the sixteenth century, which became a part of his faith and movement. Congregational singing of *kirtan* processions were organized during the Rath-yatra festivals at Puri and on occasions like Janmastami celebrations, etc. On many occasions Chaitanya's *kirtan* singing was accompanied by dance. According to the biographies of Chaitanya, dance with devotional fervour was a part of *kirtan* music. When *kirtan* was introduced by him as a fervent religious singing, dance was considered to be an integral part of the same. Chaitanya not only himself loved to sing *kirtan* but also liked to see his followers taking part in *samkirtan*. Vrindabana Dasa in his *Chaitanya Bhagavata* has mentioned that even the devotees of Navadvipa came to Puri to pay homage to Sri Chaitanya. Chaitanya advised all of his disciples to sing *nama-samkirtan* repeating '*Hare Krishna Hare Krishna Krishna Krishna Hare Hare; Hare Rama Hare Rama Rama Rama Hare Hare*'.[60]

Kirtan came to be sung by the people from house to house and then spread from town to town. It is said that the accompanying percussion instrument called *khole* was also introduced by Chaitanya. *Khole* (similar to pakhawaj, with the only difference that its body is made up of earth instead of wood) and *karatal* (two circular pieces made of brass) were the two accompanying instruments played during *kirtan*. Accompanied by these two simple rhythmical instruments, *kirtan* music was within the reach of the ordinary people among whom the message of Chaitanyaism spread through the medium of this type of devotional singing. The village folks took keen interest in this enchanting form of singing and dancing together.[61]

Chaitanya's *bhakti* movement bears a lasting impression in the socio-religious life of the people of India. His faith had a universal character and as a religious philosophy it appealed to reason with its humanism. Repeatedly asserting that the Radha-Krishna cult had a remarkable significance, expressing the highest form of love of God, he did not, however, give up his faith in the shrines associated with the Krishna legends. With a desire to complete surrender his self to his God Krishna he thus addressed Lord Jagannatha of Puri,

Here am I, and here art thou, Oh Krishna and the joy of our Union is ever new here as of old, yet my mind yearns for union with thee in Vrindaban.[62]

The above utterance relating to Chaitanya's predilection for the holy city should not be given an exaggerated importance. The temples of Durga, Siva and Ganesh and, in fact, all other shrines that he visited invoked in him spiritual emotions of the same nature. Every temple was sacred to him, as he believed his God to dwell there; every forest expressed to him the message of Vrindaban and every river the sacredness of Yamuna. Very often he forgot himself, his existence and sang thus:

Oh! when will my eyes
overflow with tears,
My voice, husky with love
Choke all utterance on my lips.
And all my limbs vibrate
with tender joy
on taking your sacred names.[63]

Chaitanya never wanted materialistic benefits or salvation. Instead of it he longed for causeless devotion and love of Lord Krishna. Thus he says,

I covet no wealth, nor retinue,
Nor even the lonely maid polsy,
Lord of the Universe, not for these
I address thee in my prayers,
to thyself supremest Master,
In my every successive life
May thou be pleased to grant me
the causeless devotion of thy love.[64]

Chaitanya expressed the fragrance of love and devotion in all his songs and prayers. Whatever may be God's behaviour he loved Him ceaselessly as is reflected in the following song,

He may embrace or tread upon
this insect clinging to his feet,
Or give me mortal pain by
banishing me from his sight.
Or in whatever other ways he may
behave to gratify his passion,
Yet is this loving cheat, none
other the darling of my heart.[65]

Chaitanya speaks of the recitation of the name of the God in the following passage:

Full many are the names
thou dost manifest,
Then thou dost imbued with
all thy power.
There is no fixed hour for
their recollections,
Such is the greatness
of thy mercy Krishna.[66]

POPULARITY OF KRISHNA AND CHAITANYA

The *bhakti* movement through *samkirtan* became very popular and had a tremendous effect on the then socio-religious order of Orissa and Bengal. The tenets of this faith were incorporated into the cult of

Jagannatha, which, over the ages, have proved its receptivity to what is there in the different faiths. The interplay of the different systems of Vaishnavism and tantricism, then existing in this part of the country, actually transformed the cult of *bhakti* into an eclectic form of Vaishnavism.[67] This reform offered enough scope to the associates of Chaitanya to mould the pattern of literature accordingly. The *panchasakhas*, particularly, played an important role in this matter and preached this new religion in such a way that every corner of Orissa was influenced by it and the literature and social life of Orissa came completely under its spell. *Gopakeli*, a part of the Oriya *Bhagavata* of Jagannatha Dasa, also made the Radha-Krishna cult more popular. Other Oriya poets wrote in the regional language which became a medium of spreading the ideas among the rural people. Achyutananda Dasa composed the *Uddhava Gita* and *Rasa Lila* which made the life and deeds of Krishna more popular and appealing to the hearts of the people of Orissa. Chaitanya's spiritual colouring of the unconventional and erotic love of Radha and Krishna, made it widely popular. The *nagar-kirtan*, centring round Chaitanya, attracted the people of all castes and creeds and through this method he reached the masses to an extent that no other devotee could do.

From one of the inscriptions of Prataprudra Dev in the Jagannatha temple one learns of the existence of the four classes of Vaishnavas who were entrusted with the performance of *nama-samkirtan* during the time of *Bara Singhara* in the temple. These are (1) Ramanujapanthi, (2) Vishnuswamipanthi, (3) Madhavpanthi and (4) Gaudiyapanthi. Chaitanya's influence was felt in all these *sampradayas*. These *sampradayas* are still attached to the temple for the performance of the *nama-samkirtan*.

The neo-Vaishnavism of Chaitanya has made Bengali as well as Orissan society what it is today. This movement left many of the lower castes unconverted, especially those living in the fringe areas covered by hills and jungles (*Kanan-basi*). But Vaishnavism, in the vast spaces of Bengal which it dominates, has produced two wholesome fruits; the ritualistic sacrifice of animals has been totally abolished and drinking of strong wine as a religious ritual, has been stopped.[68] Even greater than this, moral reformation of the upper and middle classes has been the work of Vaishnavism. It uplifted the lower ranks of society and the unlettered masses by carrying religion to their doors. The movement attempted to reduce the orthodox pattern of Brahminic domination and proclaimed the dignity of each individual in society. Of course, there were lesser number of women than men in the faith of Vaishnavism, but the cultural uplift of women was promoted by allowing them to read Sashtras. The new life breathed into Bengal, as the Vaishnava Gosains set themselves to converting the aboriginal tribes, brought illumination into their life after ages of neglect, deprivation and superstition.[69]

Chaitanya had become an incarnation of God during his lifetime. He passed away in Puri in AD 1533. His followers believed that his body and soul disappeared and mixed with Lord Jagannatha. Whatsoever may be the legend, Chaitanya left a lasting impression in the hearts of millions for his emotional devotion to and popularization of the Radha-Krishna cult, the memory of his life and teachings. The poets sang of his emotional fervour and traces. The sculptors engraved his images on the surface of stone and the painters portrayed his handsome personality and the *samkirtan* scenes where his trances and songs captivated the soul of the admiring multitude. These were often painted in lacquer on wooden boards used as palm-leaf book covers and produced for the decoration of the *Bhagavata* literature from sixteenth to early eighteenth centuries. Parents in Bengali and Oriya homes gave to their children those names by which Chaitanya was called showing how dearly they loved and cherished his memory. Gauranga, Gaura, Chaitanya and Nimai have since become very common names in Orissa and Bengal. Nadevasi—a resident of Nadiya, Nagarvasi—a resident of the city (city is here Nadiya), Nader-chand or the moon of Nadiya and its more elegant form Navadvipa-chandra now became the favourite names in which the Bengalis prided out of their great love and admiration for the Nadiya prophet.

After Sri Chaitanya, the Gaudiya Vaishnavas introduced a preliminary song called *Gaura Chandrika* in honour of the memories of Chaitanya and made a rule that it had to be sung before *samkirtan*. In his lifetime he also acquired indelible love and affection among the rich and the poor, the literate and the unlettered alike. Vasudeva Sarvabhauma, the greatest Indian logician of the age, honoured in the court of the Gajapati Prataprudra Dev of Orissa extolled the philosophy of Chaitanya. Prakashnanda, the leader of the learned *samnyasis* of Varanasi and Bharati Gosain of Chandipur (Deccan) all accepted the greatness of Chaitanya and accepted him as guru.[70]

In the inscriptions of the Govindjew temple at Vrindaban the statement is found that Rupa and Sanatan were the gurus of Raja Mansingh. It is, therefore, quite natural that the Emperor Akbar had heard a good deal about Chaitanya from his favourite general and others and conceived an admiration for him. Growse tells us that the emperor paid a visit to Vrindaban and was struck by the piety of the Vaishnava gurus.[71] It is very remarkable that Emperor Akbar thus sang in praise of Chaitanya:

Hail thee oh Chaitanya—the victor of my heart,
Mark the rhythm of his mystic dance
in lofty ecstasy quite alone.
Merrily sounds the tabor and the symbols
note keeps times,
The joyous band following him
sing and dance merrily-merrily;
He steps a pace or two on towards
in his dancing gait,
And knows no rest—intoxicated with
his own over-flowing joy.
Oh my heart's Lord, how can I express
the love I have for thee?
Shaha Akbar craves a drop from
the sea of thy piety and love.[72]

In the countryside the image of Chaitanya, as the redeemer of the fallen and a reformer of society, is held in high appreciation. In the humble huts of the peasants and other low caste people, prayers and tributes of worships are offered to him everyday. The songs 'Praise unto 'Chaitanya', 'The god-man of Nadiya', 'The friend of the fallen and one who does not believe in caste' are often sung in chorus. Govinda Dasa, a poet who flourished in the sixteenth century thus sang in praise of Chaitanya:

He gives love of God to men
without their seeking
Where is the heart so magnanimous as his !
When he danced, the lame, the blind
and the deaf danced with him,
When he wept, the eyes of the world
were blinded with tears.
When he called 'Krishna Krishna' aloud
the sound was caught by multitude,
And it reverberated in air

from direction to direction.
It is for this that I believe him
to be God
And surely His spirit was in him,
Just as the reflection of the sun
as in the mirror.[73]

While referring to Chaitanya's influence upon the masses in Orissa, we should note that it did not spread throughout Orissa. It was popular only in the coastal Districts of Balasore, Cuttack, Puri, Ganjam and in the adjoining Districts of Keonjhar, Mayurbhanj, Dhenkanal and Koraput. Prabhat Mukherjee mentions fifty-eight Chaitanya *maths* and temples in the above-said Districts. Towards the end of nineteenth century, the worship of six-handed Gauranga and in the first half of the twentieth century, the worship of Gauranga-Vishnupriya became popular. The six-handed Gauranga images are worshipped in the Jagannatha temple precincts, Puri, Old Bhubaneswar, Sohala (Saragarh, Sambalpur District), Balisahi (near Ali, Kendrapara District), Baladevjew temple (Kendrapara District), Kesonda Math (Tenda kuda, Cuttack District), Barabati (near Balasore). In 1885, the images of the six-handed Gauranga, Nityananda, and Advaita were installed within the Jagannatha temple premises by Patachhata Ananta Mahapatra, a temple priest. S. Mukherjee, built a temple in 1950s, in which he also installed the images of Gauranga, Nityananda and Advaita. The image of Nityananda is worshipped in the Shada-bhuja temple at Barabati near Balasore. The Vishnupriya-Gauranga images are worshipped at Vishnupriya-Gaura Math, Sambalpur; Gaura-Govinda Math, Anandpur (Keonjhar District); Gaura-Govinda Math, Ghodabara (Cuttack District), Jhankarpal, (Sambalpur District), Ganabharpanka (Sambalpur District). In all these temples, Lakshmipriya, the first wife of Visvambhar (Chaitanya), is worshipped.[74]

The *bhakti* and reform movement of Chaitanya was enormously successful in eastern India. Chaitanya came to Orissa at a time when there was religious ferment in the sixteenth century and the non-Brahmins challenged the monopoly of the Brahmins in intellectual pursuits. Besides, eastern India had already witnessed continuous invasion of Muslims and Muslim administration had already been established in Bengal by that time. A kind of menace and political instability had made the people of Orissa and Bengal to think of anarchy and to search for peace. The emergence of Sri Chaitanya's

44. D.C. Sen, *Chaitanya and His Age*, University of Calcutta, Calcutta, 1922, p. 283.
45. Ibid., p. 285.
46. Ibid., p. 280.
47. Ibid., p. 281.
48. Idem.
49. M. Mansingh, *History of Oriya Literature*, Sahitya Akademi, New Delhi, 1962, p. 89.
50. Sri Chaitanya, *Sikshastaka*, Canto I.
51. Kaviraj Krishnadasa, *Chaitanya Charitamrita* (*Madhya Lila*), Chap. VIII, p. 623.
52. Romila Thapar, *A History of India*, vol. I. Penguin Books, Harmondsworth, 1966, pp. 312–13.
53. M.N. Ghosh, *A Brief Sketch of the Religious Beliefs of the Assamese People*, Methodist Publishing House, Calcutta, 1896, p. 6.
54. R.M. Nath, *The Background of Assamese Culture*, A.K. Nath, Shillong, 1948, p. 132.
55. Satish Chandra, *Historiography, Religion and State in Medieval India*, Har-Anand Publications, New Delhi, 1996, p. 112.
56. S.C. Goswami, *Introducing Assam Vaishnavism*, P.C. Goswami, Gauhati, 1946, p. 20.
57. Jayananda, *Chaitanya Mangal*, Asiatic Society, Calcutta, 1971, pp. 50–2.
58. Ishwar Dasa, op. cit., Chap. 61, p. 384.
59. D.K. Mukherjee, op. cit., p. 121.
60. Ibid., p. 123.
61. Ibid., p. 124.
62. D.C. Sen, op. cit., p. 158.
63. Sri Chaitanya, *Sikshastaka*, canto VI.
64. Ibid, canto: IV.
65. Ibid., canto: VIII.
66. Ibid., canto: II.
67. H.C. Das, op. cit., pp. 381–2.
68. J.N. Sarkar (ed.), *The History of Bengal*, vol. II (AD 1200–1757), University of Dacca, 1972, p. 221.
69. Ibid., p. 222.
70. D.C. Sen, op. cit., 1917, pp. 4–5.
71. D.C. Sen, op. cit., 1922, p. 318.
72. Translated from Hindi and quoted in D.C. Sen, op. cit., (on pre-introduction page). 1922.
73. Ibid., p. 319.
74. P. Mukherjee, op. cit., 1979, pp. 113–16.
75. Shashi Joshi and Bhagawan Josh, *Struggle for Hegemony in India: Culture, Community and Power*, vol. III (1920–1947), Sage Publications, New Delhi, 1994, p. 124; see also J.T.O. Cornnell, 'Vaishnav Perceptions of Muslims in Sixteenth Century Bengal', in Milton Israel and N.K. Wegle (eds.), *Islamic Society and Culture: Essays in Honour of Professor Aziz Ahmad*, Manohar, New Delhi, 1983, pp. 294–5.

CHAPTER 5

Conclusion

THIS PROCESS of the State formation in late ancient and early medieval Orissa synchronized with conflicts and with efforts at their resolution in Orissan society at various levels. Orissa was principally a tribal State and the process of State formation gradually developed with the expansion of Sanskritic culture, growth of land-grants to Brahmins, officials and temples. Simultaneously there was integration of the tribes and the features of tribal life, instead of their being totally decimated, their assimilation and not their 'sustained displacement' was the hallmark of this process of integration. A new syncretic culture flourished with an ongoing exchanges of the cultural traits between the 'Aryans' and 'tribals', in which the former dominated, but it could not succeed in displacing the latter altogether. In the new socio-political structure the ruling chiefs of the local tribes were admitted as Kshatriyas, but the vast majority of their tribal kinsmen were degraded to the status of the Sudras. The Kshatriyaized members of the tribes fought and commanded the battles for the kingdom and defended the borders, while their Sudraized kinsmen supported the maintenance of the court circle (i.e. priests, officials and soldiers) and the construction of gigantic royal temples of the Hindu Rajas with their agricultural surplus. In this way, the State formation was accomplished, the Sanskritic culture was spread over, and the king achieved his legitimated authority both inside and outside of his kingdom.

The generous land-grant in early Orissa deeply influenced the process of development of the state and society. Land-grants to Brahmin priests and to many Brahmin and non-Brahmin officials led to the process of extension of agriculture and rural expansion. This had the attendant consequence of the transformation of the autochthonous tribes into Sudra castes simultaneously along with their peasantization.[1] The postulation that in the early medieval period in course of Sanskritization in the backward areas the local tribal people were transformed into Sudras and their chiefs absorbed as Kshatriyas into the Brahaminic-fold seems to be valid in the Orissan situation.[2] We have earlier discussed that early Orissa had two-tiered varna structure with the absence of viable Kshatriya and Vaishya varnas. But in course of time many functional castes emerged with the exigencies of time. The most remarkable development was the emergence of a distinguished functional caste, namely, the Karanikas or Kayasthas during the period of the Somavamsis.[3] They did exist and proliferate occupying possibly at instances an ambivalent position in the seemingly two-tier varna structure. It seems that during the Somavamsi and Ganga rules with the extension of land-grants and development of feudal system, the Kayastha-Karanas as a distinct caste came to emerge. Many of them were appointed as scribes, some of them rose to high positions, occupied both civil and military posts, received land-grants, held Nayakships and feudatory status.[4] Because of changes in economic and social life due to agricultural and rural expansion, power and status of the near groups of the dominant landowning elite, there emerged new functional social groups such as landlords, priests, civil and military officials, Karanikas, traders, peasants, artisans, etc., cutting across the traditional varna system. This period is characterized by the formation of State based on peasantization of the tribes, not surprisingly, therefore, the evidence of cleavage is wanting. It is asserted that the social tensions emerged when there was State intervention in rural settlements and communal rights either for making grants or for enlarging its revenue base.[5] However, it appears reasonable to infer that the relations between the non-producing landowning elite on the one hand and the actual Sudraized toiling peasantry on the other were not entirely harmonious. Thus, their degrading status, acute sense of deprivation of economic, social and cultural life vis-à-vis the ambit of the Brahminical order that conjointly shaped the consciousness of the marginalized sections of society led to the launching of a protest movement against the dominant class, authoritarianism and oppression. The leadership of this movement was initiated by a team of the *Sudramunis* chiefly from amongst the non-Brahmins of Orissa. *Sudramuni* Sarala Dasa (late fifteenth century), the pioneer of the movement came from a Sudraized peasant community, known as Chasha (cultivator) and nowadays claimed to be Khandaits. Sudramunis Balarama Dasa, Achyutananda Dasa and Ananta Dasa although were born in the Karana families they have identified themselves to be *Sudramunis*. Yashovanta Dasa was born in the cultivator Khandait family whereas only Jagannatha Dasa was born in the Brahmin family of the *puran panda* profession. Although they worked separately their mission was one and the same.

There were also other factors behind the creation of conditions for the acceptability of the teachings of these masters. The fifteenth-sixteenth centuries witnessed in Orissa a vast empire, founded by Gajapati Kapilendra Dev stretching from the Ganges to the Kaveri. Political stability, the sense of patriotism and love of one's own language and literature facilitated the poets of the soil to write in their own language and create their own literature. Sudramuni Sarala Dasa, the pioneer of this movement, rendered the most distinguished epics like the *Mahabharata*, the *Vilanka Ramayana* and *Chandi Purana* in the regional language of the people. Sarala *Mahabharata* was not a mere translation of the Sanskrit original; rather it was a unique literary document, with information on and suggestions for the social organization, politics, religion and economy, of the late fifteenth-century Orissa, narrated along with the bare skeleton of the events and the stories of Sanskrit *Mahabharata*.

Influenced by the teachings and writings of Sarala Dasa, the *panchasakhas* dedicated themselves to combat with their pens for the educational and cultural uplift of the deprived sections of the society. They strove for a new social order by removing the social barriers that separated man from man and community from community. Four of the *panchasakha* were Sudras; only Jagannatha Dasa was a Brahmin. They lodged a protest against caste, untouchability, indignity of Sudras and women, and above all, against all exploiting feature of the Brahminical order. Puri, the great pilgrimage centre and the heart of the Jagannatha culture, was the nucleus of their movement. They criticized the prevailing religious ethos through their writings, discourses and propagation. Balarama Dasa and Achyutananda Dasa, the most outspoken and radical of the *panchasakhas*, challenged the Brahmins of the *muktimandap* of Jagannatha temple and asserted the Sudras' right to access to the Vedic literature and Dharmasastras. Amongst a lot of literary creations, Balarama Dasa's

Jagamohan Ramayana, and *Lakshmi Purana*, Jagannatha Dasa's *Bhagavata*, and Achyutananda's *Harivamsa* are the most notable. Their writings are the major early contributions to the literature of Orissa.

The pattern of literature left by Sarala Dasa and the *panchasakhas*, judged from many viewpoints, are non-flattering in character. They do not sing the praise of the uncommon glorious deeds of heroism of the then illustrious Oriya kings, Kapilendra Dev, Purushottam Dev and Prataprudra Dev. Some lines composed in their eulogy are met with in some inscriptions, but they were all engraved at the instance of the rulers themselves and their ministers, on the occasion of recording some religious or semi-religious acts. Kapilendra Dev strongly resisted the invaders and organized a good government in the country, but nothing relating to his prowess and wisdom appears in any of these literary work. The incidents of the Kanchi-Kaveri expedition of Raja Purshottam Dev was recorded in the *Madalapanji* by those of the scribes of the Jagannatha temple, who had to look up to the Raja for his favour. It is also on a wall of the audience hall of the temple at Puri that a pictorial representation of the incidents appear. However, the *bhakta-kavis* of medieval Orissa composed their epics in the regional language, far away from the court without enjoying any political patronage. Theirs was the literature for the people. In tune with the medieval Indian mystic tradition, the *panchasakhas* proclaimed that the liberalizing knowledge was in one's heart itself we have to search for it, grow up to it and translate it into life. They declared that knowledge of the divine is not at all a remote thing, but is in the very temple that is in each one of us.

The period of Chaitanya's long stay in Puri was remarkable for *bhakti* ideology and movement in Orissa. He was welcomed by King Prataprudra Dev and his concept of *bhakti* received fillip with the extension of royal patronage. He popularized the cult of Radha-Krishna based on the *prema-bhakti*. Complete surrender of the self to a personal deity with *gopibhava* was the essence of the *prema-bhakti*, he preached. By preaching the love between man and man and between man and God he endeavoured to bring out the unity of humanity, leading to social integration and universal brotherhood. His association with the *panchasakhas* added momentum. The *panchasakhas* had enough knowledge of Sanskrit, but they preferred to write in the spoken language of the people, through which their feeling, thought and message could reach the common folks. Chaitanya also preached his philosophy in Oriya, sang Oriya songs and accepted disciples irrespective of caste and creed. His acceptance of Yavan Haridasa, a Muslim and Kanai, a sweeper of Puri as his disciples, and his unhesitant expression of love and affection to them, shows his broad social outlook and egalitarian attitude. In the countryside, Chaitanya is remembered as the redeemer of the fallen and a reformer of society.

In Chaitanya's devotional cult and in his *saṁkirtan* movement there was immense appeal for the rural masses. His *kirtan* introduced a new type of emotional and devotional worship, the essence of which was singing and dancing together as parts of prayer. Chaitanya emphasized universal love and brotherhood as the first step to attain communion with God. Though he did not care for rituals, he did not discard the sacred scriptures and idolatry. He disregarded all distinctions of caste and creed so far as the religious institution was concerned. Of course, he did never allow himself and his followers to have any type of social relation with women, but he never opposed the cultural uplift of women and their right to *sanyas*. The Vaishnavism propounded by him very soon acquired nearly the status of a 'dominant religious cult'. Together with the king, many State officials, military commanders and Samantas also embraced the faith of Chaitanya. The simple and lucid compositions of the *leela* (deeds) of Krishna, for example, the *Bhagavata* of Jagannatha Dasa and the *Harivamsa* of Achyutananda Dasa, propelled the themes of love and devotion and the movement to spread over the country.

Medieval Orissa witnessed two different trends of Vaishvanism which gained momentum particularly during the period of Gajapati Prataprudra Dev. When the Gaudiya Vaishnavas propagated *prema-bhava* to effect reform in society under the authority of Sri Chaitanya, the Utkaliya Vaishnavas under the *Sudramunis* advocated *sudra-bhava* to be the primary channel for communion with God: '*Knowledge could not be the preserve of any particular section of society nor it could be expressed in a particular language*' was the revolutionary message of the *Sudramunis*. They challenged the legitimacy of the prevailing Brahminical social order with the sources from within the Brahminical religious texts (i.e. *Mahabharata*, *Ramayana* and *Harivamsa,* etc.). Their advocacy for radical social reform, in fact, challenged the socio-political hegemony of the contemporary elite (the king, priests and the landlords). The king thus invited Sri Chaitanya, an unorthodox Brahmin saint and extended patronage to him. Although the position of the priests declined with the ascendancy of the Gaudiya Vaishnavism, they prepared themselves to encounter the challenges of the *Sudramunis*. We have observed earlier that King Prataprudra Dev invited Sri Chaitanya only to check the growing power of the priests of the Jagannatha temple, Puri. If he really intended to bring out changes in the ritual structure, in which his own position was lower than of the priests, then he could have acceded to the ascendancy of the *Sudramunis* in place of the Brahmin priests. He did not do this. Instead, he looked for a compromise which he saw in the ideology of Sri Chaitanya. The king believed in preserving and protecting the existing *dharma* but he could not also have ignored the challenge of the *Sudramunis*. Sri Chaitanya who came from a Brahminical background, had radical ideas, but with the difference, namely, the *prema-bhava* vis-à-vis the *sudra-bhava*, thus offered the solution.

The period also witnessed political instability and violence due to constant threats from the northern and southern sides. On the one hand the Sultan of Bengal aspired to make inroads to Orissa and on the other the ruler of Vijyanagar empire was knocking at its southern door. There were also other reasons, besides royal patronage for greater acceptability of Sri Chaitanya's mission. The people in Orissa, many of whom had lost members of their families in continuous wars craved for tranquillity and peace, which they found in Sri Chaitanya's teachings.

However, the ascendancy of Vaishanavism could not eclipse completely the other sects, namely, Saivism, Saktism, Saur and Ganapatyabad. In this way, Orissa became the centre of the confluence of various sects, cults and philosophies. Multi-faceted development took place in the subsequent period with the growth of discourses on the philosophies of various religions in Orissa.

The tradition of the *bhakta-kavis* of Orissa declined after the *panchasakhas*. They were divided into numerous branches and sub-branches. All the branches realized and propagated to be the root of the main tree and they could not see anything except maintenance of self-identity and separatist ideas. They measured the strength of their power by the number of followers. The five seats (*gadis*) of the *panchasakhas* lost closeness among them and remained busy in a self-enclosed world of false vanity.[6]

With the decline of the Gajapati empire Orissa was divided into numerous principalities and the Rajas or the 'feudal' chiefs became powerful and oppressive. They patronized Gaudiya Vaishnavism as earlier, but did not allow the radical *bhaktas* to emerge in their estates. The *panchasakhas* had encountered persecution of the king and priests, nevertheless, they did not come to the side of the authority. But, their followers could not tolerate the oppressive rule of the local Rajas, and therefore, they went away to forests and lived in caves. They preferred to meditate and write in the lines of the *panchasakhas* for propagating their ideas in the locality.[7] There were some devotees who secretly followed their path and visited their monasteries on festive occasions.

In the seventeenth and eighteenth centuries, the *bhakta-kavis*, who created the *nirguna*-literature under the impact of the writings of the *panchasakhas* were Chaitanya Dasa (seventeenth century), Dwaraka Dasa (seventeenth century), Debananda Dasa (seventeenth century), Hadi Dasa (eighteenth century) and Arakshita Dasa (eighteenth century). They devoted themselves in practice of *yoga* and worship of *sunya*. However, the anti-caste and anti-authoritarian pronouncements are quite audible in most of their writings.

Chaitanya Dasa (seventeenth century) was born in a Sudra gardener's family in the village of Khadial of Sambalpur District. In the history of Oriya literature, Chaitanya Dasa was the first poet from western Orissa who contributed to the growth of Oriya literature. He composed *Nirguna Mahatmya* and *Vishnugarbha Purana*. He was a worshipper of *sunya* and thus he sang in his *Vishnugarbha Purana* (Chap. III).

He is unknown figure
without image and colour.
Having no existence
thus a Great Void.
He is not handsome
but imageless body,
He remains Void
in the void itself.

Dwaraka Dasa was born in AD 1662 and like *panchasakhas* he declared himself to be a Sudra, although he was born in a Karana family. He was deeply influenced by Balarama Dasa and Jagannatha Dasa of sixteenth century. He made the people believe that he appeared in the world as Balarama Dasa in his previous birth and composed the twelfth and thirteenth volumes (*skandhas*) of the

Bhagavata, which was completed with the eleventh volume by Jagannatha Dasa himself. He criticized idol-worship in his *Parache Gita* and wondered how the people were confused and failed to recognize the God who remained always within their self. The influence of the *panchasakha* ideology is quite conspicuous in the writings of Dwaraka Dasa. He thus writes:

Unknowingly the ignorant people
do not worship soul but others,
Leaving me they worship the idols,
Do not know that I am the soul
They worship happily the paintings,
idols of wood, stone or metal
Do not know me with illusion
I exist in their body
but they fail to recognize.[8]

Anti-caste pronouncement is very much striking in the same work of Dwaraka Dasa. He has criticized the ignominious position of the people in the unjust caste-based social order. To him, the true devotee of any caste or out-caste is nearest to God and even a Brahmin could not come to a par with his position. Thus he puts God's words:

Who is devoted to me
May he be Brahmin, Kshatriya,
Vaishya or Sudra,
May he be born of illicit love
A Brahmin is not equal to him
Told before you, Oh Arjuna !
All the nirguna's are my devotees
irrespective of castes or out-castes,
They are my dear devotees.[9]

The *Baichandra Gita* of Debananda Dasa (seventeenth century) was another important work of this period. Poet Debananda has described the whole work in the form of question-answer between Shri Rama and sage Vasistha. He has lucidly described the erotic love between Krishna and the *gopis* in this work. However, the poet's emphasis on the life and character of the *gopis* in relation to Krishna suggests the influence of Jagannatha Dasa. He has followed both the theme and *nabakshari brutta* of Jagannatha Dasa. Thus he writes:

All the daughters of the sages,
Numbered about sixteen thousand
they are on deep meditation,
To gain your love and grace.
They will be born at Gopa
And will remain as your maiden.
You will sport with them in different colour
Playing the flute on river bank
or enjoying in Sri Vrindaban
You will make Rahasa (the Autumn festival)
Accompanying with the
cowherd boys and girls.[10]

Like the *panchasakhas*, Debananda Dasa also emphasized both *bhakti* and *jnana*, which were inseparable in perfect devotion. To him, there was no distance between *bhakti* and *jnana*. Thus he sang:

Who could proceed on this way
Without perceiving bhakti inside
Who can go ahead,
There is no salvation without bhakti
When will bhakti arise,
Knowledge will prevail upon you.[11]

Hadi Dasa, a *bhakta-kavi* of eighteenth century was born in AD 1772 in the village of Champapur, near Chhatia of the Cuttack District. He was born in a poor artisan's (blacksmith) family. In his numerous writings he identified himself to be Achyutananda Dasa (sixteenth century) in his previous birth and also composed a number of *bhajans* and *padas* in the name of Achyutananda Dasa and Ananta Dasa. He composed *Ananta Gupta Gita*, *Sankhanabhi*, *Gruhasama*, *Bhavanabar*, *Nilamadhab Gita*, *Kshetra Mahatmya* and *Lakshmidhar Vilasa*. Hadi Dasa not only took the name of Achyutananda Dasa for his precedence, he was indeed deeply influenced by the philosophy of the *panchasakhas*. In his writing, the Philosophy of *sunya* and imagelessness of the God are quite conspicuous. Thus, he writes in his *Sankhanabhi*:

He is in the mind still mindlessness
He remains voidless after showing the void.
He is not at a place but at the placelessness,

He is not in knowledge but in ignorance.
He is not an idol but remains void.
He cannot be perceived in thought, thus unthinkable
He remains in the endlessness.
And also roams around the endlessness.
The Lord is like this
And who is able to speak of Him.[12]

Arakshita Dasa (AD 1772–1803) was an extraordinary poet and reformer in the religious traditions of Orissa. Like Gautam Buddha, a prince of southern Orissa, Arakshita Dasa left his palace at the age of eighteen and wandered in search of divine truth by acquainting himself with poverty, misery and suffering. After eighteen years of strenuous religious tour he established his monastery on the Olasuni hill of the Cuttack District. He was contemporary of the *bhakta* Hadi Dasa, who also established his monastery at Chhatia, 30 km away from Olasuni. Arakshita Dasa condemned caste and he accepted food from Brahmin to Candala unhesitantly. He composed *Mahimandal Gita* with *nabakshari brutta*, considered to be a remarkable work on *Nirguna* literature.

Arakshita Dasa criticized the fraud *sanyasis*, who depended on *kaupin* and beard, but not on *bhakti*. He did not believe that *bhakti* was to arise itself if one accepted a person as guru (preceptor). He vehemently opposed the tradition of *gurubada*, and to him this system of 'hero-worship' may lead to exploitation and closeness of mind. So, thus he sang in his fearless voice:

No bhakti lies in the hands of a guru,
Where does the guru come from ?
Nothing but a human being,
So, I did not serve the guru,
Worshipped my God alone.[13]

Like the *panchasakhas*, Arakshita Dasa condemned idol-worship, rituals and pilgrimage which were not the right means of obtaining the grace of God. He begged for devotion in his prayer which was the essence of worship and God realization. In his words:

You will get nothing
If you search Him in the
Wood, Stone and Rudraksha beads,
Neither in rituals, nor in piligrimage

Oh Lord of Void, that is Vaikuntha
Oh father, I beg bhakti for you.[14]

Arakshita Dasa called upon the people not to confuse God with the images of brass, wood and stone. He advised them to realize the existence of God with their self and accept the method of *bhakti* to worship him. Thus he wrote in his *Mahimandal Gita*:

God exists in this body
Ignorant mind does not know this,
Worships brass, wood and stone
taking them to be Gods[15]

It is a phenomenon of great significance that Bhima Bhoi, a poet and reformer of the nineteenth century, who was born in the Kondh tribe, became the progenitor of a religious system which disowns caste system and idolatry. The old texts relating to the *Mahima* cult and the literary works of Bhima Bhoi were more in the genre of medieval *bhakti* literature. His writings were more in the line of medieval mysticism than philosophical speculations. In the writings of Bhima Bhoi, the '*Sunya Parambrahma*' is characterized more precisely by the concepts *alekha* (infigurable), *nirguna* (without attributes), *nirakara* (formless), *anadi* (eternal), *niranjana* (pure or without support) and *mahima* (radiance, glory) all of which already appear in the medieval *panchasakha* literature for describing *Sunya Brahma* or as synonymous for Him.

Achyutananda of the *Panchasakha* group also spoke of *Ekakshara Brahman*, the Brahman that is unique and does not ever face dissolution. He describes it as *Alekha swarupa*, i.e. the unwritten one.

Bhima Bhoi's revolutionary ideas and his *Sunya* philosophy are reflected in his writings and his statement on caste system is quite revealing. Thus he sang:

Caste is not asked to the people
Who are divided into
thirty-six clans and fifty-two professionals.
Caste is just like water
Which differs from one to another
Oh wise men; give justice on it.
You will find one person one caste
if you inquire into the whole Universe

They are made into hundreds
for the creation of the World.[16]

The tone of social protest and anti-authoritarian feelings of Bhima Bhoi is clearly reflected in his writings. He said that they (the followers of *Mahima*) were neither subjects to the king nor borrowers to the moneylender; therefore they did not fear anybody.

Thus he sang:

We are not subjects to the King
nor borrower to the moneylender,
We go there wherever the Guru takes to us
can any body prevent us from ?[17]

In this stanza of Bhima Bhoi, the oppressive character of those kings and the exploitative money lending system of contemporary society are quite conspicuous. Bhima Bhoi characterized God to be *Sunya* and formless. He cherished the religion which characterized the formlessness of God. He sang in his *Stuti Chintamani*:

He reveals in the temple of the Void,
The one without shape and form,
No, you can never see His two feet
but do submit to the one
His house is in that nameless unknown realm,
Oh wise men, remember there
Neither it is too warm, nor too cold[18]

In *Stuti Chintamani* and many of his *bhajans*, Bhima Bhoi gave powerful expression to not only the mystic ideas of personal salvation but also redemption of man in society from a cruel destiny. His poetry had not merely the meditative philosophical quality of *panchasakha* literature but it also had the lyricism and musical quality which was associated with earlier poets like Gopal Krishna, Banamali or Kabisurya Baladeva Rath. In extremely lyrical lines Bhima Bhoi brought forth the essence of the well-known *mahima* cult in the celebrated lines quoted below, for example. His heart was filled with love and compassion having seen the sorrow and misery of living beings. He was even prepared to consign his soul to the hell if it could save humanity. Thus he sang for the redemption of mankind:

Boundless is the anguish
and misery of the living,
Who can see it and tolerate
Let my soul be condemned to hell,
But let the Universe be redeemed[19]

The impact of the Chaitanya movement on State system is a matter of interest. The Gangas and the Suryavamsi kings established Brahman *sasanas* and patronized Brahminism. The trend of the religion took a new shape with the advent of Sri Chaitanya during the reign of Prataprudra Dev. Vaishnavism took the place of Brahminism, which was never tolerated by the Brahmin priests. Nevertheless, it had a remarkable impact on comtemporary State systems and brought out a change in the cultural life of the people.

First of all, King Prataprudra Dev extended royal patronage to Sri Chaitanya, his followers and helped in propagation of the new cult. No doubt, the king remaining at the apex of politics and administration, upheld a significant religious commitment, and his patronage to Chaitanya movement corroborates the influence of the latter on him. Secondly, with the royal acceptance the neo-Vaishnavism appeared to be a 'dominant religious cult'. The State officials and the feudal chiefs (the Rajas) accepted and patronized this faith. Thirdly, the neo-Vaishnavism swayed over other religious sects and beliefs of the contemporary period. Between the two trends of Vaishnavism, the Utkaliya stream of Vaishnavism under the banner of the *pancha-sakha*s and the Gaudiya stream of Vaishnavism under guidance of Sri Chaitanya, maintained their distinct identities, but the Gaudiya Vaishnavism became more impressive, widespread and dominant with the patronage of the royal court at the centre, i.e. Puri and the 'feudal' courts in the peripheries.

Ray Ramananda was an important official of Prataprudra Dev, who held the office of the governor of Rajmuhendry, then a part of the Gajapati empire. He was not only an administrator, but also a poet, dramatist, scholar and a great exponent of the *premabhakti*. Chaitanya and Ramananda, both were influenced by each other, and ultimately Ramananda resigned from his job at the instance of Chaitanya and stayed in Puri.[20]

When Prince Birabhadra, the young and inexperienced son of Prataprudra Dev took over the office of the governor of Rajmuhendry after Ramananda, the internal administration was seriously affected.

However, in Puri a lot of measures were taken to organize and propagate the faith of Sri Chaitanya. A religious council namely, *Gaura Parishad*, was formed under the authority of the king and Pundit Sarvabhauma. Ramananda and some others remained *parshads* (members) of the council. Ramananda was the chief organizer of the Council and he was also paid his salary, although he resigned from his job.[21]

Another incident corroborates the impact that Chaitanya had on the internal administration of the State. Once, Gopinatha Badajena, Governor of Midnapur in the northern Orissa, fell in arrears of the State revenue to such an extent that Prataprudra ordered his execution. But after some days the king himself pardoned him only to keep Sri Chaitanya peaceful and undisturbed in Puri.[22] Of course, Chaitanya did not interfere in this affair; the king did it by his own consideration. To keep a saint undisturbed, a corrupt official was not only pardoned but was also reinstated to his earlier job. This impact on administration was deliberate and even it was welcomed by the king at the cost of the royal treasury and maintenance of law and order.

Some historians have also pointed to the negative impact of the Chaitanya movement. They hold the view that the Bhakti movement of Chaitanya was responsible for the decline of medieval Orissa. According to R.D. Banerjee,

> Suddenly from the beginning of the 16th century, a decline set in the power and prestige of Orissa with the corresponding decline in the military spirit of the people. The decline is intimately connected with the long residence of the Bengali Vaishnava saint Chaitanya in the country. If we accept one tenth of what the Bengali and Sanskrit biographies of the saint state about his influence over Prataprudra Dev and the people of the country, we must admit that Chaitanya was one of the principal causes of the political decline of the empire and the people of Orissa.[23]

The argument put forth by R.D. Banerjee has been unhesitantly supported by H.K. Mahatab in his *History of Orissa*, vol. I and Mayadhar Mansingh in his *History of Oriya Literature*.

Can the decline of medieval Orissa be linked with the great Vaishnava saint Sri Chaitanya? On account of its acceptance by the royalty, the religion preached by him had become a fashionable cult, and important officers of the State had embraced the new faith with uncommon zeal. However, Chaitanya never asked the ruling elements to give up their responsibility for the protection of the State. Although Ray Ramananda resigned from the office of the Governor of Rajmuhendry and joined the Chaitanya movement, a suitable and efficient person could have been appointed in his place. It is not possible that a system will break down because of the absence of one individual. Prataprudra Dev did try to retrieve the fortune of the Gajapati House. But he lacked both military and diplomatic skill and could not add to or recover what he had lost. The medieval Orissa declined in AD 1568, i.e. thirty-five years after Chaitanya passed away (AD 1533). King Prataprudra Dev was engaged in warfare to protect the boundaries of his empire. Numerous factors were responsible for the decline of medieval Orissa, not one isolated reason that Chaitanya's religious movement was able for the end of the mighty Gajapati empire.

It may be argued that Prataprudra Dev was not a stubborn fighter like his grandfather, Kapilendra Dev. He need not have given up military campaign, although he possessed a religious bent of mind. His defeat was due to the simultaneous attacks from two frontiers, i.e. Bengal from the north and Vijayanagar empire from the south. In 1509, he had gone to the south, on account of the hostile preparations of Krishnadev Raya. The invasion of Hussain Shah of Bengal in 1511 compelled him to march up to the northern frontier of Orissa to expel the enemy. He again went back far south to the banks of the Nellore river to guard his southern frontier. In 1512 he returned to his capital. These expeditions exhausted his army. Hussain Shah's raid into northern Orissa indirectly helped Krishnadev Raya to gain a decisive victory over Prataprudra Dev. At the same time it must be remembered that the king of Vijayanagar was an able commander and his well planned Orissa campaigns which began in 1513 give an indication of his brilliant and forceful personality. He could easily overpower his adversary.[24]

Again, Prataprudra Dev was responsible for neglecting the defence of the military outposts in the Godavari-Krishna *doab*. Quli-Qutb Shah of Golkonda encountered little resistance when he seized Kondapalli, probably in 1531. The whole of the Godavari-Krishna *doab* was lost to Orissa shortly after the death of Prataprudra Dev. The sense of frustration caused by the humiliating peace with Krishnadev Raya, and the assassination of his only competent son Virabhadra by Govinda Vidyadhar had a deeply tragic impact upon Prataprudra's mind.[25] He eschewed militarism for which Chaitanya could hardly be blamed. Prataprudra left to his weak successors a territory which was held by the Ganga kings in their palmy days.

The weak successors and treacherous officers added fuel to the process of decline of medieval Orissan empire, founded by Kapilendra Dev.

A quietist movement of social equality, brotherhood and love alone can hardly be held responsible for weakening the political structure of a kingdom. A variety of social, economic, political and military factors must share the responsibility.

After Sri Chaitanya, the doctrine of his neo-Vaishnavism having closely assimilated into the *sahajiya* cult, influenced the growth of erotic literature, patronized by the 'feudal' courts. This doctrine had also two other directions, namely, performance of music, and singing and worship of Lord Krishna and Radha. Contemporary literature on the one hand was confined to the court and the performance of song and music was confined to the *gotipua nacha* (dance of young boys being dressed as girls); *thiapala* (performance of Puranic themes through song, dance and musical instruments by five men) and *daskathia* (similar to *thiapala*, but performed by two men) entertained the people in different manner. This tradition is still current in rural Orissa.

The *gotipua* dance was introduced by the Gaudiya Vaishnava community from the time of Ray Ramananda, because of their aversion to see the dance performed by women. So they introduced this dance to be performed by the young boys being dressed like girls.[26] Since the late sixteenth century, the *gotipua* dance was taught in an *akhada ghar* (house where song, dance and actions were taught and performed) generally patronized by a local zamindar. The dance was then held in the spacious drawing room of the local zamindar, or in the premises of the temple or in a monastery. The *gotipuas* acted, danced and sang to entertain the audience with different themes. This tradition continued till the first half of the twentieth century and gradually it declined under the impact of the theatre, cinema and radio. The *gotipua* tradition flourished mainly in Cuttack, Puri and Ganjam Districts of the State. The *gotipuas* moved throughout Orissa and outside to perform this dance and music. Odissi dance was derived from the *gotipua* dance and in fact, all the famous Odissi dance teachers were *gotipua* dancers during their early young age.[27]

The *suanga*, a kind of drama, played a vital role in entertaining the people and in moulding the character of the society and culture of Orissa, The *Lakshmi-Narayan Vachanika* of Sarala Dasa is considered to be the first Oriya *suanga* literature. In sixteenth century, the *Lakshmi Purana* of Balarama Dasa, was performed in form of *suanga*, as a source of folk entertainment. It influenced the people and generated self-respect among the women, and the common men as well.[28] The *suanga* acted as a vehicle of expression: it did not merely entertain people, it also expressed the thought of the people, their consciousness, experience of freedom and expectations.

The *pala* is an improved form of the folk-play which developed out of the cultural contacts between the tribal *sabari* dance of Orissa and the *sahajiya* cult. It developed into the present form of *pala* with the cultural interaction between the Vaishnavas of Orissa and Bengal on the one hand and Islam on the other during sixteenth century.[29] Rameswar, Ramadasa, Bishweswara, Ramakrishna and Kavichandra Ayodhya Ray wrote a number of *pala* books during this time. In seventeenth century Kavi Karna also composed a number of *pala* books in the mixed language of Oriya and Bengali. In the *Vidyadhara Pala* Chaitanya was highly honoured and described to be an incarnation of God. In the *Abhina Madan pala* some stray references to the Rangani port and conflict between the Oriyas and Marathas are available. In the *Sadananda Saudagar Pala*, the names of two ports, namely, Ranganighat and Hinguli ghat have been mentioned. In seventeenth and eighteenth centuries, a number of *pala* books were composed by Kavi Vallabha, Bhruguram, Dwija Vasudeba, and Dwija Vishwanatha in the mixed language of Oriya and Bengali.[30]

There has been a peculiar development of *sola pala* (celebration of sixteen years of age of children with feast and performance of *pala* generally in Orissa and Bengal) out of Hindu-Muslim cultural interaction and assimilation. *Sola palas* have a significance in as much as all of them aim at promoting religious tolerance between the Hindus and the Muslims. They were used to propagate the worship of Satyapir who, according to the philosophy of the *pala*, is identically the same as Satyanarayan. The language of this *pala* is a novel blending of Arabic and Persian words with Oriya and Bengali,[31] which undoubtedly suggests the indelible faith of these linguistic groups in the concept of co-existence. This synthesis of language helped create an atmosphere congenial to the very idea of peaceful co-existence, interdependence, mutual help and cooperation among various linguistic and ethnic communities.

The cultural interaction that took place between two neighbouring provinces of Banga and Kalinga, did not remain confined to Puri or to areas close to Bengal. It had a far-reaching consequence which became evident from the manuscript of the *Dwarika pala* purported to have been written by Dhananjaya Bhanja, the grandfather of Kavisamrat Upendra Bhanja. Dhananjaya also utilized the story of *Lakshmi Purana* of Balarama Dasa and delineated it with a unique literary touch. The readers of *Dwarika pala* will be convinced that it is not just a *brata-katha* (the story of initiation) but a real literary creation.

I have mentioned earlier that some erotic court literature developed under the impact of the Gaudiya Vaishnavism. In seventeenth century Raja Govinda Bhanja of Keonjhar in his *Bhakti Vinod* described the erotic love of Radha and Krishna and in *Charan Sudhanidhi* he characterized Chaitanya as the incarnation of Krishna. In eighteenth century the character of Radha becomes the central theme in the works like *Purnatama Chandrodaya* of Brundavati Dasi, *Preeti Chintamani* and *Vidagdha Chintamani* of Abhimanyu Samantasimhar, *Gopibhasha* of Janardana Dasa, *Chora Chintamani, Nama Chintamani* and *Prema Tarangini* of Sadananda Kabisurya Brahma, which illustrate the impact of Chaitanya on the later poets.[32]

Chaitanya's teaching brought about a phenomenal change in the concept of Radha-Krishna cult which was exalted by the contemporary and later poets. The Chaitanya faith had also an effective impact on the vassal chiefs of the declined Gajapati empire, who patronized the Radha-Krishna cult in their respective principalities by following the selective mentality of their monarch. The king and the vassal chiefs organized the *melana* (get-together) festivals on the occasion of Holi, where the deities of Radha and Krishna from different regions were brought to a large ground with the purpose of the get together of idols of Radha and Krishna. This festival is still current in Orissa.

The growth of *Bhagavata ghara* or *tungis* in the villages, which brought about a significant change in socio-religious and cultural life of the people of Orissa, bear testimony to Jagannatha Dasa's impact. The first *Bhagavata ghara* was established at the *Satalahari math* in the heart of Puri town by *Atibadi* Jagannatha Dasa in the first part of the sixteenth century.[33] The tradition comes down that Dasia Bauri, a *bhakta-kavi* of early seventeenth century and Bhima Bhoi, distinguished *bhakta-kavi* of nineteenth century, who acquired knowledge of old time Oriya literature by merely listening to Jagannatha Dasa's *Bhagavata* and other Puranas in the *Bhagavata ghara* of their villages,[34] which indicates the extent of influence of this institution.

The *Bhagavata ghara* was a multi-purpose institution in the village. The *Bhagavata* which was written on palm-leaves, generally known as the *pothis* (manuscript), was kept in this house located in the middle or in the corner of the village. The people assembled in the evening where the *Bhagavata* was read and discussed. The village folks got relaxation after the day's labour by listening to the stories and morals of the *Bhagavata*. A number of lessons and morals featured in *Bhagavata*, which tallied with the character of the Oriya people. The house was used for a number of other purposes by the inhabitants of that village. It was a temple, a school, a club, a library, a guest-house and a *panchayat,* the place to settle rural disputes. It was, indeed, the nerve centre of village life even during pre-industrial days of the last century. The people of Orissa were keenly interested in educating their sons who could recite the *Bhagavata* at the time of their death. It was a popular belief that the soul could attain Vaikunthapur (the heavenly abode of Lord Vishnu) if the person listened to *Bhagavata* at the time of his death. The students who could recite the *Bhagavata* well, were believed to have got good education. Thus, there was widespread of primary education in Orissa. The *Bhagavata* became a link between the value system of the people and spread of education in Orissa. The Oriyas regulated their food habits, social practices and religious activities by its teachings. Many lines from the *Bhagavata* acquired the status of socio-religious sanction and entered into the deeper psyche of the people. On every conceivable occasion, an Oriya could recite some lines from the *Bhagavata*. Perhaps, no other epic is quoted so extensively and so often as the *Bhagavata*.

Sankardev from Assam saw for himself the tremendous impact of the *Bhagavata ghara* in the life of Orissa and started the institution of *Nama ghara* in Assam. In the darkest days of the Oriya people when they lay dismembered and scattered as neglected and exploited minorities, their language and identity were systematically extirpated by neighbours. It was this *Bhagavata* of Jagannatha Dasa, and the institution like *Bhagavata ghara* that kept their Oriya identity alive, enabling them even in hostile and inhospitable pockets, to be united again as a homogeneous people after centuries of suffering. Even today the *Bhagavata* may be found in a hundred thousand homes outside the political boundaries of Orissa—in Bengal, Bihar, Madhya Pradesh and Andhra Pradesh—as the commonest and the surest symbol of Oriya identity.[35]

The period of our study signified an era of cultural and literary development in eastern India. Particularly in Orissa the contributions of Sudramuni Sarala Dasa, the *panchasakhas* and Sri Chaitanya's movement were of great significance, in reconstructing the society and culture of the people. In their own way, each of them tried to reform society and became an individual who would have the inner strength to fight against injustice and Brahminical orthodoxy. The torchbearers of this movement were the *Sudramunis* accompanied and supported by Jagannatha Dasa and Sri Chaitanya, the two distinguished unorthodox Brahmin devotees of the period. Although this social movement against the injustice and dominance was initiated by the *Sudramunis* of Orissa, the role of Sri Chaitanya and Jagannatha Dasa provided a unique dynamism for the enormous success of a significant tradition. It was possible for the utilization of 'wide-ranging social mobilization, skills of recursive learning and capacity to respond to threats and opportunities in the ever changing milieu with adequate foresight and effectiveness' of the traditional elite. (Saberwal 1996: 242).

We have discussed how the movement of Sri Chaitanya was successful with the availability of royal patronage and his acceptance by the vassal chiefs. Undoubtedly a link between high and low was established with the rise of Sri Chaitanya and Jagannatha Dasa. The Oriya *Bhagavata* of Jagannatha Dasa was popularized due to 'the long durability of the Brahmical order and its ability to transmit its tradition, including its texts' (Saberwal 1996: 227). It may be stated here that the composition of Jagannatha Dasa was not a radical departure from the set pattern of writing. He used both Sanskrit words and local idioms (the blending of *tatsam* and *tadbhav* words) in his *Bhagavata* that was acceptable to the contemporary *Puran pundits*. So looking at the inevitability of the movement of the *Sudramunis* and their rendering of major epics into Oriya, the *Puran pandas* accepted the Oriya *Bhagavata* in place of its Sanskrit counterpart, recited it in each village making *Bhagavata tungis* or *gharas*. Besides, one of the mobilizational techniques of Jagannatha Dasa was that he wrote very often at the end of the each chapter that the narration was by Bipra Jagannatha, probably with the intention of indicating to the reader that the Oriya version of the *Bhagavata* was written by a Brahmin scholar. During that time the Puranas and epics were beginning to be written in Oriya by the *Sudramunis,* which aroused criticism and anger from the elite, so Jagannatha Dasa might have wished to make it clear that it was written in Oriya by a Brahmin scholar which would make it acceptable. And that, in fact, popularized *Bhagavata* in each and every village where the Brahmins were the upholders of religion, worship, learning and education. Last, but not the least, spread of Vaishnavism (the cult of Radha and Krishna) led to popularization of the Oriya *Bhagavata* containing the life and deeds (*leela*) of Krishna. Jagannatha Dasa by preaching Vaishnavism from the temple premises of Lord Jagannatha, one of the great centres of Hindu religion and philosophy, enhanced his name and glory and that in turn further added to the popularity of the *Bhagavata*.

The *Sudramunis* with great difficulty carried out a sustained campaign to protect the common people from injustice, dominance and deprivation; their message was for self-respect and dignity for the commoners of society. In the process, the *bhakta-kavis* had to face the opposition, criticism and even conspiracy of the orthodox pundits who induced the king to put them through various tests. As we have observed earlier, many of them were banished from their home during the period of Prataprudra Dev. Balarama Dasa was banished to Samagara pata, Jagannatha Dasa to the sea-shore Balibantar and Achyutananda to Banki Muhan. In spite of these repressive measures, the movement could not be curbed fully, even if, it had to compromise eventually with the Brahminical system in many ways. That they all became parts of the Brahminical order which shows the remarkable flexibility of Brahmnism and it must be emphasized that the *Sudramunis* succeeded in changing the direction of the established order.

NOTES

1. Suvira Jaiswal, 'Studies in Early Indian Social History: Trends and Possibilities', *Indian Historical Review*, vol. VI, nos. 1 and 2, 1980a, p 25.
2. R.S. Sharma, *Sudras in Ancient India*, 3rd edn., Motilal Banarsidass, Delhi, 1990, pp. 340–4; see also H. Kulke, 'Early State Formation and Royal Legitimation in Late Ancient Orissa', in M.N. Das (ed.), *Sidelights on History and Culture of Orissa*, Vidyapuri, Cuttack, 1977, pp. 110–14; and B.P. Sahu, 'Social Morphology and Physiology of Early Medieval Orissa (*c.* AD 400–1000)', *PIHC*, 44th Session, 1983, p. 135.
3. *EI*, vol. XXIX, pp. 188–9.
4. *EI*, vol. III, p. 224; vol. XXXII, pp. 311–16; see also *JAHRS*, vol. VI, p. 208 and S.K. Panda, 'Changes in the pattern of Social Stratification in Medieval Orissa (*circa* AD 1100–1600)', in H.S. Patnaik and A.N. Parida (eds.), *Aspects*

of Socio-Cultural Life in Early and Medieval Orissa, Utkal University, Bhubaneswar, 1996, p. 32.

5. B.D. Chattopadhyaya, *Aspects of Rural Settlements and Rural Society in Early Medieval India*, K.P. Bagchi & Co., Calcutta, 1990, p. 10
6. Chittaranjan Das, *Sant (Bhakti) Sahitya*, Orissa Sahitya Akademi, Bhubaneswar, 1982, pp. 523–4.
7. Ibid., pp. 325f.
8. Dwaraka Dasa, *Parache Gita*, Chap. X, ed. A.B. Mohanty, Prachi Publications, Cuttack, 1929, p. 18.
9. Ibid., Chap. VII, p. 12.
10. Debananda Dasa, *Baichandra Gita*, Arunodaya Press, Cuttack, 1909, Chap. XIX, p. 91.
11. Ibid, Chap. XIX, p. 92.
12. Hadi Dasa, *Sankhanabhi*, Chap. VII. See R.K. Sahoo, *Orissar Dharma O Sahityaku Hadi Dasanka Dana* (Oriya), Gopabandhu Sahitya Mandir, Cuttack, 1980.
13. Arakshita Dasa, *Mahimandala Gita*, Mohanta Sri Lachhman Das, Olasuni, Cuttack, 1970, Chap. 47.
14. Ibid., Chap. 13.
15. Ibid., Chap. 38.
16. Bhima Bhoi, *Stuti Chintamani*, Prachi, Bhubaneswar, 2nd rpt., 1940, *boli* 70.
17. Idem.
18. Ibid., boli 7.
19. Ibid., boli 9.
20. Kaviraj Krishnadasa, *Chaitanya Charitamrita* (*Madhya Lila*), Chap. VIII.
21. Sarala Debi, *Ray Ramananda*, Orissa Sahitya Akademi, Bhubaneswar, 1963, pp. 30–1.
22. Idem. See also H.K. Mahatab, *History of Orissa*, vol. I, Prajatantra Prachar Samiti, Cuttack, 1959, p. 329.
23. R.D. Banerjee, *History of Orissa*, vol. I, R. Chatterjee & Co., Calcutta, 1930, pp. 330–2.
24. P. Mukherjee, *History of the Chaitanya Faith in Orissa*, Monohar, New Delhi, 1979, pp. 80–1.
25. Sarala Debi, op. cit., p. 32.
26. D.N. Patnaik, *Odissi Nrutya*, Orissa Sangit Natak Akademi, Bhubaneswar, 1974, pp. 53f.
27. For example, Shri Pankaja Charan, Kelu Charan, Debi Prasad and Mayadhara started their career from the *gotipua* dance. The famous Oriya singer Bhikari Charan Bal and renowned violin player Sunakar Sahoo once had acquired good name in the field of *gotipua* dance. Vide ibid, pp. 60f.
28. Raicharan Das, *Prustha Bhumi* in the *Orissara Jatara* of Dhiren Dash, Orissa Sangita Natak Akademi, Bhubaneswar, 1981, pp. 130f.
29. Nilakantha Das, *Oriya Sahityara Krama Parinama*, vol. I, Navabharata Granthalaya, Cuttack, 1948, pp. 116–19.
30. Raicharan Das, op. cit., pp. 133–4.
31. The linguistic synthesis of Oriya, Bengali, Arabic and Persian of the *Sola Pala* may be seen in the following passage:

Ehirupe janamile prabhu Satyapir,
Duniya Keramat Karite Jahir.
Fakirer bese prabhu rajake dekhila,
Pandaver Govinda se jena sakha haila.
Rajake dekhia bat bale Satyapir,
Kuthae tumi jao raja kiser khatir.
Raja bale landa Fakir Chhinda Kantha gay,
Jetha ichha mora jai tor kiba jay.
Dewan balen raja kahe kara rosh,
Jijnasha kariya bat karinu ki dosh.

Vide B.P. Panda, 'Contribution of Oriya Poets to Medieval Bengali Literature', in H.K. Mahatab et al. (eds.), *Glimpses of Orissan Art and Culture*, Orissa State Museum, Bhubaneswar, 1984, pp. 308–9.

32. A.K. Deb, *The Bhakti Movement in Orissa*, Punthi Pustak Calcutta, 1984, p. 62.
33. B.B. Shukla, *Bhagabata Ghara and Village Panchayat in Medieval Orissa* (1510–1803 AD), Bharati Publications, Cuttack, 1986, p. 44.
34. Banshidhar Mohanty, *Bhaktakavi Baligan Dasa*, 1st edn., Jagannatha Publishers, Bhubaneswar, 1986, pp. 2–8; Sitakanta Mahapatra, *Bhima Bhoi*, Sahitya Akademi, New Delhi, 1983, p. 9.
35. M. Mansingh, *History of Oriya Literature*, Sahitya Akademi, New Delhi, 1962, pp. 98–9.

Glossary

Ajivikas:	A heterodox sect of the Buddha's time.
Agnistoma:	The name of a sacrifice.
Agraharas:	The land-grant enjoyed by the Brahmins.
Apabhramsa:	Changed form of the original word.
Asana:	Sitting posture.
Atavika:	The forest dwellers .
Avijita Anta:	Unconquered tribes in border of Kalinga.
Bhagavata:	A cult of devotion to Vishnu.
Bhakta-kavi:	One who composed devotional poems, in the medieval times.
Bhakti:	Devotion.
Bhattarpe:	One divine title of the king.
Bhoga:	Offering to deity.
Brahmadeya:	The land donated to a Brahmin.
Brahmavidya:	Metaphysical themes.
Chalanti Pratima:	Small idol of the main deity who is taken to different places on festivals or rituals.
Candala:	People of the lowest rank in Hindu Social Order.
Chaukidari:	Watchmanship.
Dadu-panthi:	Followers of Dadu Dayal.
Daita:	The progenies of Vidyapati (the Brahmin minister of the legendary king Indradyumna) and Lalita (daughter of the Sabar chief Vishwavasu).

Dakshina: A gift in cash or kind to a priest.
Dandi brutta: Where in a colophon letter numbers are not equal but recited with the same lyric.
Dharamsastras: Social and religious codes of Hinduism .
Ekamra: (One mango), other name of Bhubaneswar.
Gajapati: Medieval Orissan kings assumed the title Gajapati for their possession of huge elephantry.
Garbhagriha: The inner place of the temple where the idol is installed for worship.
Golaka: Other name of the tree sahada(Strebulus Asphera).
Guru: Preceptor.
Hingula: Goddess of Fire.
Jnana: Philosophical knowledge
Karma: Action or deeds in the life.
Kaupin: An inner garment like *kachha*.
Kendra: A musical instrument of one string of ware.
Khalsa: Pure.
Kutumbin: Large family holder.
Linga: Phalus or male sexual organ.
Madalapanji: Temple Chronicle of Lord Jagannatha.
Mathas: Monasteries, school attached to a temple.
Maya: Illusion.
Muni: Worshipper of deities.
Natha Yogis: Follower of Gorakshanath, they practised yoga and moved different places.
Nayaka: A military title like commander.
Nirguna: Belief in God without human attributes.
Nityaloka: Abode of eternity.
Paikas: Oriya milita, enjoyed landgrants and fought for kings.
Pauti: One amount almost 70 kg of grain.
Parakiya: Physical relation with a woman other than wife.
Paraloka: The belief in the place where the people live after death.
Praja: Subject class.
Prakrit: Regional dialect.
Premabhakti: Love based devotion.

Pundits:	Priests or learned people generally of the Brahmin community.
Puranas:	Stories of life and deeds of different Gods and Goddesses.
Sabar/Saura:	Name of a tribe who, as per the legend, first worshipped Lord Jagannatha.
Sadhakas:	One who practised yoga or meditation.
Saguna:	Belief in God with human attributes.
Sahajiya:	Faith in getting *nirvan* by involving in extra-marital affairs.
Sampraday:	One religious group or association.
Samraja:	Overlord or chief.
Sanja:	Rent i.e. crop sharing system.
Sasana/Brahmapura:	Brahmin Settlements.
Siddhacharyas:	Religious preceptors of the early medieval Orissa who emerged from the popular background.
Sramana:	Buddhist monks.
Srikshetra:	Other name of Puri, where Goddess Lakshmi resides.
Suddhadvait:	Pure monism.
Sudhi:	Rituals and sacredness.
Sudramuni:	The devotee and writer of puranas of the Sudra Community.
Sunya:	Void.
Suryavamsi:	Solar dynasty.
Vajrayana:	Tantrik form/division of Buddhism.
Varna:	(colour) Four fold division of the Hindu Social Order e.g. Brahmin,Kshatriya, Vaishya, Sudra.
Varnashrama dharma:	Practise of the duties of four varnas in society.
Vedanta:	Last part of the Vedas.
Vishistadvait:	Faith in one God only i.e. monism.
Yajna:	Sacrifice.
Yavan:	Used in Indian sources for the people of Western Asia.

Appendix

Facsimile cover pages of a few Medieval Oriya books printed in Bengali script

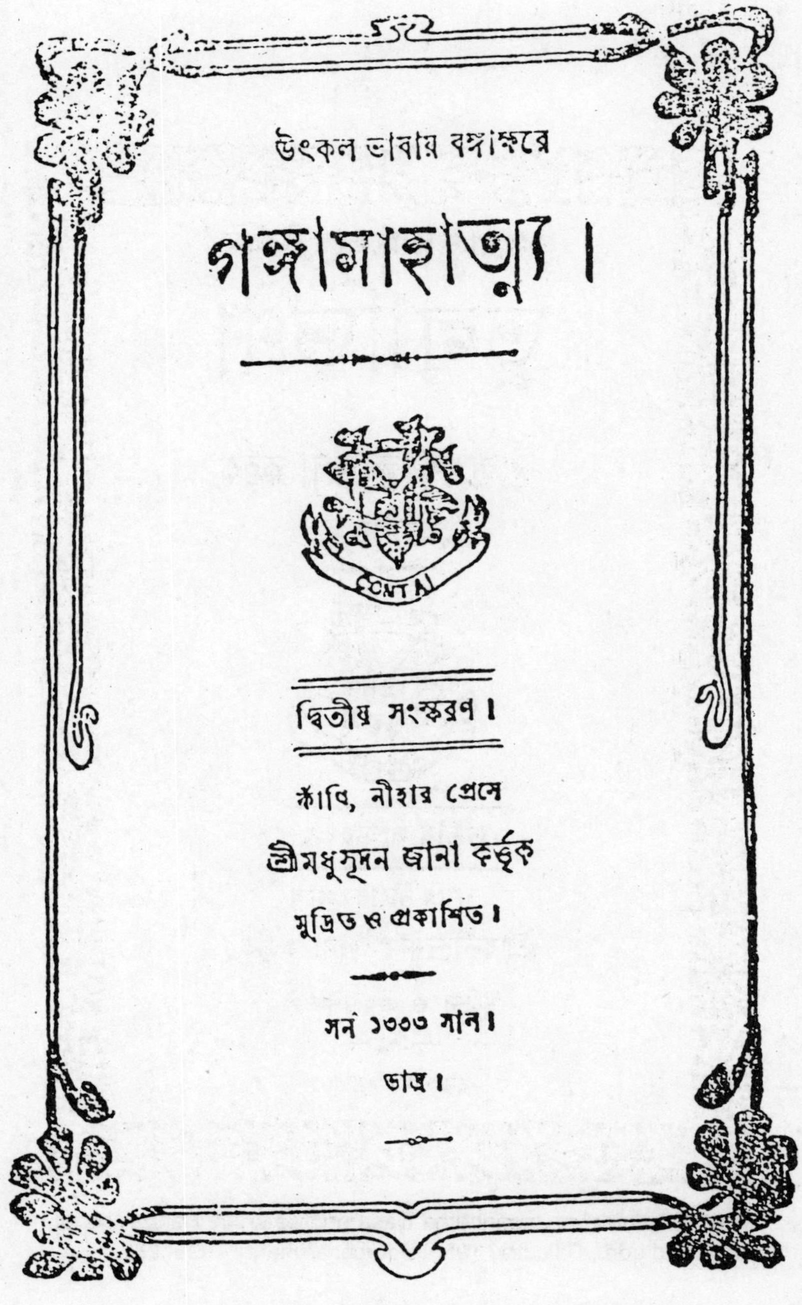

উৎকল ভাষায় বঙ্গাক্ষরে

গঙ্গামাহাত্ম্য।

দ্বিতীয় সংস্করণ।

কাঁথি, নীহার প্রেসে

শ্রীমধুসূদন জানা কর্ত্তৃক

মুদ্রিত ও প্রকাশিত।

সন ১৩৩৩ সাল।

ভাদ্র।

The "*Ganga mahatmya*" of Purushottam Dasa in the Bengali script, 2nd edn., Calcutta, 1926. Source: Mohanty 1995: 233.

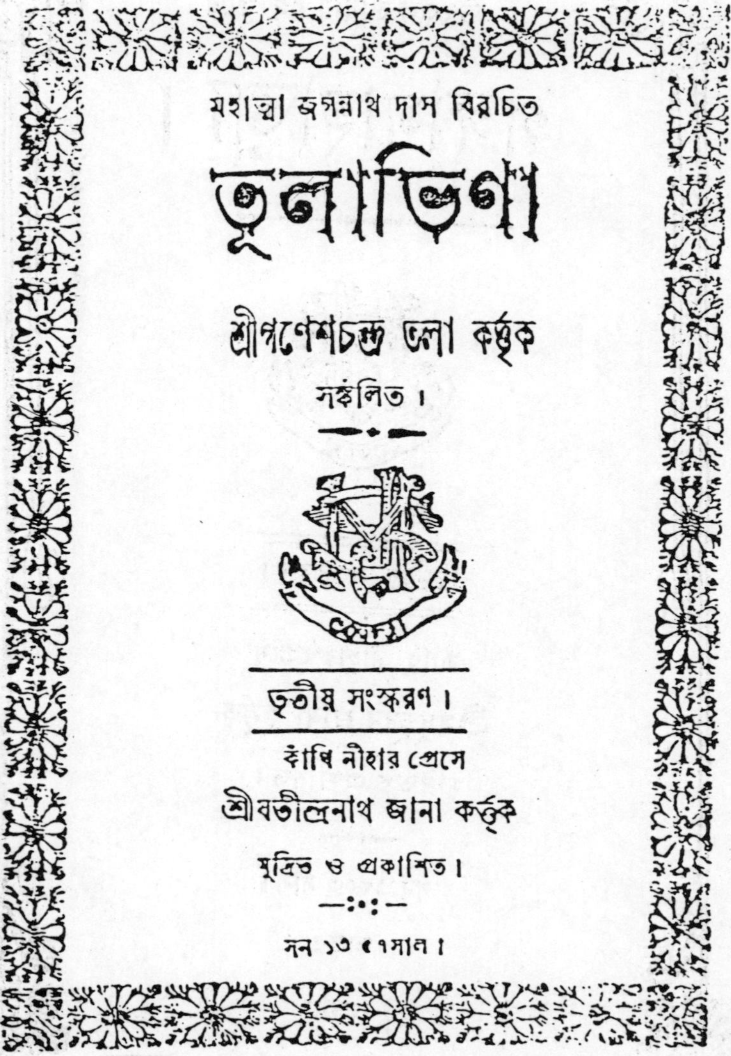

মহাত্মা জগন্নাথ দাস বিরচিত

তুলাভিণা

শ্রীগণেশচন্দ্র ডলা কর্ত্তৃক

সঙ্কলিত।

তৃতীয় সংস্করণ।

কাঁথি নীহার প্রেসে

শ্রীযতীন্দ্রনাথ জানা কর্ত্তৃক

মুদ্রিত ও প্রকাশিত।

সন ১৩৫৭ সাল।

The "*Tulabhina*" of Jagannatha Dasa printed in the Bengali script, 3rd edn., Calcutta, 1950. Source: Mohanty 1995: 282.

উৎকল ভাষায় বঙ্গাক্ষরে

রাসলীলা

কাঁথি নীহার প্রেস হইতে প্রকাশিত।

সপ্তবিংশ সংস্করণ।

কাঁথি নীহার প্রেসে
শ্রীযতীন্দ্রনাথ জানা দ্বারা
মুদ্রিত।

সন ১৩৫৮ সাল।

The Oriya "*Rasalila*" in the Bengali script, 27th edn., Calcutta, 1951. Source: Mohanty 1995: 283.

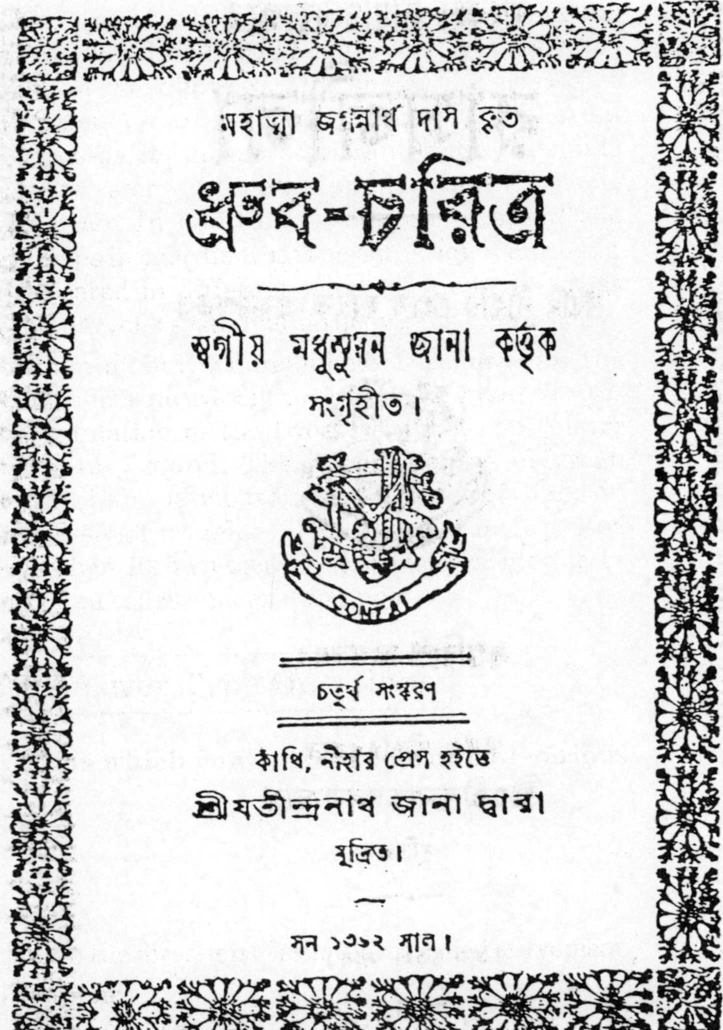

মহাত্মা জগন্নাথ দাস কৃত

ধ্রুব-চরিত্র

স্বর্গীয় মধুসূদন জানা কর্ত্তৃক

সংগৃহীত।

CONTAI

চতুর্থ সংস্করণ

কাঁথি, নীহার প্রেস হইতে

শ্রীযতীন্দ্রনাথ জানা দ্বারা

মুদ্রিত।

সন ১৩৬২ সাল।

The "*Dhruba Charitra*" of Jagannatha Dasa in the Bengali script, 4th edn., Calcutta. 1955. Source: Mohanty 1995: 284.

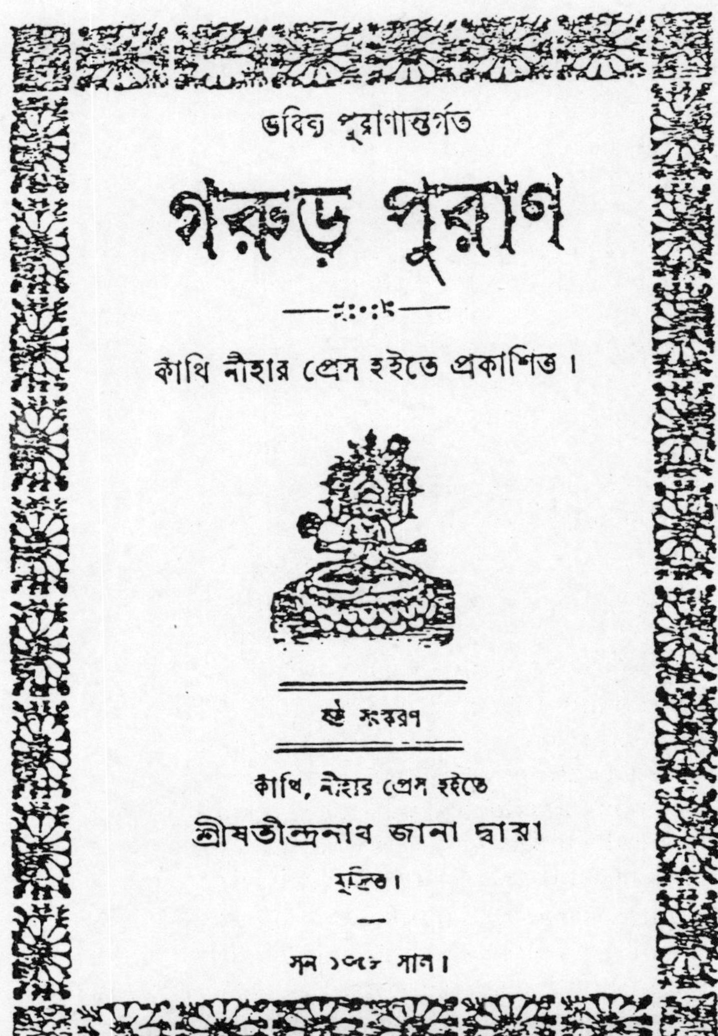

ভবিষ্য পুরাণান্তর্গত

গরুড় পুরাণ

কাঁথি নীহার প্রেস হইতে প্রকাশিত।

ষষ্ঠ সংস্করণ

কাঁথি, নীহার প্রেস হইতে

শ্রীযতীন্দ্রনাথ জানা দ্বারা

মুদ্রিত।

সন ১৩৫৮ সাল।

The Oriya "*Garuda Puran*" in the Bengali script, 6th edn., Calcutta, 1951. Source: Mohanty 1995: 286.

Bibliography

PRIMARY SOURCES

Inscriptions, Plates and Grants

Epigraphia Indica (*EI*), vols. III, VI, VII, VIII, XII, no. 36, XXII, XXIV, XXVII, XXVIII, XXX, XXXIII, pt. 3, XXXVI, XXXIX.

Alipur Plates of Narasinghadev II, dated 1294, *EI*, XXI.

Arasavali Plates of Vajrahasta III, dated AD 1600, *EI*, XXXII.

Banapur Copper Plate of Dharmaja, III, *EI*, XI.

Chikkalavalasa Plates of the Ganga King Vajrahasta III, dated AD 1059; *EI*, XXXIII, pt. III.

Jagannatha Temple Inscription of Purushottamdev, dated AD 1470 and 1485.

Koni Copper Plate of Anantavarman Chodagangadev, dated AD 1082, *JAHRS*, vol. I, no. I.

Mallen Plates of Narasimhadev II, dated AD 1294; *EI*, XXI.

Murupoka Grant of Chodagangadev, dated AD 1084, *JAHRS*, vol. XII.

Nagari plates of Anangabhima Dev III, dated AD 1231; *EI*, XXVII, pts. V and VI.

Orissa Museum Plates of Anangabhima Dev III, dated AD 1211–38, *OHRJ*, XII.

Orissa State Museum Manuscripts, B/10, Orissa State Museum, Bhubaneswar.

Puri Plates of Narasimha Dev IV, dated AD 1384 and 1385.

Raghudevapur Grant of Kapilendra Dev, dated AD 1456, *EI*, XXXIII.

Rajguru, S.N. (ed.), *Inscriptions of Orissa* (*IO*), vol. I, pt. II, Orissa State Museum, Bhubaneswar, 1958.

South Indian Inscriptions, vol. IV, no. 761, *Saka* 1387 (Sanskrit); vol. V, no. 1035. B33.

Talacher Plate of Sivakara III, *EI*, XI.

Archaeology

Panigrahi, K.C., *Archaeological Remains at Bhubaneswar*, Orient Longman, Calcutta, 1961.

Vasu, N., *Archaeological Survey of Mayurbhanja*, vols. I and II, Calcutta University, Calcutta, 1911.

Sanskrit

Goswami, Raghunatha Dasa, *Stabavali*, Radharaman Press, Murshidabad, 1922.

Goswami, Rupa, *Stabamala*, Radharaman Press, Murshidabad, 1880.

Gupta, Murari, *Chaitanya Charitamritam*, Amrita Bazar Patrika Office, Calcutta, 1931.

Jayadeva, *Gitagovinda Mahakavyam*, Orissa Sanskruta Akademi, Bhubaneswar, 1999.

Kavi, Karnapura, *Chaitanya Charitamritam*, Radharaman Press, Murshidabad, 1884.

Ray, Ramananda, *Jagannatha Vallabha Natakam*, Radharaman Press, Murshidabad, 1921.

Persian

Abul Fazal, *Ain-i-Akbari*, vol. I (tr. H. Blochmann), Asiatic Society of Bengal, Calcutta, 1873.

Al-Biruni, *Tarikh-ul-Hind* (tr. Edward C. Sachau), Atlantic Publishers, New Delhi, 1990; Also edited by Q. Ahamad, *Al-Bruni's India*, National Book Trust, New Delhi, 1983.

Minhaj-ud-din-bin-Siraj-ud-din, *Tabaquat-i-Nasiri* (tr. Major H.G. Raverty), Gilbert & Rivington, London, 1881.

Shams-i-Shiraj, *Tarikh-i-Firoz Shahi*, Bib. Ind., Calcutta, 1890.

Bengali

Dasa, Lochan, *Chaitanya Mangal*, Ramanarayan Vidyaratna, Murshidabad, 1913.

Dasa, Vrindaban, *Chaitanya Bhagavata*, Hari Das Seth, Calcutta, 1923.

Jayananda, *Chaitanya Mangal*, Bangiya Sahitya Parishad, Calcutta, 1901, rpt. in 1971, Asiatic Society, Calcutta.

Kaviraj, Krishnadasa, *Chaitanya Charitamrita* (*Adi Lila, Madhya Lila*), Cuttack Printing Company, n.d.

———, *Chaitanya Charitamrita* (*Antya Lila*), Orissa Jagannatha Company, Calcutta, 2nd edn., 1965.

Mazumdar, B.B., *Sri Chaitanya Chariter Upadan*, Calcutta University, Calcutta, 1959.

Oriya

Bhoi, Bhima, *Stuti Chintamani*, 2nd rpt., Prachi, Bhubaneswar, 1940.

———, *Brahmanirupan Gita*, Orissa Jagannatha Company, Cuttack, 1967.

Chaini, R.K. (ed.), *Achyutananda Rachanavali* (*Kavita Khanda*), Achyutananda Smruti Samsada, Cuttack, 1989.

——— (ed.), *Achyutananda Rachanavali* (*Tattva Sahitya Khanda*), Achyutananda Smruti Samsada, Cuttack, 1990.

Dasa, Achyutananda, *Sunya Samhita*, Arunodaya Press, Cuttack, 1914.
———, *Virata Gita*, Rajendra Prakasani, Berhampur, n.d.
———, *Harivamsa*, Dharmagrantha Store, Cuttack, 1970.
———, *Gopalanka Ogala*, Orissa Jagannatha Company, Cuttack, 1990.
———, *Sri Guru Bhakti Gita*, Cuttack, pts. I and II., Prachi Samiti, Bhubaneswar, 1970.
———, *Mahagupta Padmakalpa*, Siddheswari Pustakalaya, Cuttack, n.d.
———, *Kalikalpa Gita*, Siddheswari Pustakalaya, Cuttack, n.d.
———, *Garuda Gita*, Orissa Jagannatha Company, Cuttack, n.d.
———, *Brahmasankuli* (*Prathama Kalpa*), ed. A.B. Mohanty, Mukur Press, Cuttack, 1926.
Dasa, Arakshita, *Mahimandala Gita*, Mohanta Sri Lachhman Das, Olasuni, Cuttack, 1970.
Dasa, Balarama, *Vedantasara Gupta Gita*, Union Printing Works, Cuttack, 1910.
———, *Jagamohan Ramayana*, vols. I-VII, Dharmagrantha Store, Cuttack, n.d.
———, *Lakshmi Puran*, Sanyasi Pustakalaya, Berhampur, n.d.
———, *Chhatish Gupta Gita*, Dasarathi Pustakalaya, Cuttack, n.d.
———, *Bata Avakasha*, Prachi Samiti, Bhubaneswar, n.d.
———, *Virata Gita*, Cuttack, 1969.
———, *Bhava Samudra*, Dharmagrantha Store, Cuttack, 1972.
Dasa, Bhagawan, *Gauranga Bhagavata*, Dharmagrantha Store, Cuttack. 1967.
Dasa, Bhima, *Bhakti Ratnavali*, pts. I and II, Vishnupuri, Cuttack, 1964.
Dasa, Chaitanya, *Nirguna Mahatmya*, edited by A.B. Mohanty, Prachi Samiti, Bhubaneswar, 1927.
Dasa, Debananda, *Baichandra Gita*, Arunodaya Press, Cuttack, 1909.
Dasa, Dibakara, *Jagannatha Charitamruta*, Bada Oriya Math, Puri, 1963.
Dasa, Dwaraka, *Parache Gita*, ed. A.B. Mohanty, Prachi Publications, Cuttack, 1929.
Dasa, Ishwar, *Chaitanya Bhagavata*, 1st edn., Utkal University, Bhubaneswar, 1953.
Dasa, Jagannatha, *Srimad Bhagavata* (*Skandha* I–XII), Orissa Jagannath Company, Cuttack, n.d.
———, *Padmakalpa Tika*, Dutta Press, Cuttack, 1930.
———, *Tulabhina*, Sri Maheswar Swain, Cuttack, 1970.
Dasa, Jashovanta, *Premabhakti Brahma Gita*, Prachi Samiti, Bhubaneswar, n.d.
———, *Tika Govindachandra*, Dharmagrantha Store, Cuttack, n.d.
Dasa, Nilambara, *Deula Tola Suanga*, quoted by B.M. Padhi, '*Panchasakha Sahityare Sri Jagannatha*', in B. Mohanty (ed.), Konark, Panchsakha Special, Orissa Sahitya Akademi, Bhubaneswar, 1971, pp. 85–93.
Dasa, Rama, *Dardhyata Bhakti*, pts. I and II, Dharmagrantha Store, Cuttack, 1913.
Dasa, Sarala, *Mahabharata*, edited by A.B. Mohanty, Directorate of Culture, Orissa, Bhubaneswar, 1968.
Dasa, Vrindaban, *Chaitanya Bhagavata*, Utkal University, Bhubaneswar, n.d.
Mohanty, A.B. (ed.), *Madalapanji*, Prachi Samiti, Bhubaneswar, 1940.
Patnaik, D.K. (ed.), *Brahma Puran*, Orissa Oriental Text Series (Oriya–23), Directorate of Tourism and Cultural Affairs, Orissa, Bhubaneswar, 1978.

SECONDARY SOURCES

English

Alam, Muzaffar, 'Assimilation from a Distance: Confrontation and Sufi Accommodation in Awadh Society', in R. Champaklakshmi and S. Gopal (eds.), *Tradition, Dissent and Ideology: Essays in Honour of Romila Thapar*, Oxford University Press, Delhi, 1996.

Ambedkar, B.R., *Who were the Shudras? How They came to be Fourth Varna in the Indo-Aryan Society*, Thacker & Co., Bombay, 1946, rpt., 1947.

———, *The Untouchables: Who were They and Why They Became Untouchables*, Amrit Book Depot, New Delhi, 1948.

Appadurai, Arjun, 'King, Sects and Temples in South India, 1350–1700 AD', *IESHR*, vol. XIV, no. I, 1977.

Banerjee, A.K., *Philosophy of Gorakhnath*, Mahanta Digvijayanath Trust, Gorakhpur, 1961.

Banerjee, P., *Early Indian Religions*, Vikas, New Delhi, 1973.

Banerjee, R.D., *History of Orissa*, vols. I and II, R. Chatterjee & Co., Calcutta, 1930.

Behera, S.C., *Rise and Fall of the Sailodbhavas,* Punthi Pustak, Calcutta, 1982.

Bhandarkar, R.G., *Vaishnavism, Saivism and Minor Religious Systems*, J. Trubner & Co., Strassburg, 1913.

Carpenter, J.E., *Theism in Medieval India*, Oriental Reprint, New Delhi, rpt., 1977.

Chakravarti, Ramakanta, *Vaishnavism in Bengal*, Sanskrit Pustak Bhandar, Calcutta, n.d.

Chakravarty, M.M., 'Notes on the Geography of Orissa in the 16th Century', *Journal of Asiatic Society of Bengal*, 1916.

Chandra, Satish, 'Historical Background to the Rise of the Bhakti Movement in Northern India', in Sabitri Chandra Sobha, *Social Life and Concepts in Medieval Hindi Bhakti Poetry—A Socio-Cultural Study* (Introduction), New Delhi, 1983.

———, *Historiography, Religion and State in Medieval India*, Har-Anand Publications, New Delhi, 1996.

Chatterjee, A.N., '*Sri Krishna Chaitanya: A Historical Study on Gaudiya Vaishnavism*', Associated Publishers, New Delhi, 1985.

———, 'Sri Chaitanya and His Sect', *PIHC*, 41st Session, Bombay, 1980, pp. 289–96.

Chatterjee, S.K., *Jayadeva*, Sahitya Akademi, New Delhi, 1990.

Chattopadhyaya, B.D., *Aspects of Rural Settlements and Rural Society in Early Medieval India*, K.P. Bagchi & Co., Calcutta, 1990.

———, 'Political Processes and the Structure of Polity in Early Medieval India', in H. Kulke (ed.), *The State in India (1000-1700 AD)*, Oxford University Press, Delhi, 1997.

Cornell, J.T.O., 'Vaishnav Perceptions of Muslims in Sixteenth Century Bengal', in Milton Israel and N.K. Wegle (ed.), *Islamic Society and Culture: Essays in Honour of Professor Aziz Ahmad*, Manohar, New Delhi, 1983.

Das, Biswarup, 'The Migration of Brahmins to Orissa', *Proceedings of the Orissa History Congress* (*POHC*), Berhampur, 1977.

——, 'Development of Radha-Krishna Cult in Orissa', *Proceedings of Indian History Congress (PIHC)*, vol. I, 1978.

——, 'Kayasthas and Karanas in Orissa', *PIHC*, 41st Session, Bombay, 1980, pp. 940–44.

Das, Chittaranjan, *Studies in Medieval Religion and Literature of Orissa*, Visva Bharati, Calcutta, 1951.

——, *A Glimpse into Oriya Literature*, Orissa Sahitya Akademi, Bhubaneswar, 1982a.

——, *Balarama Dasa*, Sahitya Akademi, New Delhi, 1982 b.

Das, D., *The Early History of Kalinga*, Calcutta, 1977.

Das, H.C., *Cultural Development in Orissa*, Punthi Pustak, Calcutta, 1985.

Das, K.B. and Mahapatra, L.K., *Folklore of Orissa*, National Book Trust, New Delhi, 1990.

Das, M.N. (ed.), *Sidelights on History and Culture of Orissa*, Vidyapuri, Cuttack, 1977.

Das, R.K., *Legends of Jagannatha Puri*, Pragati Udyoga, Bhadrak, 1978.

——, 'Social Protest in Medieval Orissa', in *PIHC*, 41st Session, Bombay, 1980, pp. 340–9.

Dash, G.N., 'The King and Priests: An Analysis of the Gita Govinda Tradition', *Visva Bharati Quarterly*, LX 3, Calcutta, 1976.

——, 'The Evolution of the Priestly Power: The Ganga Vamsa Period', in A. Eschmann et al. (eds.), *The Cult of Jagannatha and the Regional Tradition of Orissa*, Manohar, New Delhi, 1986.

——, 'The Evolution of the Priestly Power: The Suryavamsa Period', in A. Eschmann et al. (eds.), *The Cult of Jagannatha and the Regional Tradition of Orissa,* Manohar, New Delhi, 1986.

Dey, S.K., *Early History of the Vaishnav Faith and Movement in Bengal*, Firma KLM Pvt Ltd, Calcutta, 1961.

Deb, A.K., *The Bhakti Movement in Orissa*, Punthi Pustak, Calcutta, 1984.

Eschmann, A. et al. (eds.), *The Cult of Jagannatha and the Regional Tradition of Orissa*, Manohar, New Delhi, 1986.

Fathullah, Mujtabasi, *Aspects of Hindu-Muslim Cultural Relations*, National Book Bureau, New Delhi, 1978.

Ghosh, M.N., *A Brief Sketch of the Religious Beliefs of the Assamese People*, Methodist Publishing House, Calcutta, 1896.

Goswami, B.K., *The Bhakti Cult in Ancient India*, Varanasi, 2nd edn., 1956.

Goswami, S.C., *Introducing Assam Vaishnavism*, P.C. Goswami, Gauhati, 1946.

Gupta, P.C., *Literature and Society: Selected Essays*, Peoples Publishing House, New Delhi, 1983.

Gurukkal, Rajan, 'Non-Brahman Resistance to the Expansion of the Brahmadeyas: The Early Pandya Experience', *PIHC*, 45th Session, 1984, pp. 161–3.

Habib, Irfan, *Agrarian System of Mughal India*, Asia, New Delhi, 1963.

——, 'The Historical Background of the Popular Monotheistic Movement of the 15th–17th centuries', in B. Prasad (ed.), *Ideas in History*, Asia, Bombay, 1969.

——, *Essays in Indian History: Towards a Marxist Perception*, Tulika, New Delhi, 1995.

Hussain, Yusuf, *Glimpses of Medieval Indian Culture*, Asia, Bombay, 1957.

Jaiswal, Suvira, *The Origin and Development of Vaishnavism*, Munshiram Manoharlal, New Delhi, 1967.

———, 'Studies in the Social Structure of the Early Tamils', in R.S. Sharma and V. Jha (eds.), *Indian Society: Historical Probings,* 2nd edn., Peoples Publishing House, New Delhi, 1977.

———, 'Studies in Early Indian Social History: Trends and Possibilities', *Indian Historical Review,* vol. VI, nos. 1 and 2, 1980a.

———, 'Changes in the Status and Concept of the *Sudra Varna* in Early Middle Ages', *PIHC*, 41st Session, Bombay, 1980b, pp. 112–21.

Jha, D.N., 'Temples as Landed Magnets in Early Medieval South India', in R.S. Sharma and V. Jha (eds.), *Indian Society: Historical Probings*, Peoples Publishing House, New Delhi, 1974.

Joshi, S., and B. Josh, *Struggle for Hegemony in India: Culture, Community and Power*, *vol. III* (*1920–47*), Sage Publications, New Delhi, 1994.

Kapoor, O.B.L., *The Philosophy and Religion of Sri Chaitanya*, New Delhi, 1977.

Kennedy, M.T., *The Chaitanya Movement*, Oxford University Press, 1925.

Kosambi, D.D., *Myth and Reality*, Popular Prakashan, Bombay, 1962.

Kulke, Hermann, 'Kshatriyaization and Social Change: A study in Orissa setting', in S. Devadas Pillai (ed.) *Aspects of Changing India: Studies in the Honour of Prof. S.G. Ghurye*, Bombay, 1976.

———, 'Early State Formation and Royal Legitimation in Late Ancient Orissa', in M.N. Das (ed.), *Sidelights on History and Culture of Orissa*, Vidyapuri, Cuttack, 1977.

———, 'Fragmentation and Segmentation versus Integration? Reflections on the Concepts of Indian Feudalism and the Segmentary State in Indian History', *Studies in History*, vol. IV, no. 2, 1982, pp. 237–63.

———, *Kings and Cults: State Formation and Legitimation in India and South East Asia,* Manohar, New Delhi, 1993.

———, (ed.), *The State in India* (*1000–1700* AD), Oxford University Press, New Delhi, 1997.

Lahiri, Aloka, *Chaitanya Movement in Eastern India,* Punthi Pustak, Calcutta, 1993.

Law, B.C., *Tribes in Central India*, 2nd edn., Poona, 1973.

Mahatab, H.K., *History of Orissa*, vols. I and II, Prajatantra Prachar Samiti, Cuttack, 1959.

Mahapatra, Sitakanta, *Bhima Bhoi*, Sahitya Akademi, New Delhi, 1983.

———, *Jagannatha Dasa*, Sahitya Akademi, New Delhi, 1989.

Majumdar, A.K., *Bhakti Renaissance*, Bharatiya Vidya Bhavan, Bombay, 1965.

———, *Chaitanya: His Life and Doctrine*, Bharatiya Vidya Bhavan, Bombay, 1969.

Majumdar, R.C., *The History and Culture of the Indian People*, vol. VI, Bharatiya Vidya Bhavan, Bombay, 1960.

Malik, S.C. (ed.), *Indian Movements: Some Aspects of Dissent, Protest and Reforms*, Indian Institute of Advanced Studies, Simla, 1978.

Mallik, B.K., 'Some Aspects of Social Protest and Reform in Medieval Orissa (*circa* AD 1500–1600)', *Orissa Historical Research Journal*, vol. XXXIV, nos. 3 and 4, Bhubaneswar, 1989, pp. 139–64.

———, *Medieval Orissa: Literature, Society, Economy*, Mayur Publications, Bhubaneswar, 1996.

———, 'Samkirtan Movement in Eastern India (*circa* AD 1500–1600)', in S.C. Padhy and S.K. Panda (eds.), *Society, Culture and Polity in Eastern India,* Berhampur University, Berhampur, 1999.

———, 'Dissent and Protest in Medieval Orissa: A study of the Role of Saint-poet Achyutananda Dasa', in *PIHC*, 58th Session, Bangalore 1998.

Mansingh, Mayadhar, *History of Oriya Literature*, Sahitya Akademi, New Delhi, 1962.

Mazumdar, B.C. (ed.), *Typical Selections from Oriya Literature*, vol. I, Calcutta University, Calcutta, 1928.

Mishra, K.C., *The Cult of Jagannatha*, Firma KLM Pvt Ltd, Calcutta, 1971.

Misro, R.C., 'Brahmanas as Created Landholders in Early Medieval Orissa: An Epigraphic Study (*circa* AD 400–1000)', in H.S. Patnaik and A.N. Parida (eds.), *Aspects of Socio-Cultural Life in Early and Medieval Orissa,* Utkal University, Bhubaneswar, 1996.

Moon, Vasant (ed.), *Dr. Babasaheb Ambedkar: Writings and Speeches*, vol. VII, Govt. of Maharashtra, Bombay, 1990.

Mukherjee, D.K., *Chaitanya*, National Book Trust, New Delhi, 1970.

Mukherjee, Prabhat, *The Oriya Preachers of Gaudiya Vaishnavism*, *Mayurbhanja Chronicle*, XIV, 1944-45.

———, Influence of Vaishnavism in Medieval Orissa, *PIHC*, 1949.

———, *A Study of Vaishnavism in Ancient and Medieval Bengal*, Calcutta, 1966.

———, *History of the Chaitanya Faith in Orissa*, Manohar, New Delhi, 1979.

———, *The History of the Gajapati Kings of Orissa*, Kitab Mahal, Cuttack, 1981.

Nath, R.M., *The Background of Assamese Culture*, A.K. Nath, Shillong, 1948.

Panda, B.P., 'Contribution of Oriya Poets to Medieval Bengali Literature', in H.K. Mahatab et al., (eds.), *Glimpses of Orissan Art and Culture*, Orissa State Museum, Bhubaneswar, 1984.

Panda, S.K., 'Nayaka System in Medieval Orissa', in K.K. Dasgupta et al. (eds.), *Sraddhanjali: Studies in Ancient Indian History*, Delhi, 1988.

———, 'From Kingdom to Empire: A Study of the Medieval State of Orissa under the Later Eastern Gangas (AD 1038–1434)', *Indian Historical Review,* vol. XVII, nos. 1 and 2, 1990, pp. 48–59.

———, *Medieval Orissa: A Socio-Economic Study*, Mittal Publication, New Delhi, 1991.

———, 'Changes in the Pattern of Social Stratification in Medieval Orissa (circa AD 1100–1600)', in H.S. Patnaik and A.N. Parida (eds.), *Aspects of Socio-Cultural Life in Early and Medieval Orissa,* Utkal University, Bhubaneswar, 1996.

———, *The State and Statecraft in Medieval Orissa under the Gangas,* K.P. Bagchi & Co, Calcutta, 1997.

Panigrahi, K.C., *Chronology of Somavamsi and Bhaumakaras of Orissa*, Madras, 1961.

———, *Sarala Dasa*, Sahitya Akademi, New Delhi, 1975.

———, *History of Orissa*, Kitab Mahal, Cuttack, 1989.

Patnaik, D.P., 'Aryanization of Orissa', *OHRJ*, vol. VII, no. I, Bhubaneswar, 1958.

Patnaik, P.K., *A Forgotten Chapter of Orissan History* (1568–1828), Punthi Pustak, Calcutta, 1979.

Rajguru, S.N., *History of the Gangas*, pt. I, State Museum, Orissa, Bhubaneswar, 1968.

———, *History of the Gangas*, pt. II, State Museum, Orissa, Bhubaneswar, 1972.

Rath, Banamali, 'Development of Oriya Literature (AD 1434–1803)', in P.K. Mishra and J.K. Samal (eds.), *Comprehensive History and Culture of Orissa*, vol. 2, pt. II, Kaveri Books, New Delhi, 1997.

Ray, N.R., *The Sikh Gurus and the Sikh Traditions*, Punjabi University, Patiala, 1970.

Rao, C.V. Ramachandra, 'The Later Eastern Gangas: The Suryavamsa Gajapatis and Telugu Language and Literature', in H.C. Das et al. (eds.), *Krsna Pratibha: Studies in Indology*, vol. II, Sundeep Prakashan, Delhi, 1994.

Rout, L.N., *Socio-Economic Life in Medieval Orissa* (*AD 1568–1751*), Punthi Pustak, Calcutta, 1988.

Saberwal, Satish, 'Tradition and Resilence: Mobilizational Energy in the Brahmanical Order', in R. Champaklakshmi and S. Gopal (eds.), *Tradition, Dissent and Ideology: Essays in Honour of Romila Thapar*, Oxford University Press, Delhi, 1996.

Sah, A.P., *Life in Medieval Orissa*, Chaukhạmbha Orientalia, Varanasi, 1976.

Sahoo, K.C., *Literature and Social Life in Medieval Orissa*, Pustak Sadan, Ranchi, 1971.

Sahu, B.P., 'Some Aspects of Early Orissan Economy and Society', *PIHC*, 41st Session, Bombay, 1980, pp. 122–32.

———, 'Social Morphology and Physiology of Early Medieval Orissa (*c*. AD 400–1000)', *PIHC*, 44th Session, 1983, pp. 133–44.

———, 'Ancient Orissa: The Dynamics of Internal Transformation of the Tribal Society', *PIHC*, 45th Session, 1984, pp. 148–60.

Sahu, N.K., *Buddhism in Orissa*, Utkal University, Bhubaneswar, 1961.

———, *History of Orissa*, vols. I and II, Bharatiya Publishing House, Delhi, 1980.

Sarkar, J.N. (ed.), *The History of Bengal*, vol. II (AD 1200–1757), University of Dacca, 1972.

Sen, D.C., *Bengali Language and Literature*, University of Calcutta, Calcutta, 1911.

———, *Chaitanya and His Companions*, University of Calcutta, Calcutta, 1917.

———, *Chaitanya and His Age*, University of Calcutta, Calcutta, 1922.

Sen, Sukumar, *History of Bengali Literature*, Sahitya Akademi, New Delhi, 1960.

Sengupta, A., *A Critical Study of the Philosophy of Ramayana*, Varanasi, 1967.

Shah, Ghanashyam, *Protest Movements in Two Indian States: A Study of the Gujarat and Bihar Movements*, Ajanta, Delhi, 1997.

———, *Social Movements in India: A Review of the Literature*, Sage Publications, New Delhi, 1990.

Sharma, Krishna, *Bhakti and the Bhakti Movement: A New Perspective*, Munshiram Manoharlal, New Delhi, 1987.

Sharma, R.S., *Social Change in Early Medieval India* (*c*. *AD 500–1200*), Devraj Chanana Memorial Lecture, Peoples Publishing House, Delhi, 1969.

———, '*Problem of Transition from Ancient to Medieval in Indian History*', *The Indian Historical Review*, vol. I, no. I, March, 1974.

———, *Indian Feudalism*, (*circa* AD *300–1200*), 2nd edn., Macmillan, New Delhi, 1980.

———, *Sudras in Ancient India*, 3rd edn., Motilal Banarsidass, Delhi, 1990.

Shukla, B.B., *Bhagabata Ghara and Village Panchayat in Medieval Orissa (1510–1803 AD)*, Bharati Publications, Cuttack, 1986.

Singh, Amar, 'Guru Nanak in Orissa', in M.N. Das (ed.), *Sidelights on the History and Culture of Orissa*, Vidyapuri, Cuttack, 1977.

Sircar, D.C., *Studies in the Religious Life of Ancient and Medieval India*, Motilal Banarsidass, Delhi, 1971.

Subramanyam, R., *The Suryavamsi Gajapatis of Orissa*, Andhra University, Waltair, 1957.

Subudhi, U., *The Bhaumakaras of Orissa*, Punthi Pustak, Calcutta, 1978.

———, 'A Study of the Brahmanas of Ancient and Early Medieval Orissa from Epigraphic Sources (*c.* 350–1100 AD)', in *POHC*, 1980, pp. 18–24.

Tagore, Rabindranath, *One Hundred Poems of Kabir*, Macmillan, London, 1915.

Tarachand, *Influence of Islam on Indian Culture*, Asia, Allahabad, 1963.

Thapar, Romila, *A History of India*, vol. I, Penguin Books, Harmondsworth, 1966.

———, *Ancient Indian Social History: Some Interpretations*, Orient Longman Limited, New Delhi, 1978.

———, *Past and Prejudice*, National Book Trust, New Delhi, 1979.

Tripathy, K.B., *The Evolution of Oriya Language and Script*, Orissa Sahitya Akademi, Bhubaneswar, 1962.

Vaudeville, Charlotte, *Kabir Granthavali (Dohan)*, Institute Francis D' Indologie, Pondichery, 1957.

———, 'Kabir and the Interior Religions', in *History of Religions*, Chicago, 1969.

———, *Kabir*, vol. I, Clarendon Press, Oxford, 1979.

Westcott, G.H., *Kabir and the Kabirpanth*, Christ Church Mission Press, New Delhi, 1986.

Zelliot, Eleenor, *From Untouchable to Dalit and Essays on Ambedkar Movements*, Manohar, New Delhi, 1992.

Oriya

Acharya, Chintamani, 'Bhaktakavi Jagannatha Dasa O Nabakshari Mahabharata', Naba Bharata, vols. II, IV, and XI, 1941.

Behera, S.C., 'Panchasakha Sahityara Ketoti Bibhava', *Utkal Sahitya*, vol. III, no. *VII*, 1963.

Das, Chittaranjan, *Achyutananda O Panchasakha Dharma*, Visva Bharati, Santi Niketan, 1951.

———, *Sant (Bhakti) Sahitya*, Orissa Sahitya Akademi, Bhubaneswar, 1982.

Das, Harihara, 'Panchasakha Sahityara Angika O Pranadharma', *Dagar*, XXII, VII, January 1960.

Das, Madhusudan, 'Gupta Gita O Balarama Dasa', in B.M. Mohanty (ed.), *Orissara Sadhu Sant*, vol. I, Cuttack, 1982.

Das, Nilakantha, *Oriya Sahityara Krama Parinama*, vol. I, Nababharata Granthalaya, Cuttack, 1948.

———, *Atma Jeevani*, Cuttack Students Store, Cuttack, 1973.

Dash, Dhiren, *Orissara Jatara*, Orissa Sangita Nataka Akademi, Bhubaneswar, 1981.

Dash, S.N., *Oriya Sahityara Itihasa*, Grantha Mandir, Cuttack, 1963.

Debi, Sarala, *Ray Ramananda*, Orissa Sahitya Akademi, Bhubaneswar, 1963.

Mishra, Binayak, *Prachina Utkal*, Orissa Sahitya Akademi, Bhubaneswar, 1990.

Mishra, N., 'Bharatiya Sahityara Milan Bhumire Rama Sahitya: Kambann O Balarama Dasanka Ramayan', *Jhankar*, vol. VIII, no. I, 1956.

———, 'Dandi Ramayanara Lokadharma O Loka Bibhava', *Utkal Sahitya* (Nuaprastha), vol. II, no. I, 1962.

Mishra, Nilamani (ed.), *Oriya Koili Sahitya*, Directorate of Cultural Affairs, Bhubaneswar, 1973.

———, *Bhaktakabi Salabega*, Grantha Mandir, Cuttack, 1979.

———, *Bhakta Baligan Dasa: Jibani O Rachana*, Grantha Mandir, Cuttack, 1981.

Mishra, S., 'Panchasakha Parampara', *Jhankar*, vol. XI, no. XII, March 1960.

———, 'Jagannathamruta: Eka Adhyayana', *Jhankar*, vol. XVI, no. VIII, November 1964.

Mishra, Srinibas, 'Parabarti Kavi Mananka Upare Jagannatha Dasanka Prabhava', *Jhankar*, vol. II, no. XI, 1951.

Mohanty, Banshidhar (ed.), *Konark* (The Panchasakha Special), Orissa Sahitya Akademi, Bhubaneswar, 1971.

———, *Bhaktakavi Baligan Dasa*, 1st edn., Jagannatha Publishers, Bhubaneswar, 1986.

Mohanty, D., *Panchasakha Oriya Sahitya*, Cuttack, 1978.

Mohanty, J.B., (Bharadwaj), 'Balarama Dasa O Tahanka Aprakasita Rachana', *Saptarshi*, vol. II, no. VI, 1973.

Mohanty, P.M., 'Mahapurusha Yashovanta Dasa', in B.M. Mohanty (ed.), *Orissara Sadhu Sant*, vol. I, Cuttack, 1982.

Mohanty, Surendra, *Oriya Sahityara Adiparva*, Cuttack Students Store, Cuttack, 1963.

———, *Oriya Sahityara Madhyaparva*, Cuttack Students Store, Cuttack, 1973.

———, *Oriya Sahityara Madhyaparva O Uttar Madhyaparva*, 6th edn., Cuttack Students Store, Cuttack, 1995.

Nanda, Gopinatha, 'Dandi Ramayan', *Konarka*, vol. I, Orissa Sahitya Akademi, Bhubaneswar, 1960.

Panigrahi, K.C., *Ithasa O Kimbadanti*, Utkal University, Bhubaneswar, 1962.

———, *Sarala Sahityare Aitihasika Chitra*, Prajatantra Prachar Samiti, Cuttack, 1989.

Parida, A.N., 'Kaivarta Gita: Eka Samkshipta Adhyayan', in K.S. Behera (ed.), *Sagar O Sahitya*, Dasarathi Pustakalaya, Cuttack, 1993.

Patnaik, D.N., *Odissi Nrutya*, Orissa Sangit Natak Akademi, Bhubaneswar, 1974.

Rajguru, S.N. and R.N. Dash, *Orissara Samskrutika Itihasa* (AD *1100–1568*), Orissa Sahitya Akademi, Bhubaneswar, 1986.

Rath, Dinabandhu, *Bhaktakavi Sri Achyutananda Dasa: Sahitya Vichar*, Friends Publishers, Cuttack, 1970.

———, *Sarala Mahabharatare Samajika Jeevan*, Friends Publishers, Cuttack, 1974.

Sahoo, K.C., 'Balarama Dasa O Vedantasara Gupta Gita', *Jhankar*, vol. XIX, no. I, 1967.

———, 'Panchasakha Prabachan Nehuen', *Diganta*, vol. IX, nos. I–III, 1967–8.

———, *Sarala Mahabharata: Sampadana O Alochana*, Friends Publishers, 1st edn., Cuttack, 1978.

——— (ed.), *Charikhani ba Sabdabrahma Samhita of Achyutananda Dasa*, Books and Books, Cuttack, 1979.

———, *Kavi Balarama Dasa*, Orissa Sahitya Akademi, Bhubaneswar, 1988.

———, *Prachina Sahitya,* Janasakti Pustakalaya, Cuttack, 1992.

Sahoo, Ratnakar, *Orissara Dharma O Sahityaku Hadidasanka Dana,* Gopabandhu Sahitya Mandir, Cuttack, 1980.

Sahu, L.N., 'Achyutananda Dasa Gauda Khandayat Nuhanti', *Utkal Sahitya*, vol. XXXIII, no. II, 1936.

Sahu, N.K., *Oriya Jatira Itihasa*, 1st edn., Orissa State Text Book Publications Bureau, Bhubaneswar, 1974.

Sahu, R.K., 'Bhavanabarara Kavi Hadidasa, Achyutananda Nuhanti', *Jhankar*, vol. XIV, no. VIII, November 1967.

Samantaray, Natabar, *Sakhahina Panchasakha*, Swadhina Press, Berhampur, 1975.

Swain, P., 'Panchasakha Sahitya', *Nabapatra*, vol. IV, no. II, 1967.

Tripathy, K.B., 'Bhaktakavi Jagannatha Dasanka Bhashara Bhabishyata', *Jhankar*, vol. VIII, no. I, April 1966.

———, *Prachina Oriya Abhilekha*, Orissa Sahitya Akademi, 2nd edn., Bhubaneswar, 1988.

Index